The A-Z of Eating

For Molly and Theo, who were cooking at the same time

FIG TREE

UK | USA | Canada | Ireland | Australia
India | New Zealand | South Africa

Fig Tree is part of the Penguin Random House group of companies
whose addresses can be found at global.penguinrandomhouse.com.

Penguin
Random House
UK

First published 2016
001

Text copyright © Felicity Cloake, 2016
Photographs copyright © Helen Cathcart, 2016
Illustrations copyright © Giulia Garbin, 2016

The moral right of the copyright holders
has been asserted

Design by Giulia Garbin
Printed in China

A CIP catalogue record for this book is available from the British Library

ISBN: 978–0–241–00313–8

www.greenpenguin.co.uk

The A–Z of Eating

A Flavour Map for the Adventurous Cook

Felicity Cloake

Photographs by Helen Cathcart

PENGUIN
FIG TREE

G

is for **Garlic** page 91

Confit garlic, thyme and Parmesan tart /
Hot and sour seafood soup with black garlic aïoli /
Brined and slow-cooked lamb with flageolet
beans, white wine and garlic / Duck fat garlic
bread / Georgian griddled chicken on toast /
Grand aïoli for heretics

H

is for **Hot** page 105

Blackened jalapeño and avocado slaw /
Sweet sriracha cakes / Red lentil and tomato
soup with harissa / Green chilli, New Mexico
style / Lemongrass and chilli tofu /
Meatball curry / Mexican chilli chocolate mousse

I

is for **Ice** page 119

Simple banana and peanut butter ice /
Salted brown butter and buttermilk ice cream /
Avocado and double lime sorbet / Rum punch
ice cream / Simple persimmon, lime and ginger
sorbet / Frangelico and espresso granita shots /
Ricotta ice cream terrine with fig molasses

J

is for **Junk** page 133

Sweet paprika cheesy chips / Buttermilk onion
rings / Vietnamese crispy pork and prawn
pancakes (bánh xèo) / Texan queso dip /
Homemade butterscotch 'Angel Delight' /
Marathon pie

K

is for **Kale and other greens** page 145

Spinach soup with spiced anchovy butter toasts /
Spicy cashew kale crisps / Fava e cavolo nero /
Spinach, ricotta and feta tart with
hard-boiled eggs / Homemade orecchiette with
sausage and kale / Chard gratin with
a Gruyère crumb

L

is for **Leaves** page 161

Nice salad / Green herb cauliflower 'tabbouleh' /
Three pea salad with lemon butter dressing /
Black kale salad with anchovy dressing /
Chicory with beetroot, goat's cheese and walnuts /
Mustard leaves and little gem with bacon
vinaigrette and toasted walnuts

 **M**

is for **Malt** page 177

Moules marinières écossaises / Single malt loaf /
Rye and porter porridge with bacon, leeks and
cheese / Malted milk creams / Triple chocolate
malt cake / Black and white shake

 **N**

is for **Noodles** page 189

Japanese carbonara / Baked ziti with sausage
and kale / Spicy peanut butter noodles with
sprouting broccoli / Beetroot noodles with goat's
cheese, toasted walnuts and baby kale / Spätzle
with cheese and onion / Spaghetti with courgette
noodles and Parmesan / Vietnamese bún chả

 **O**

is for **Octopus and other
cephalopods** page 205

Cambodian stuffed frog-style squid /
Coconut squid / Black risotto with eggs /
Braised octopus with chickpeas and coriander /
Maryland-style octopus sandwich

 P

is for **Potatoes** page 219

Baked potato soup / Chorizo baked potatoes
with avocado crema / Aloo tikki Scotch eggs /
Northern potato salad / Potato, black kale and
anchovy pie / Aligot / Tattie scones à la Arnold
Bennett / Potato and cauliflower curry with
coconut and cashew cream

 Q

is for **Quiver** page 237

Tricolore jellies / Goat's cheese custards with
honey-glazed hazelnuts and black olive toasts /
Jelly cherry jubilee / Gooseberry and
buttermilk pots / Caribbean milk punch jelly /
Almond and rosewater blancmange

 **R**

is for **Rhubarb** page 253

Mackerel and samphire tartare with pickled
rhubarb / Pork rillettes with rhubarb chutney /
Persian lamb and rhubarb stew / Rhubarb Bircher
muesli / Rhubarb and marmalade sticky pudding /
Rhubarb and custard trifle with an amaretto
syllabub / Rhubarb gin granita

S

is for **Smoke** page 267

Charred squash soup with zhoug and toasted pumpkin seeds / Muhammara / Smoked cod's roe and beetroot dip / Kentucky pulled lamb / Kichri-kedgeree / Smoky black dal with eggs / Smoked mackerel and charred cauliflower gratin with smoked chilli breadcrumbs / Bacon and split peas with a quick mustard pickle

T

is for **Toast** page 281

Burnt toast powder / White beans on toast / Duck and sherry pâté with pickled figs and pistachios / Southern cheese on toast / Salmon and coriander tartare with avocado and wasabi cream on toasted rye / Mexican torta with black beans, chorizo, avocado and goat's cheese crema

U

is for **Umami** page 293

Shrimp and grits with bacon and Parmesan / Courgette fritters with bagna cauda hollandaise / Ox cheeks braised in Marmite / Chargrilled Caesar salad / Crunchy soy-braised pig's tails / Broccoli and edamame salad with Korean dressing / Dashi pickles / Green lamb kebabs

V

is for **Violets and other edible flowers** page 309

Crab with ricotta and lemon zest and an elderflower and cucumber salad / Fig and goat's cheese olive oil flatbread with lavender honey / Geranium and apple snow / Marzipan violets / Scandi saffron buns / Shrikhand, or spiced saffron and pistachio yoghurt / Rose petal vodka

W

is for **Wild** page 323

Roast new potatoes with wild garlic dressing / Scrambled eggs with crab and samphire / Wild garlic bread / Michaelmas mess / Almond rice pudding with blackberry and apple compote / Bramble old-fashioned

X

is for **Xmas** page 337

Bread and walnut sauce / Georgian aubergine rolls with walnut sauce and pomegranates / Brussels sprout, hazelnut and lemon zest salad with goat's cheese / Spiced pumpkin and Parmesan pie with chestnuts / Turkey mole poblano / Tangerine and pomegranate salad with spiced Pedro Ximénez syrup and Marcona almonds

Y

is for **Yeast** page 351
Georgian cheesebread (khachapuri) /
Buckwheat pikelets / Pissaladière /
Marmite and cheese mini doughnuts /
German plum bread with almond cream /
Wholesome loaf

 Z

is for **Zest** page 363
Slow-roast tomato pasta with lemon salt, ricotta
and basil / Mediterranean ceviche / Peach
and mozzarella salad with crispy lemon zest
and basil / Candied peel / Pistachio and pink
grapefruit cake / Chocolate orange cheesecake /
Pomelo sour

Introduction

This is a book for people who are beyond cookbooks. For those brave souls who feel they have a fairly firm grasp on the basics, who know it's easier to make tomato sauce than to go out and buy a jar (even if they don't always bother), for whom fish holds no fear and baking birthday cakes is a cause for celebration, not panic – in other words, people who can already cook. (Or who, like me, feel they're on their way there at least.)

This is not a book to teach you how to fry an egg, or make a hollandaise; I reckon I've covered that all fairly comprehensively elsewhere. It's a rough guide when you're hungry for inspiration, not instruction, one I hope will make you look at familiar ingredients in a new way, and welcome new ones with open arms – in the chapters that follow, I've picked out twenty-six food ideas I love, each of which has something special to offer the adventurous cook. From basics like yeast and eggs to delicate wild flowers and decadent jellies, all deserve a place in your personal culinary arsenal.

Much as I enjoy tackling the classics for my Perfect column in the *Guardian* it's been a real treat for me to cook with a completely free hand here, and an eye-opener too, shaking me out of well-worn gastronomic grooves and encouraging me to look beyond the more obvious possibilities of some of my favourite ingredients.

God knows how much garlic bread I've put away over the years without once wondering how it would taste made with something other than butter – the duck fat version on page 98 was a very happy revelation. And who would have thought Guinness would make such great jelly (page 248), or that chilli sauce would pair so well with marshmallows (page 111)?

Although I selected these ingredients for their culinary potential, in the course of writing this book I've been surprised and delighted anew by just how versatile many of them are. So, in a sense, we go hand in hand together here – I hope you enjoy the ride.

A few practicalities

Though I won't offer an inventory of useful kitchen equipment here so as not to repeat myself (there's a complete list in *Perfect Too*), I do feel strongly enough about a handful of things to recommend them for getting the best results from the recipes that follow.

Measuring spoons: They're cheap, they last for ever, and they're essential for baking in particular. Teaspoons and tablespoons vary wildly in size depending on their design; measuring spoons do not.

Stick blender: More of an investment this, but a less significant one than the countertop variety, and far easier for soups, sauces and purées. Electric beaters are also very handy for anything more than a small amount of cream or mayonnaise, and cheaper and more versatile than a stand mixer.

Cooking thermometer: Why faff about trying to guess oil temperatures with breadcrumbs, the stages of molten sugar with a glass of water, and the progress of your roast pork by violating it with a skewer, when you can harness the wonders of modern technology and know for sure? Digital varieties with a probe on a lead are the most practical (or the point and shoot ones are even better if you can run to one).

Decent food processor: These don't come cheap, but they're almost infinitely useful. Make sure you get one with a small bowl for smaller amounts. I'd also suggest a pestle and mortar for crushing and a mandoline for super-thin slicing; invaluable for the potato pie on page 229 or the pissaladière on page 357. (Always use the guard supplied for the last; I lost a fingertip to perfect dauphinoise.)

Oven thermometer: Few ovens, if any, are the same temperature from top to bottom, and many vary quite considerably from that shown on the dial. An oven thermometer will give you a good idea of how yours performs, and allow you to adjust cooking temperatures accordingly. My oven has a fan in it to help distribute the heat more evenly; if yours doesn't, then you'll need the higher conventional temperatures in the recipes that follow, or indeed the relevant gas mark if it's gas fired. Bear in mind that, baking aside, the temperature or cooking times are rough guides only; you should be the one to decide when your food is ready based on how it looks and smells. Trust your instincts.

All eggs in this book are medium unless otherwise specified. And all recipes are fair game for playing about with – please feel free to use them as a starting point for some new favourites of your own. Happy cooking!

is for Almond

I've thought long and hard about it (seriously), and almonds are definitely my favourite nut. Pistachios have their considerable merits, and it's surprisingly tough to imagine life without the humble peanut, but neither can touch the almond for elegance and versatility.

No nut slips so easily between the sweet and the savoury, or blends as happily into a rich Indian curry as a delicate French pastry, or indeed makes such an addictive accompaniment to a salty sherry. Truly the almond is the king of nuts. (Or perhaps the queen. Those lovely curves are decidedly feminine.)

Almonds are a booming business, in demand worldwide, but only happy in a very narrow climatic region, with mild wet winters and warm summers – and they're priced accordingly. California is the world's largest producer, followed by Spain and Italy, though they're cultivated from Afghanistan to Australia and I have heard boast of fruiting trees in UK gardens.

Strictly speaking, they're not a true nut at all, but a drupe, part of the *Prunus* family, where their closest relative is the peach – look at an unshelled almond and a peach stone, and you'll see the resemblance. We prize most drupes for their juicy flesh, but that of the almond is thin and fibrous; instead, the real prize, the kernel, is hidden inside the pit. But this family has a dark side too: bitter almonds are laced with cyanide, and just a handful can prove fatal (though the flavour is so pungent that few people are likely to eat more than one). That said, the same highly aromatic quality that proved so useful to Agatha Christie's amateur detectives makes this variety popular for flavouring purposes: as hydrocyanic acid breaks down upon heating, they're perfectly safe to use in cooking. A little is usually added to marzipan (as in the marzipan violets on page 316) and amaretti biscuits to round out the flavour, and anything sold as pure almond extract is likely to have been made from them too. Beware of artificial flavourings, which are only worth a look if you're catering for a nut allergy, and don't confuse almond extract with sweet almond oil, which is better for massage than marzipan.

Almonds have health benefits too – they're a high-protein snack rich in healthy monounsaturated fats, which is why they fill you up annoyingly fast (though they taste so good it's tempting to power through and finish the bowl anyway), and an excellent source of vitamin E, which is good for peachy skin. (There's also some evidence to suggest the latter slows the onset of Alzheimer's disease, but this is not yet conclusive at the time of writing.)

Cooking

Almonds have been part of the Arabic and European culinary tradition for thousands of years – the original medieval blancmange, or 'white food', was made from shredded chicken, rice, sugar and almond milk (for a modern version, see page 251) – and they're still an important ingredient in the confectionery industry in the form of marzipan.

Soft and malleable, this was once a wildly popular choice for sculptural table centrepieces. If you'd like to render a marzipan manticore of your own, it's incredibly easy to make a basic version at home from ground almonds, sugar and egg (see the marzipan violets, page 316).

You may be lucky enough to find young green almonds in Middle Eastern grocers which, crunchy as a cucumber and refreshingly sour, can be eaten whole, but you're more likely to find the dried variety in most shops. Keep the skins on whenever possible – blanched almonds may be better for cooking, but if you're just popping them into your gaping maw, your body will thank you for it. Toasting always improves the flavour.

Spicy almond butter dressing

serves 6

3 tablespoons almond
    butter
Juice of 1 lime
2 teaspoons keçap manis sauce
    (see intro)
1 teaspoon soy sauce
1 garlic clove, crushed
½ a small red chilli, deseeded
    and finely chopped

This sweetly nutty salad dressing works particularly well on a colourful Asian-style coleslaw of grated carrot, shredded red cabbage, cucumber ribbons and pepper slices, and it's also rather good with a cold rice noodle salad topped with chicken, pork or prawns, and a fistful of chopped coriander, mint or Thai basil.

If you can't find almond butter in the supermarket, health food shops almost always have it (like the peanut variety, it's great in a banana sandwich, or spread on slices of apple) – note that it may well need stirring back together before use. Keçap manis is a thick, treacly Indonesian soy sauce often stocked in the speciality ingredients aisle, as well as Asian supermarkets.

1. Whisk together the almond butter, lime juice, keçap manis and soy sauce with enough warm water to make it smooth and pourable – exactly how much will depend on the consistency of your almond butter.
2. Mix in the garlic and red chilli and taste, adding a little more keçap manis if you'd like it sweeter, soy sauce if you'd prefer it saltier, or lime for sourness.

Chilled almond soup with mojo rojo

serves 4

200g blanched almonds
100g fresh white breadcrumbs
200ml olive oil
4 tablespoons natural yoghurt
1 teaspoon honey
A squeeze of lemon juice

For the mojo rojo:
4 dried ancho or other
    small red chillies
½ teaspoon cumin seeds
1 teaspoon coarse salt
1 teaspoon smoked paprika
2 small garlic cloves
50ml olive oil
1 teaspoon sherry vinegar

A late but enthusiastic convert to the cult of the chilled soup, once I'd mastered the art of gazpacho, ajo blanco, a punchy garlic soup thickened with ground almonds, and another stroke of Spanish genius, was next on my hit list. But, much as I love garlic (see page 91), I wanted to celebrate the natural sweetness of the nuts too.

This version separates the two, replacing the more usual grape garnish with a fiery chilli-red condiment from the Canary Islands, mojo rojo, which looks very fetching pooling against the smooth whiteness of the soup. Its pungency will vary according to the variety of dried chilli you use – it should be fiery, but not, of course, inedible.

1. Toast the almonds in a dry frying pan until beginning to colour. Set aside to cool. Meanwhile, soak the dried chillies for the sauce in hot water for 20 minutes.
2. Roughly chop the almonds and put into a food processor with the breadcrumbs and 400ml of cold water and whiz until smooth. Add the oil and yoghurt and whiz again until smooth. You can pass it through a sieve at this point if you're a perfectionist, but I have to admit I'm not averse to the odd shard of almond in my soup.
3. Stir in the honey and a squeeze of lemon juice and season to taste, then chill until ready to serve.
4. Toast the cumin seeds in a dry frying pan until fragrant, then allow to cool. Put into a pestle and mortar with the salt and crush finely, then add the smoked paprika and garlic and crush again. Add the drained chillies, having first removed any stalks (or transfer the lot to a mini chopper or the small bowl of a food processor if you have one), and crush or whiz until you have a smoothish paste. Stir in the oil and vinegar and check the seasoning.
5. When you're ready to serve, divide the soup between shallow bowls and dollop a few small blobs of mojo across the surface – it's powerful stuff, so don't go overboard. Put the rest on the table for people to help themselves to.

Sicilian almond and tomato pesto

serves 4–6

120g blanched almonds
400g sweet cherry
    tomatoes
2 small garlic cloves,
    crushed
A handful of mint,
    leaves only
4 tablespoons extra virgin
    olive oil

I was beside myself with excitement when I happened upon a jar of Sicilian *pesto alla trapanese* in the Polish-run Italian deli down the road – it felt as if it had been placed there by God, specifically to catch my almond-loving eye, and even at £4 a jar, I was sold.

But, good as it was, like all such sauces, it's even better fresh. Already lighter and more summery than traditional Genovese pesto, thanks to the addition of tomatoes and almonds, in a further nod to that sunny island's Arab heritage I've used mint rather than basil, and left out the cheese, although I do like to grate a little pecorino over the top before serving. (OK, quite a lot.)

If it's not tomato season, and you're faced with a tray of sour orange gobstoppers, replace some of them with a jar of semi-dried tomatoes instead (or the baked versions on page 365), or the pesto will be watery and bland.

1. Heat the grill to maximum. Toast the almonds on a greased baking tray for a couple of minutes until just beginning to colour, being careful they don't burn. Spread out on a cold surface to cool, and meanwhile, put the tomatoes on the baking tray and grill until beginning to char.
2. Once the almonds are cool, very roughly chop and put into a food processor with the crushed garlic. Whiz until most are fairly finely chopped, with a few larger shards, then add the tomatoes and mint and pulse until just combined. Pour in the oil and whiz again, then season to taste and use as you would ordinary green pesto.

Chicken korma

serves 4–6

4 tablespoons double cream
1 teaspoon saffron
1 tablespoon rosewater
4 tablespoons ghee
6 green cardamom pods,
    lightly crushed
2 cinnamon sticks,
    lightly crushed
4 cloves, lightly crushed
8 chicken thighs,
    skinned and boned,
    or 1 small chicken, jointed,
    skinned and boned
2 onions, finely sliced
2 tablespoons finely
    grated ginger
6 garlic cloves, crushed
100g ground almonds
1 teaspoon sugar
½ teaspoon ground nutmeg
250ml natural yoghurt
½ teaspoon salt
3 black cardamom pods,
    seeds only, ground
    (optional)

Mild and creamy, korma tends to be viewed as a starter curry in this country, the preserve of children and the spice-shy elderly, when in fact its delicate nutty flavour made it one of the most celebrated dishes in the repertoire of the Mughal court. A favourite at imperial banquets, its sugary British incarnation bears little resemblance to the nutmeg, saffron and rosewater heavy original.

This version differs from the cashew-based one I wrote for the *Guardian*, being slightly sweeter and somewhat less thick. It's still best served with plain basmati rice or naan though, with perhaps a sharp vegetable pickle, and some fruit afterwards.

1. Heat the cream gently in a small pan or the microwave until hot, but not simmering, then stir in the saffron and half the rosewater. Set aside.
2. Heat half the ghee in a large lidded frying pan or casserole dish on a medium-high heat and fry the whole spices until aromatic. Scoop out with a slotted spoon and set aside.
3. Brown the chicken, in batches, until golden, adding more ghee if necessary, then set aside. Add the onions to the pan, turn the heat down slightly and cook until soft and starting to brown.
4. Add the ginger and garlic and cook for a couple of minutes, then add another spoonful of ghee, stir in the almonds, sugar and nutmeg, and return the spices to the pan.
5. Stir in the yoghurt, along with 150ml of water and the salt, and mix to make a gravy. Put the chicken back into the pan and simmer gently for about 40 minutes, until the meat is cooked through and the gravy thick and rich.
6. Stir in the crushed black cardamom if using, plus the saffron-infused cream, and season to taste, adding the remaining rosewater if necessary (they vary greatly in strength).

Salted almond toffee

makes about 45 toffees

150g salted almonds,
    roughly chopped
225g caster sugar
45g soft light brown sugar
170g butter
260g golden syrup
480ml double cream
1 teaspoon vanilla extract
1 teaspoon salt

This is a homage to my granny's love of bags of brazil nut toffee – given that she was never shy of the salt cellar either, I hope she would have approved.

I think it's so worth buying a digital thermometer for any number of culinary tasks that I haven't bothered with the instructions for checking the set otherwise, but you can easily find them online.

1. Tip the chopped almonds on to a small baking tray lined with greaseproof paper. Slowly bring the sugars, butter, golden syrup and half the cream to the boil in a large pan, stirring until the sugars have dissolved.

2. Very gradually stir in the remaining cream, being careful not to disturb the boil. Simmer until it reaches 130°C on a digital or sugar thermometer, then quickly stir in the vanilla and salt. Tip on to the tray, smooth out quickly and leave to set. Once it's firmed up a bit, cut into squares and leave to harden completely.

Almond, honey and fig cake

makes 1 x 20cm cake

4 tablespoons honey
1 tablespoon lemon juice
8 whole dried figs

For the cake:
300g ground almonds
2 teaspoons baking powder
A pinch of salt
3 large eggs
120ml honey
120ml olive oil

I'm a sucker for a dense, moist almond cake – my standard recipe, the sticky orange version in my second book, *Perfect Host*, also includes semolina flour, but this one is all nut, which makes it satisfyingly sweet and squidgy. It's more of a dessert cake than a teatime slice, with a vaguely southern Mediterranean or Middle Eastern feel to it thanks to the olive oil and dried figs. You can continue the theme by serving it with thick Greek yoghurt, although I like the tanginess of crème fraîche. Interested parties should note that this is both gluten and dairy free.

1. Stir the 4 tablespoons of honey into 4 tablespoons of boiling water and add the lemon juice and figs. Leave to soak for at least an hour.
2. Heat the oven to 160°C/fan 140°C/gas 3 and grease and line a 20cm cake tin.
3. Put the almonds, baking powder and salt into a large mixing bowl and whisk to combine and break up any clumps. Whisk together the eggs, honey and olive oil in a separate bowl, then stir into the dry ingredients.
4. Pour into the prepared tin and arrange the figs on top, reserving the soaking liquid. Bake for 40–50 minutes, until golden brown on top, and firmish.
5. Use a cocktail stick to poke a few small holes in the top of the cake and pour over the fig soaking liquid, waiting for the cake to absorb each dose before adding more. Allow to cool completely before removing from the tin.

B

is for Blue Cheese

I must admit, I hesitated before choosing blue cheese for B. Not because I don't love it (my mum claims she once found the infant me casually munching a wedge of Stilton I'd grabbed from the supermarket shelf), but because so many other, apparently sane people do not.

The fact is, blue cheese tastes like nothing else on earth, and although you're under no obligation to love the stuff, I think all decent cooks should at least have a passing acquaintance with its rich, tangy, gorgeously savoury flavour. One day you'll realize what you're missing.

Those mouldy bits

The bit that seems to freak many people out about blue cheese is the mould, though I suspect few know that we have the comfortingly familiar-sounding penicillium to thank for it, rather than anything nasty. This was traditionally introduced by leaving cheese in caves where such fungi grow naturally, but these days is injected straight into the curd (though Roquefort, the world's oldest blue cheese, is still matured in the same damp *grottes* it has been for centuries, carefully watched over by attendants who, according to the late Alan Davidson, 'enjoy particularly good health as a result of sharing this strange environment with the cheeses'. Retirement plan sorted).

The veining is created by piercing the cheeses with needles loaded with the relevant penicillium, encouraging mould to develop along these paths of least resistance and then spread outwards, which is why, when you buy a large chunk of Stilton, you may notice tiny holes in the rind.

Most blue cheeses have been injected with *Penicillium roqueforti* or *Penicillium glaucum*. As well as creating the veins, these moulds produce lipase enzymes which break down the fats in the milk into fatty acids and thus flavour. Quite a lot of flavour in fact; those suspicious of blue cheese should start with a mild variety like Dolcelatte, St Agur or Cambozola (which resembles a slightly spotty Brie) and work slowly upwards to a decent Roquefort.

The three kings

Somewhat appropriately for a food often associated with Christmas time, the classic blue cheeses of Europe are known collectively as the three kings. King Emperor, in my opinion, is our very own Stilton, a hard cow's milk cheese from the English Midlands, but Roquefort, a softer ewe's milk cheese from the south-west of France, and the northern Italian cow's milk Gorgonzola also have their charms. In general, I favour the creaminess of the last for cooking, although the other two work well in dishes which make a virtue of their unapologetic saltiness.

It's no coincidence that festive favourite Stilton is at its best in December, when the cheeses made with the rich summer milk are matured to perfection. Although to qualify for the name they must be aged for a minimum of nine weeks, older 'vintage' varieties will have a far superior flavour. According to Paxton & Whitfield, who have been pushing cheese since 1742, ripe Stilton should be neither white nor crumbly but creamy both in colour and in consistency.

Roquefort, meanwhile, which is matured for at least three months in those famous caves, should, like Stilton (and indeed all blues), be well marbled, but the colour of the cheese itself will be paler thanks to the sheep's milk involved, with an almost buttery sheen.

Gorgonzola comes in two forms: piccante (or naturale) and dolce. Piccante is the traditional drier, more pungent sort, while the dolce is a younger, unpressed, creamier version introduced in the post-war period in response to market demand for milder cheeses (interesting research could no doubt be conducted into the effect of politics on people's taste buds). The dolce is whiter and more moist in texture, while the piccante is closer to a dark ivory; in fact, the colour of the cheese is a good indication of its strength.

Other favourites of mine include Dorset Blue Vinney, which is slightly sharper and spicier than Stilton, Tipperary's 'voluptuously creamy' Cashel Blue (I can't improve upon Neal's Yard Dairy's wonderful description), the buttery Jersey milk Barkham Blue from Berkshire and an unusual goat's milk variety from Devon, Harbourne Blue. All of these can be found at specialist cheesemongers, both on the high street and online.

Storage

If your cheese has come wrapped in clingfilm or any kind of sweaty plastic, your first task should be to remove it to let the cheese breathe; you can buy waxed cheese paper online, but I rewrap mine in greaseproof paper or, at a pinch, foil.

That done, in the absence of a cool pantry or cellar, the salad drawer of your fridge is the best place for it. If there's no room, as is generally the case at Christmas time, don't panic; Paxton & Whitfield's cellars are 12°C, so anywhere dry, with a fairly cool, stable temperature, will do just fine, whether that's a garage, porch or car boot. If you're storing it for a while, putting something fresh like a carrot in with the cheese will stop it drying out.

Before serving, it's important to let it come to room temperature first, or the flavours will be muted – take it out about an hour ahead of time, but keep it wrapped so it doesn't lose moisture.

See also: Venison and port casserole with Stilton dumplings (page 54, Dumplings).

Polenta with Gorgonzola and honeyed hazelnuts

**serves 2
(but easily doubled)**

1 litre weak chicken stock
150g polenta
100g Gorgonzola, crumbled

For the honeyed hazelnuts:
40g hazelnuts, skin off
1 tablespoon runny honey,
    plus extra to drizzle

It took me quite a long time to get the point of polenta, to see that its very blandness was a virtue, a warm, comforting blank canvas for any kind of flavour you care to throw at it, whether that's delicate wafers of cured pork fat in Bergamo or vast amounts of melted cheese, sausage and egg up in the Italian Alps.

This makes a very satisfying dinner for two on a cold evening – you can serve it just as is, and eat it with a spoon, but some steamed greens (cavolo nero, for example) will salve your conscience.

1. Heat the oven to 200°C/fan 180°C/gas 6. Toss the nuts together with the honey and some salt and bake on a lined tray for 15 minutes, shaking occasionally, then leave to cool; they'll firm up as they do so.
2. Bring the chicken stock to the boil in a large pan, then sprinkle over the polenta, stirring as you do so. Cook for about 30 minutes over a very gentle heat, stirring regularly, until soft and thick. Stir in most of the cheese, reserving a little as garnish, allow it to melt, and season to taste.
3. Divide the polenta between bowls, then roughly chop the nuts and sprinkle on top along with the remaining cheese. Drizzle with a little honey to serve.

Leek and Stilton steamed pudding

serves 4–6

4 tablespoons butter
500g trimmed leeks, sliced into
    2cm rounds
A whole nutmeg, to grate
2 tablespoons flour
300ml milk
100g crumbled Stilton

Suet puddings are so much lighter than they sound, with a wonderful fluffiness thanks to this hard fat's high melting temperature, which means the pastry sets around it before it dissolves to leave a network of tiny holes in its place. There's also a pleasing theatre to cutting into one at the table to reveal the treasures concealed within.

For the suet pastry:
250g plain flour
2 teaspoons baking powder
¼ teaspoon salt
½ teaspoon English mustard
   powder
105g chopped suet (vegetarian
   or otherwise)
3 sprigs of thyme, leaves
   finely chopped
Oil, to grease

The plain leek variety, a speciality of the English north-east, was introduced to me by a *Guardian* reader – this is my variation, rich with nutmeg and cheese.

1. Melt half the butter in a large frying pan over a medium-low heat and add the leeks. Grate in a good pinch of nutmeg and season, then cook until soft but still keeping their shape.
2. Scoop the leeks out of the pan and add the remaining butter to the pan in their place. Sprinkle over the flour and cook for a couple of minutes, stirring, then gradually add the milk, stirring all the time to incorporate the flour. Cook, stirring, until it thickens into a white sauce, then mix in the cheese, and once it's melted, gently fold in the leeks.
3. Sift the flour and baking powder into a mixing bowl and add the salt and mustard powder. Rub in the suet briefly to mix, then add the thyme and enough cold water (about 150ml) to bring it to a firm dough. Pinch off a quarter of the dough and set aside, then roll out the rest to about ½cm thick. Grease a 1 litre pudding basin generously, and use the pastry to line it, being careful not to stretch it more than you have to.
4. Fill the pastry with leeks and sauce, stopping about 2cm from the top, then roll out the rest to make the lid and stick it on with a little cold water. Cover the basin with foil, leaving enough slack for the pastry to rise, and fashion a handle out of string to lift the basin out of the water.
5. Put the pudding into a large pan half-filled with boiling water, then cover and simmer for 2 hours, checking the water level regularly and topping up with more boiling water as necessary. Turn out and serve immediately.

Roquefort and honey cheesecake with walnut and pear

serves 10–12

For the base:
200g plain, finely milled
    oatcakes
70g walnuts
125g melted butter, plus
    extra to grease
3 tablespoons honey

For the topping:
400g cream cheese
200g Roquefort, crumbled
3 eggs, beaten
3 tablespoons honey
1 pear

Because it's so gorgeously rich, a little of this goes a long way, which makes it perfect to feed a festive crowd – salty sweet, with a crunchy oatcake base, it's best served still quivery and warm (emphatically not hot), preferably accompanied by a sharply dressed green salad. And don't worry that the ratio of base to topping seems unusually high – it works, I promise.

1. To make the base, whiz the oatcakes and 50g of the walnuts in a food processor until finely chopped, then drizzle in the melted butter and the honey and whiz to combine.

2. Grease a 23cm springform tin with butter, making sure the bottom half of the sides is particularly generously greased. Press the mixture down firmly into the base of the tin. Whiz the remaining walnuts until finely chopped, then add to the tin and rotate it on its side so it is coated with walnut crumbs to about halfway up. Chill for at least an hour.

3. Heat the oven to 130°C/fan 110°C/gas ½. Beat together the cheeses until well combined, then beat in the eggs, one at a time, followed by 1 tablespoon of the honey and some black pepper. Pour into the tin and bake for 1½ hours, then remove from the oven and leave to cool in the tin while you finish the topping.

4. Turn the oven up to 200°C/fan 180°C/gas 6. Thinly slice the pear, removing the stalk, and put it on a greased baking tray. Brush with half the remaining honey and bake for 15 minutes.

5. Heat the grill, brush the pear slices with the rest of the honey and grill for about 5 minutes, until beginning to brown. Arrange on top of the cheesecake and serve warm, but not hot.

Wedge salad with quick pickled onions and buttermilk blue cheese dressing

serves 4

4 rashers of smoked
   streaky bacon
A handful of pecans
200g Roquefort or other
   strong blue cheese
180ml soured cream
120ml buttermilk
4 tablespoons cider vinegar
2 teaspoons soft light
   brown sugar
1 iceberg lettuce
A small bunch of chives

For the quick pickled onions:
50ml cider vinegar
2 teaspoons soft light
   brown sugar
½ a small red onion, very
   thinly sliced

In America salads are a serious business, and the classic wedge is a case in point – perhaps the only decent use I've found for the iceberg lettuce. Its blandly juicy sweetness and frankly awesome crunch are the perfect foil for a rich blue cheese dressing that knocks the socks off that gloopy stuff they used to serve at the Deep Pan Pizza salad bar.

1. Start with the onions. Whisk together the vinegar and sugar to dissolve, then add the thinly sliced onion. Leave to sit for at least half an hour before use, though longer won't hurt – they keep well in the fridge.
2. Cook the bacon in a dry frying pan over a medium heat until crisp and brown. Set aside on kitchen paper to dry, and toast the pecans in the same pan until fragrant. Tip on to the kitchen paper and allow to cool.
3. Meanwhile, to make the dressing, crumble the Roquefort and set half aside. Put the other half into a jug with the soured cream, buttermilk, vinegar and sugar and whiz with a hand blender until smooth. Add the remaining crumbled cheese and taste; season if necessary.
4. Roughly chop the bacon and pecans. Cut the lettuce into 4 wedges. Put each on a plate and spoon over the dressing. Sprinkle over the bacon, pecans and a few of the drained onion slices, and snip over the chives to serve.

Blue cheese creamed spinach

**serves 2 generously
or 4 with other sides**

400g spinach
125ml single cream
50g creamy blue cheese,
    crumbled
2 tablespoons butter
1 garlic clove, finely chopped
A whole nutmeg, to grate

You can't go to the States without visiting a steakhouse, and you can't order an enormous t-bone without getting a mound of creamed spinach on the side. It's the rules.

Beefing it up with blue cheese makes it so delicious that you hardly need the steak – that said, it's also worth trying it tossed with pasta or gnocchi, heaped on a baked potato or polenta, or alongside a Sunday roast.

1. Blanch the spinach briefly in plenty of salted boiling water until wilted, then run under cold water to cool immediately. When cool enough to handle, squeeze out very well.
2. Simmer the cream in a small pan until it has thickened slightly and is beginning to smell faintly caramelized (almost an evaporated milk type smell). Crumble in the cheese, stir well to melt, and set aside.
3. Heat the butter in a frying pan until just beginning to brown, and sauté the garlic for a couple of minutes. Add the spinach and stir to coat, grate in a little nutmeg, and stir in the cream. Check the seasoning (it probably won't need any salt) and serve.

Poached plum crumble with blue cheese ice cream

serves 4–6

For the ice cream:
100g Dolcelatte
4 egg yolks
300ml whole milk
100g honey
200ml whipping cream
A whole nutmeg, to grate

I'll admit that cheese ice cream does tend to sort the adventurously minded sheep from the more conservative, or perhaps sensible goats, but the sweetness of the honey and the freezing temperature both work to temper the saltiness of the Dolcelatte into a rich, subtle tang which works brilliantly with the plums and walnuts. Promise.

1. To make the ice cream, which needs to be done a good few hours ahead, finely chop or crumble the cheese and put into a large heatproof bowl with a sieve set over the top. Put the egg yolks into a medium heatproof bowl by the hob, then warm the milk to a simmer in a heavy-based saucepan, stirring regularly. Meanwhile, gently heat the honey in a small saucepan until runny, then set aside.

For the crumble:
800g plums
25g soft light brown sugar
½ teaspoon ground cinnamon
50g walnut pieces, toasted in a
    dry pan until fragrant
150g spelt flour
125g cold butter, cubed
50g demerara sugar
¼ teaspoon salt

2. As soon as the milk comes to a simmer, take it off the heat and pour on to the egg yolks, whisking frantically. Return the mixture to the pan over a medium-low heat and stir until it thickens sufficiently to coat the back of a wooden spoon (it should be thick enough for you to be able to draw a distinct line in it with your finger).

3. Pour the mixture through the sieve into the cheese and stir until this has melted into the custard, then mix in the cream, honey and a generous pinch of grated nutmeg.

4. Allow to cool, then churn in an ice cream maker (or see instructions for still freezing on page 120) and freeze.

5. Heat the oven to 190°C/fan 170°C/gas 5. Cut the plums in half, remove the stones and arrange in one tightly packed layer in an ovenproof dish. Mix together the sugar and cinnamon and scatter on top of the plums. Pour 4 tablespoons of water into the dish, and bake for about 30 minutes until they are soft, but still keep their shape.

6. Meanwhile, whiz the toasted walnuts in a food processor until relatively finely chopped. Add the flour and butter and pulse briefly until the mixture resembles very coarse breadcrumbs, with a few larger lumps. Stir in the sugar and salt, sprinkle with a little cold water and rake with a fork to make a lumpy, crumbly mixture. Put this into the freezer for 10 minutes.

7.Take the plums out of the oven and keep warm, then turn the oven up to 220°C/fan 200°C/gas 7. Spread the crumble out on a baking tray and cook for 15–20 minutes, until golden.

8. Get the ice cream out of the freezer 10 minutes before you want to serve. Put a spoonful of plums and their juices on each plate, scatter with crumble, and top with a scoop of ice cream.

C
is for Caramel

The relentless rise of caramel in recent years, powered largely by the advent of the excellent salted variety, has improved life immeasurably. I've always preferred toffee to chocolate, favoured fudge over fruit pastilles, and once managed to inadvertently eat an entire tub of pralines and cream ice cream on the way to the freezer (in my head, I was just tidying up the melted bit). The addition of salt has only served to fan the flames of my passion; it gives caramel depth and balances its intense sweetness, allowing you to eat more. In short, I see salted caramel as an indisputably great leap forward for mankind.

Caramel, strictly speaking, is what you get when you heat sugar above 170°C (i.e. that scary point where it hovers between something delicious and something black, smoky and welded to the base of your pan), but the term is generally used to refer to all sorts of products of the sugar browning process, most of which occur at less terrifying temperatures.

When things begin to change colour, the flavour starts to get interesting, whether that's sugar itself, or the milk solids in a caramel sauce. Heat is the magic ingredient in all the recipes that follow, contributing acidity and, eventually, a bitterness bordering on the smoky to the basic, one-dimensional sweetness of white sugar.

It's heat that's responsible for breaking down sucrose into glucose and fructose, and then, eventually, into hundreds of different compounds, each with its own distinct flavour – bitter, yes, but also buttery, nutty and toasty. Heat can turn milk proteins rich and chewy, as in the dulce de leche recipe on page 43, and heat can transform a thin sugar solution into those rich, viscous syrups that drop ever so slowly from a spoon on to your morning porridge. In short, heat + sugar = bliss.

Making caramel

It's wise to treat anything which can reach such searing temperatures with respect, but that said, it's not a difficult skill to master. The most important ingredient here is patience; heat works in funny ways, so it's vital to give the sugar your full attention, rather than keeping half an eye on it while doing something else.

The simplest way of making caramel, by heating sugar in a dry pan, is not the easiest; the sugar tends to cook unevenly. Dissolving that sugar in water helps distribute it more evenly around the pan, which avoids this problem.

It's important not to interfere with the sugar as it melts, or you risk bringing undissolved sugar crystals into contact with dissolved ones, which can (if you're unlucky) cause the whole lot to solidify.

If this does happen, and you find yourself staring at a curiously pretty, but obstinately solid panful of crystals, the best thing to do is to take it off the heat, stir in a couple of tablespoons of hot water, and then continue stirring until you have a syrup again. You should then be able to proceed with the recipe as written. As you may have guessed, a sugar thermometer will make your life a lot easier here, saving you endless fiddling about with molten sugar and cold water. They're not expensive; if you're using a non-electronic one, ensure the bulb isn't resting on the base of the pan, as not only will this affect the accuracy of the reading, but it may cause it to overheat and shatter.

The other thing that will make the whole process less painful is filling the sink a quarter full of cold water, and boiling a kettle before you begin. The sink is to cool the caramel down rapidly if it looks like it's about to burn, and the kettle is to pour into the pan as soon as you've poured the finished caramel out – it will save you a lot of scrubbing later, although if you do burn anything to the base, putting the pan of hot water back on the heat will make slightly lighter work of it.

Lastly, lest all this talk of high temperatures hasn't hammered it home already, sugar gets very, very hot and will set on your tender flesh alarmingly quickly, so never dip a finger in it to taste, and stand back when adding cold liquid like cream for the sake of your precious eyesight.

See also: Salted almond toffee (page 21, Almond), Marathon pie (page 142, Junk).

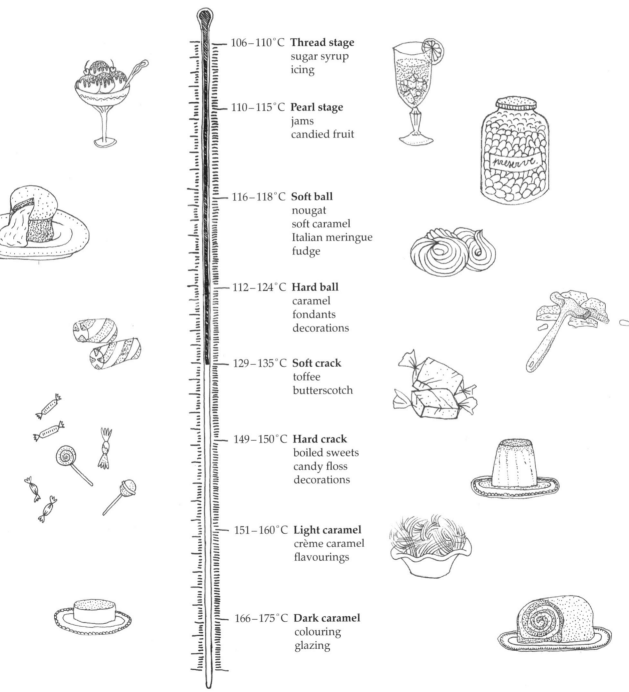

106–110°C **Thread stage**
sugar syrup
icing

110–115°C **Pearl stage**
jams
candied fruit

116–118°C **Soft ball**
nougat
soft caramel
Italian meringue
fudge

112–124°C **Hard ball**
caramel
fondants
decorations

129–135°C **Soft crack**
toffee
butterscotch

149–150°C **Hard crack**
boiled sweets
candy floss
decorations

151–160°C **Light caramel**
crème caramel
flavourings

166–175°C **Dark caramel**
colouring
glazing

Roast duck with miso caramel

serves 4–6

1 duck, approximately 2kg
1 teaspoon baking powder
Coarse salt
A splash of white wine for
  gravy (optional)

For the miso caramel:
170g white sugar
120ml double cream
2 tablespoons white miso

Fermented soy beans may not be an ideal pairing with ice cream, but the intense combination of slightly smoky sugar and umami-rich miso is heaven with rich, fatty roast duck. Although the skin won't go as earth-shatteringly crisp as the well-tanned Cantonese window-decorations in Chinatown, it will develop a burnished lacquer just as addictive.

I like it served with some plain rice and steamed greens, but am also tempted by the idea of roast potatoes or root veg cooked in its fat – if you don't go down that route, try it in garlic bread (see page 98). Note that the caramel is also very good with pork belly.

1. Remove the duck from any wrappings and lightly score the skin on the breast. Rub with baking powder and coarse salt and put into the fridge, uncovered, for at least 24 hours to dry out.
2. Take the duck out of the fridge an hour before cooking to bring it to room temperature. Meanwhile, make the caramel. Put the sugar into a wide pan and pour over 60ml of water. Bring to the boil over a medium-high heat, swirling the pan initially to help dissolve the sugar.
3. When the caramel turns a rich amber colour, take off the heat and stir in the cream until well combined, then stir in the miso. Set aside.
4. Heat the oven to 180°C/fan 160°C/gas 4. Boil a full kettle of water and pour it over the duck, then leave to drain for 5 minutes. Dry well with kitchen paper and put into a roasting tray.
5. Coat the duck with caramel (if it's too solid to spread, put it back on a gentle heat for a couple of minutes), then roast for 30 minutes. Pour off the fat and baste again with caramel.
6. Return the duck to the oven and roast for another hour, basting every 15 minutes with the caramel and pouring off fat as required, until it is a deep burnished brown. Check the temperature at the thickest part of the thigh; it should be at least 65°C for medium rare, or the juices should run clear-ish; continue cooking until you've achieved this. Allow to rest for at least 20 minutes before carving.
7. To make gravy, spoon the fat from the pan (or use a gravy separator if you have one), then heat the pan on the hob and deglaze with a little wine and some hot water. Bubble for a couple of minutes and season to taste.

Vietnamese caramel and pork hotpot

serves 4

600g pork belly, skin removed
2 tablespoons grated ginger
2 tablespoons minced garlic
4 tablespoons fish sauce
½ teaspoon ground black
    pepper
4 tablespoons white sugar
250ml coconut water
1 tablespoon soy sauce,
    to finish

Vietnamese food is justly famous for its fresh flavours, the vast bunches of herbs, tiny, vicious chillies and zingy citrus, but up near the Chinese border you'll also find plainer, heartier dishes, such as this rich, sweet clay-pot pork I was taught at a cookery school in the northern city of Hanoi. It's ridiculously easy to make, and needs nothing more than a mound of steamed rice, and perhaps a few steamed greens, on the side.

1. Cut the pork into bite-sized chunks and put into a bowl with the ginger, garlic, fish sauce and pepper. Cover and leave to marinate for about an hour.
2. Boil 100ml of water in a kettle. Put the sugar into a wide, heavy-based pan over a medium heat and leave for about 3 minutes until beginning to melt, then stir until the grains have dissolved and the sugar is golden. Pour in the boiling water, stirring all the time until the caramel has re-dissolved, then add the pork and stir to coat. Pour in the coconut water and bring to a simmer.
3. Cover, turn down the heat and cook for about an hour and a half, until the meat is falling apart and the sauce has thickened. Stir in the soy sauce and serve with rice.

Banoffee split

serves 4

150ml double or whipping
    cream
50g pecans
4 bananas
1 tub of coffee ice cream
1 tub of vanilla ice cream

Bananas and caramel, or indeed toffee, are a match made in heaven – two such sweet things shouldn't work so well together, but somehow they do.

This Mexican goat's milk version of dulce de leche, *cajeta*, has a slightly savoury, farmyardy edge which I love, but use cow's milk instead if you prefer, or indeed, substitute ready-made dulce de leche if you're short on time. With that, ice cream and bananas, you can't really go wrong.

For the cajeta *(or use
ready-made dulce de leche):*
1 litre goat's milk (or cow's
   if you're not a fan)
150g white sugar
¼ teaspoon coarse salt
¼ teaspoon bicarbonate
   of soda

1. To make the *cajeta*, put the milk, sugar and salt into a large pan over a medium-low heat and bring to a simmer. Meanwhile, dissolve the bicarb in 2 teaspoons of water.

2. Take the milk off the heat and stir in the bicarb (beware, it will bubble up, hence the large pan) then put back on the heat and simmer gently, stirring occasionally, for about 45 minutes, until it's a pale caramel colour.

3. Stir more regularly for about another 30–45 minutes, until it's a deeper, toffee colour; once it starts to thicken, stir continuously to stop it burning. It's ready when it's thickish but still easily pourable. Take off the heat so it doesn't solidify any further (if you've taken it too far, stirring in a little more milk or cream over the heat should thin it down satisfactorily).

4. To assemble the splits, whip the cream to soft peaks and toast the pecans in a dry pan. Cut the bananas in half lengthways and arrange, slightly apart, in shallow bowls.

5. Put a scoop of coffee and two scoops of vanilla in between the two banana halves, then drizzle generously with the *cajeta*. Put a small dollop of whipped cream on top of each scoop of ice cream, and a pecan on top of each dollop of cream. Roughly chop any extras and scatter around the sides with a little more caramel. Serve immediately.

Pecan, bourbon and salted caramel cookies

makes about 15

50g pecans
120g salted butter, at room
    temperature
75g soft light brown sugar
75g granulated sugar
A pinch of salt
1 egg
3 tablespoons bourbon
240g plain flour
½ teaspoon bicarbonate
    of soda
80g white chocolate chips

*For the toffee (or use 15 small
ready-made toffees):*
170g white sugar
2 tablespoons golden syrup
2 tablespoons butter,
    at room temperature
120ml double cream,
    at room temperature
1 teaspoon salt

These started off as blondies, but I couldn't get enough of the crisp, overbaked bits stuck to the sides of the pan, which led, inevitably, to the idea of cookies.

The toffee recipe makes more than you'll need for this batch, but it's harder to make in smaller quantities, and I'm sure you'll find some way to dispose of the excess.

1. If making the toffee, you'll need to start at least 4 hours before you want to bake the cookies, to give it time to set. Line a small, shallow tin or dish with greased baking paper.
2. Put the sugar and golden syrup into a medium high-sided pan over a medium heat with 2 tablespoons of water. Swirl the pan to moisten all the sugar, and heat until it has dissolved to a deep amber syrup and the temperature reaches 155°C.
3. Whip off the heat and stir in the butter until melted, quickly followed by the cream and salt. Put back on the heat and cook until the temperature gets back up to 120°C, then pour the toffee into the tin or dish and leave to set.
4. Meanwhile (ideally, do this just after you make the toffee, to give the mixture time to rest), put the pecans into a dry frying pan and toast until fragrant, then roughly chop. Beat together the butter, sugars and salt in a food mixer until well combined, then mix in the egg, followed by the bourbon.
5. Fold in the flour and bicarb, followed by the pecans and chocolate chips. Cover and chill until the toffee is set (or up to 48 hours).
6. Heat the oven to 200°C/fan 180°C/gas 6 and line a couple of baking trays with greased baking paper. Roll the dough into golf-ball sized lumps, then cut or pinch off a little nugget of toffee and tuck it into the middle. Space well apart on the trays and bake for about 15 minutes, until golden. Allow to cool on the trays for 5 minutes, then move to a rack to cool completely (yeah right).

Salted peanut caramel crispy cakes

makes about 12

200g Rice Krispies
100g roasted salted peanuts,
    roughly chopped
100g butter, diced
100g soft light brown sugar
50ml double cream
40g milk chocolate,
    broken into pieces

I have a nostalgic fondness for chocolate crispy cakes – these, based on the excellent Paul A. Young recipe for salted caramel with milk chocolate, are both deliciously sticky and dangerously light. The salted peanuts rescue them from overbearing sweetness, though feel free to substitute other nuts, or indeed chocolate chips if you'd prefer.

1. Mix together the Rice Krispies and peanuts. Grease a shallow tray roughly 28 x 18cm.
2. Melt the butter and sugar together in a wide pan until they come to a simmer. Simmer gently for 5 minutes, until amber and beginning to smoke, then take off the heat and stir in the cream, followed by the chocolate and a pinch of salt.
3. Once you have a smooth mixture, stir in the Rice Krispies and peanuts until well mixed and spoon into the prepared tray. Smooth the top and leave to set; once cool, refrigerate to help it along.

Walnut caramel cream pie

serves 6–8

For the base:
300g dark chocolate
    digestive biscuits
75g butter, melted
3 tablespoons cocoa powder

For the filling:
200g walnut pieces
400g white sugar
200g butter, cubed
200ml crème fraîche
1–2 teaspoons flaky sea salt
300ml double or whipping
    cream
¼–½ teaspoon coffee
    granules

The gorgeous love-child of a banoffee and pecan pie, this sticky, creamy confection is saved from sugar overload by the slight bitterness of the toasted walnuts and the crunchy dark chocolate base. A little goes a long way, but it's horribly addictive.

1. Roughly break up the biscuits and put into a food processor. Whiz to crumbs, then mix in the melted butter and cocoa powder along with a pinch of salt until well combined. Use to line a roughly 23cm loose-based tart tin, pressing down firmly with your fingers so the mixture goes well up the sides. Cover with clingfilm and refrigerate while you make the filling.

2. Toast the walnuts in a large dry pan, then set aside.

3. Put the sugar into a wide shallow pan along with 250ml of water, making sure all the sugar is moistened. Set over a medium heat and swirl the pan to help the sugar to dissolve, then keep a close eye on it – make sure you have the butter, crème fraîche and salt close to hand.

4. Once it's a rich amber (be careful not to let it get too dark), whip it off the heat and immediately stir in the butter, frantically whisking to melt it. Stir in the crème fraîche and salt to taste (remember to let a little cool on a spoon before tasting) – if you have bits stuck to the bottom of the pan, put it briefly back on a low heat and keep stirring.

5. Spread the walnuts across the bottom of your tart, then pour on the caramel to fill – you may not need it all, depending on the depth of your tin, but excess caramel sauce is never a bad thing to have on hand, and it will store in a jar in the fridge for a few weeks. Leave the tart to cool, then refrigerate until set.

6. Just before serving, whip the cream to soft peaks with ¼ teaspoon of coffee granules, adding a little more if you prefer a stronger flavour. Spoon artistically on top of the tart.

D

is for Dumplings

A marvellously apt-sounding name for a very satisfying culinary concept, who can fail to feel a certain warmth towards the dumpling, whether it conjures up nostalgic memories of Granny's cooking, or the clatter of dim sum trolleys on a Sunday afternoon.

Few cultures are oblivious to their charms, from the obvious examples, like Italian gnocchi and Japanese gyoza, to the lesser-known varieties: the wonderfully named *chlupaté knedlíky*, or hairy dumplings, from the Czech Republic, the meaty Anatolian *manti* and the Puerto Rican green plantain *bollitos*, to name just a few friends you may not have met yet.

As *The Oxford Companion to Food* puts it so beautifully, a dumpling is a food with 'few, indeed no, social pretensions', which evolved, in all its forms, as a way of making a little go a long way. While the nobs may have been feasting on barons of beef, the rest of us had to make do with stretching the same animal's scrawny tail out a bit further by cooking it in a stew, and then topping it with plain, starchy dumplings – or even making those dumplings a meal in themselves.

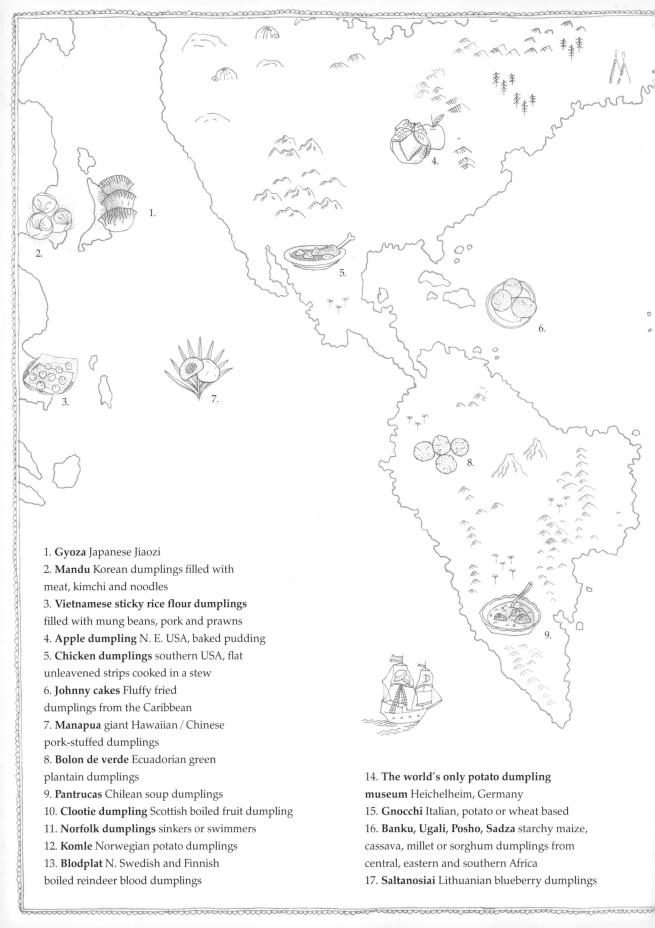

1. **Gyoza** Japanese Jiaozi
2. **Mandu** Korean dumplings filled with meat, kimchi and noodles
3. **Vietnamese sticky rice flour dumplings** filled with mung beans, pork and prawns
4. **Apple dumpling** N. E. USA, baked pudding
5. **Chicken dumplings** southern USA, flat unleavened strips cooked in a stew
6. **Johnny cakes** Fluffy fried dumplings from the Caribbean
7. **Manapua** giant Hawaiian / Chinese pork-stuffed dumplings
8. **Bolon de verde** Ecuadorian green plantain dumplings
9. **Pantrucas** Chilean soup dumplings
10. **Clootie dumpling** Scottish boiled fruit dumpling
11. **Norfolk dumplings** sinkers or swimmers
12. **Komle** Norwegian potato dumplings
13. **Blodplat** N. Swedish and Finnish boiled reindeer blood dumplings

14. **The world's only potato dumpling museum** Heichelheim, Germany
15. **Gnocchi** Italian, potato or wheat based
16. **Banku, Ugali, Posho, Sadza** starchy maize, cassava, millet or sorghum dumplings from central, eastern and southern Africa
17. **Saltanosiai** Lithuanian blueberry dumplings

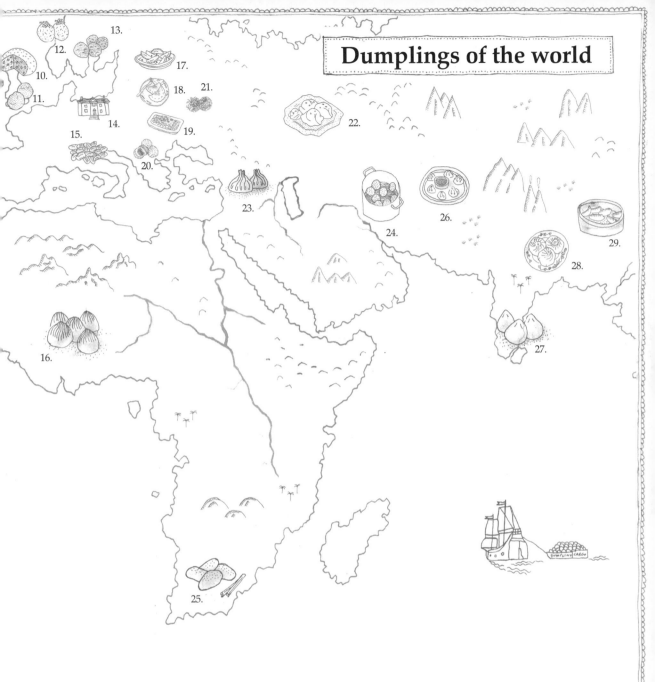

Dumplings of the world

18. **Polish pierogi** stuffed with potato, meat, cheese, sauerkraut, etc.
19. **Brynzové halušky** Slovak potato dumplings with sheep's cheese
20. **Gombóc** Hungarian plum and potato dumpling
21. **Chlupaté knedlíky** Czech potato 'hairy dumplings'
22. **Pelmeni** Russian dumplings filled with meat, fish or mushrooms and often served with sour cream
23. **Khinkali** soupy, meaty Georgian dumplings, often with sheep's cheese

24. **Gondi** Iranian Jewish meat and chickpea dumplings served in soup
25. **Sous kluitjies** South African cinnamon dumplings
26. **Manti** steamed and boiled dumplings popular throughout Central Asia and as far west as Turkey, usually stuffed with sour cream and yoghurt
27. **Kozhukattai** South Indian steamed coconut and rice flour dumplings
28. **Momos** Nepalese / Tibetan steamed dumplings, often filled with fat mutton
29. **Jiaozi** Chinese boiled, steamed or fried dumplings, often stuffed with minced pork and cabbage

They still fulfil much the same function today; though we may often cook dumplings because we love them (indeed, like the Yorkshire pudding element of a Sunday lunch, many of us are secretly more excited about these cheap and cheerful sides than the pricier star attraction), they do also permit a certain thriftiness with the other ingredients, allowing you to bypass further carby accompaniment if desired.

Back when many households baked their own loaves, dumplings would have been no more than small pieces of ordinary bread dough. Whatever they're made from nowadays, whether cornmeal or breadcrumbs, suet or olive oil, the basic principle of the dumpling remains the same: they're a starchy filler whose very blandness is perfectly designed to soak up the flavours of their cooking liquid or sauce. Submit to the dumpling's warm embrace. You will not regret it.

Canederli alla tirolese with Parmesan broth

serves 3–4

For the broth:
50g Parmesan rinds
(see intro)
750ml good chicken stock
2 garlic cloves, squashed
2 large handfuls of baby
spinach (optional)

For the dumplings:
A knob of butter
75g speck, smoked pancetta or
streaky bacon, finely chopped
½ an onion, finely chopped
1 leek, finely chopped
150g crustless sourdough
(or other sturdy, chewy
bread), cut into small cubes
1 tablespoon chopped parsley
1 tablespoon chopped chives
2 eggs, beaten
40g plain flour

Mountain fare from the South Tirol, a gorgeous region where Austria and Italy collide, home to spectacular skiing, epic walking, and the kind of rib-sticking food that's half the point of doing either. These are a great way to use up stale bread, and endlessly versatile in terms of flavouring, while the savoury broth will dispense with those odds and ends of cheese cluttering up the fridge door (you can use any other hard cheese rind, as long as it hasn't been waxed or cloth bound – Gruyère is another good candidate). Thrifty and tasty; you can't say smugger than that.

1. To make the broth, put the rinds into a medium saucepan with the stock, the garlic and 750ml of water. Bring to a simmer, then turn down the heat and simmer gently for about an hour, stirring occasionally to make sure the rinds don't weld themselves to the bottom of the pan.

2. Meanwhile, heat the butter in a frying pan and add the speck. Cook for a couple of minutes until the fat starts to run, then add the onion and leek. Season and cook until soft.

3. Tip into a large bowl and add the bread, herbs and eggs. Stir well, then mix in the flour. You should have a mixture firm enough to shape into balls – if not, add a little more flour. (If, on the other hand, it's too dry, add a splash of milk.) Season, then, with wet hands, form into dumplings about the size of a walnut, shaping them well until smooth (doing this with wet hands will help them stay together).

4. Bring a pan of well-salted water to the boil, turn down the heat to a gentle simmer and add the dumplings. Cook for 15 minutes.

5. Strain the broth to remove the cheese rinds and garlic, then bring back to a simmer. Just before the dumplings are ready, add the spinach, if using, and as soon as it wilts, divide the broth and leaves between bowls. Put the dumplings in the middle, and serve.

Venison and port casserole with Stilton dumplings

serves 4–6

500g braising venison
2 tablespoons plain flour,
    seasoned with salt
    and pepper
2 tablespoons lard or oil
100g lardons or bacon chunks
2 small red onions, sliced
2 sprigs of thyme, leaves only
2 carrots, peeled and finely
    diced
6 baby turnips, trimmed and cut
    into chunky wedges
300ml port
300ml beef stock

For the dumplings:
100g plain flour
1 teaspoon baking powder
50g suet
75g Stilton, crumbled
Leaves from a couple of sprigs
    of thyme, chopped

This rich, fruity sauce studded with sweet root vegetables proves the perfect pair for venison's savoury, almost earthy flavour, while fluffy suet dumplings are, of course, the ideal accompaniment to just about any stew. This is definitely one for chilly evenings; I'd be tempted to add some sautéd Savoy cabbage or other greens on the side to help mop up the glorious gravy.

1. Cut the venison into chunks if it's not been done already, and toss in the seasoned flour.
2. Heat the fat in a large lidded casserole dish over a medium-high heat until smoking and brown the venison in batches, being careful not to overcrowd the pan. Scoop out and set aside. Heat the oven to 170°C/fan 150°C/gas 3.
3. Turn the heat down under the pan and add the bacon. Cook until the fat begins to render, then stir in the onions and cook until soft. Add the thyme, carrots and turnips and cook for a couple of minutes more.
4. Return the meat to the pan, pour in the port and stock and scrape the base of the pan to dislodge any nice crusty flavourful bits of flour. Bring to a simmer, then put in the oven and bake for 2 hours.
5. Forty minutes before it's finished cooking, mix together the flour, baking powder, suet, crumbled Stilton and thyme in a bowl. Season and add just enough cold water (about 70ml) to bring the mixture together. Roll into six dumplings and plop on top of the stew. Replace the lid and put back into the oven for the remainder of the cooking time, by which point the dumplings should be cooked through and fluffy.

Queenie and samphire crystal dumplings

makes about 25

A dash of neutral oil
100g smoked streaky bacon,
    finely chopped
3 garlic cloves, crushed
100g samphire, finely chopped
25 queen scallops, roe on
    (about 150g, shelled weight)
Chilli oil and Chinkiang
    rice vinegar, to serve

For the dumpling skins:
125g wheat starch
60g tapioca flour
¼ teaspoon fine salt
240ml boiling water
4 teaspoons neutral oil

Though a fully paid-up member of the ancient and honourable cult of the Roast, a Sunday devoted to the delights of the dim sum trolley is never a Sunday wasted. What the ceremony lacks in goose fat and roast potatoes it more than makes up for with endless cups of tea to soothe a groggy head, and a welter of buns and dumplings to tickle the jaded palate.

Pick of the bunch, in my book, are *har gow*, sometimes known as crystal dumplings for their gloriously delicate, translucent skin, through which glows the luminous pink of plump minced prawns. But even more colourful than the prawn is the electric orange roe of the scallop, the diminutive queen variety of which is the perfect size for the purpose. Salty samphire and rich fatty bacon are the perfect accompaniments.

Depending on where you live, you may need to order the sweet little queenies from a fishmonger – make sure they have the roe still attached (in extremis you can cut the bigger ones to size, but it seems a shame). The tapioca flour and super-fine wheat starch are essential for the stretchy, slightly chewy, nearly see-through texture of the wrappers, and will be easy to find in an oriental supermarket, or online.

(Note that this is not the traditional method of shaping the wrappers, but I find it the easiest with the dough. If you are more adept, more authentic instructions can easily be found online, along with numerous excellent videos demonstrating crimping technique better than mere words could ever explain it.)

1. Start by making the filling. Heat a frying pan with a splash of oil on a medium heat and fry the bacon until it begins to release its fat. Add the garlic and fry for a minute or so, stirring so it doesn't catch, then drop in the samphire and stir-fry for a minute until coated with the fat. Set aside, off the heat.

2. Put the wheat starch, tapioca flour and salt into a mixing bowl and stir in the water and the oil to make a soft, pliable dough. Knead until smooth; it shouldn't be at all dry, or sticky (if it is, add a tiny bit more water or flour as necessary). Divide in half and put one half under a damp cloth.

3. Roll out the dough on a lightly floured surface as thinly as possible. Use a cutter about 10cm in diameter to cut out circles, then cover these with a damp cloth and repeat with the remaining dough and any scraps that can be re-rolled.

4. Bring a pan of water with a steamer in or over it to the boil. Meanwhile, fill the dumplings. Put a scant teaspoon of the bacon mixture in the middle of the dumpling, then add a scallop. Fold over and press to seal completely, then crimp. Repeat.

5. Steam the dumplings in batches for about 5–6 minutes until translucent, and serve immediately, with chilli oil and rice vinegar to dip.

Chickpea and spinach dumplings in a tomato and yoghurt sauce

serves 4

For the dumplings:
250g spinach
½ teaspoon cumin seeds
2 garlic cloves
½ teaspoon salt
1 tablespoon grated ginger

These nutty chickpea flour dumplings have their origins in Rajasthan, in north-western India, which, along with a princely number of handsome palaces and cities, is home to the vast Thar desert, where I once spent a couple of miserable days atop a camel. It's a magnificently bleak place, where, as with many such magnificently bleak places, very little grows in the way of vegetables, and these thrifty dumplings are the result.

2 small green chillies, deseeded and finely chopped
2 teaspoons melted ghee
250g chickpea (gram) flour

For the sauce:
3 tablespoons ghee
½ teaspoon black mustard seeds
½ teaspoon cumin seeds
1 Indian bay leaf (the sort with 3 central veins)
1 onion, finely chopped
2 garlic cloves, finely chopped
½ teaspoon turmeric
½ teaspoon asafoetida
½–1 teaspoon chilli powder
½ teaspoon ground coriander
1 x 400g tin of plum tomatoes, roughly chopped
350ml natural yoghurt
Coriander, to finish

The spinach is my addition; not only do the flavours work very well together, but it lightens the texture a little, and as the dumplings need no bread or rice accompaniment, makes them into a complete meal. That said, the tanginess of the sauce means the dish is even nicer with a sweet chutney on the side.

1. Blanch the spinach in a large pan of salted water for about 10–20 seconds, until wilted, then drain and run under cold water to cool. Squeeze out as much moisture as you can, then spread out to dry. Roughly chop.

2. Toast the cumin seeds for the dumplings in a small dry pan until fragrant, then tip into a mixing bowl. Crush the garlic, salt, ginger and chillies into a paste, then add to the bowl along with the ghee, flour and spinach. Add just enough water to bring together into a firm dough; it probably won't need more than 50ml.

3. Turn out on to a lightly floured surface and roll into smallish dumplings; they're quite dense, so about the size of a walnut is ideal. Set aside and put a large pan of salted water on to boil while you make the sauce.

4. Heat the ghee in a large frying pan over a medium-high heat and add the mustard and cumin seeds and the bay leaf. Once the seeds begin to pop, add the onion and turn down the heat, then cook until softened. Add the garlic and cook for another couple of minutes, then stir in the ground spices and cook for another minute, stirring.

5. Add the tomatoes and cook until the oil begins to separate and pool around the edge of the pan. Meanwhile, once the water has come to the boil in the other pan, plop in the dumplings, stirring once to stop them sticking. Once they bob to the surface, cook for 5 minutes, then cut one open to see if it's cooked through. Once it is, drain the entire pan and set aside.

6. Whisk the yoghurt with 250ml of cold water, then stir energetically into the sauce and keep stirring until it comes to a simmer – if you don't, you risk it curdling.

7. Add the drained dumplings and simmer gently for about 5 minutes, until they're heated through. Serve topped with roughly chopped coriander.

Southern chicken and jalapeño dumplings

serves 4–6

8 bone-in, skin-on
    chicken thighs
500ml chicken stock
50g butter
4 rashers of smoked streaky
    bacon, finely sliced
1 onion, finely chopped
50g flour
350ml milk
1 tablespoon cider vinegar, or
    to taste
100g sweetcorn kernels
    (tinned is fine, but make sure
    they're unsweetened)

*For the jalapeño cornmeal
dumplings:*
100g plain flour
100g fine or medium cornmeal
    (polenta)
2 teaspoons baking powder
½ teaspoon salt
15g cold lard or butter
1 egg, beaten
75ml milk
1 green jalapeño chilli,
    deseeded and finely
    chopped (optional)

Thick, creamy and intensely savoury, with little pops of sweetness from the corn, this is pure unadulterated comfort for those dreary days that demand a warm duvet of a dinner.

Proper Southern dumplings are wide, flat strips of dough, almost like noodles, but I prefer these cornmeal ones, which will merge as they cook to form a fluffy, cobbler-like topping. Good served with spring greens, Savoy cabbage or broccoli.

1. Put the chicken into a large pan and cover with stock. Bring to a simmer, then turn down the heat and poach gently for about 15–20 minutes, until cooked through. Scoop the chicken out with a slotted spoon and set aside to cool, reserving the cooking liquid.
2. Melt a knob of the butter in a large lidded ovenproof pan and fry the bacon and onion until beginning to brown. Scoop out and set aside. Heat the oven to 200°C/fan 180°C/gas 6.
3. Melt the rest of the butter in the same pan, then whisk in the flour. Cook for a couple of minutes, then little by little whisk in the stock the chicken was cooked in, followed by the milk, until you have a smooth sauce. Bring to a simmer, allow to thicken, then stir in the vinegar and season to taste, adding more vinegar if you think it needs it.
4. Strip the chicken meat from the bones and skin, and tear into large chunks. Stir into the sauce along with the bacon and onion and the sweetcorn. Cover and bake for 40 minutes.
5. Meanwhile, make the dumplings. Whisk together the flour and cornmeal in a bowl with the baking powder and salt, and then cut the fat into the bowl in small pieces. Rub in with your fingertips, then stir in the egg and milk (and the chilli if using) to make a dough.
6. Once the chicken has been in the oven for 20 minutes, take it out and dot teaspoonfuls of the dumpling dough on the surface. Cover and put back into the oven for the remaining 20 minutes, until the dumplings are crisp on top.

Spotted dick

serves 6–8

225g plain flour
2½ teaspoons baking powder
A pinch of salt
2 tablespoons soft light
    brown sugar
1 teaspoon mixed spice
125g suet
150g currants
25g candied peel
175–200ml milk

At school, where we were spoilt for choice in the matter of hot stodgy puddings every day of the week, spotted dick was never met with enthusiasm, but some years later I've come to appreciate its unassuming charms. Rich and comfortingly fluffy, it has a tangy vine-fruit sweetness that makes it an excellent partner for some thick yellow custard (Bird's for maximum authenticity).

I haven't dared mess with the recipe too much, except for adding some mixed peel, because I love the citrussy bitterness and a little spice – otherwise, it's a fairly canonical version that will be recognizable to anyone educated in Britain. Nostalgia of the most currant kind.

1. Whisk together the flour, baking powder, salt, sugar and spice, then stir in the suet, followed by the currants and peel. Add just enough milk – probably about 175ml – to allow it to come together into a dough.
2. Shape the dough with floured hands into a sausage shape about 20cm long and wrap loosely in greaseproof paper. Twist the ends to seal and secure with string, then put into a steamer and cook for 90 minutes, topping up the water as necessary. Slice to serve.

E

is for Eggs

I've waxed lyrical about the joys of eggs before; the single most useful ingredient you can keep in your kitchen, they also have the benefit of being quite absurdly good value.

With a box of eggs in the house, you need nothing more than heat and a pinch of salt for a satisfying meal – add butter or olive oil and a sprinkle of herbs or spices and you have a veritable feast. And think of all the wonderful recipes where they're cast as best supporting actor; adding richness to sauces and custards and lightness to meringues, soufflés and sponges. Uninspiring leftovers? Stick a fried egg on top to see them undergo a miraculous three-minute makeover.

In fact, much as I hate the word in a culinary context, there's no other way to say it; eggs make everything sexy. It's something about the vaguely pornographic way the golden yolk spills out on to the plate, which has made it as much an internet phenomenon as grumpy cats and sweary toddlers, but with far more justification.

All of us, vegans aside, can appreciate the beauty of a well-cooked egg. It's the Rosetta Stone of the kitchen – the key that unlocks so many of the secrets of cooking.

Little wonder that many chefs test potential employees by asking them to make an omelette. A simple dish, on the plate in less than two minutes, but one that requires real skill, care and finesse – a chewy chammy leather of an egg pancake is easy enough, but a perfectly fluffy *baveuse* beauty takes practice.

The nutrition bit

Eggs are officially good for you. The average medium-sized egg contains about 70kcal, which isn't much given how filling they are. Most of these are in the yolk, but as this is also the most nutritious, and delicious, part of the egg, I wouldn't recommend switching to egg-white omelettes except in cases of dire need: a meringue is a far better use for excess whites.

Eggs are a complete source of easily digested protein, which means they contain all eight amino acids our bodies need, and which we can't make ourselves, and at a far lower cost than many other, meat-based 'complete' alternatives. In fact, eggs are so protein rich that they're used as the benchmark against which all other sources are based.

They also contain most of the vitamins known to science, with the notable exception of vitamin C (just add orange juice), and are a particularly good source of vitamin B12 and riboflavin, which help maintain blood and nerve cells, ward off certain types of anaemia, and allow the body to absorb other nutrients. And, just when you thought that was enough of all the nutrition stuff (almost too much of a good thing, these eggs), they also contain handy amounts of iodine for your thyroid, the antioxidant selenium and phosphorus for bone health.

Lastly (I promise), eggs are a decent source of the long chain omega-3 fatty acids so important for brain function and vision, which is particularly useful if you're not a fan of the oily fish we're all constantly encouraged to eat more of. (Start every day with kippers and a poached egg and you're all but guaranteed a Nobel prize.)

But, though eggs may be simple, that doesn't mean that you can't teach your grandmother anything on the subject.

Choosing and storing

Most of the recipes in this chapter assume you're using hen's eggs, but it would be very easy to swap in duck or goose eggs, both of which have a larger ratio of yolk to white and a higher protein content, which makes them taste richer and produces particularly light, well-risen cakes. In volume terms a duck egg is roughly equivalent to a large hen's egg (though they look bigger, the shells are thicker), while a goose egg will replace two large hen's eggs.

A word on choosing eggs – pale blue and speckled eggs look very pretty, but they taste just the same as the ordinary brown variety. The colour of an eggshell is determined by the breed that laid it (and, fact fans, can often be guessed by the colour of the chicken's earlobe, though this is not an absolute rule – the cream Legbars that lay those blue eggs have whitish earlobes) and is no indication of the quality of the egg within. Even the colour of the yolk is down to the chicken's diet, rather than any particular nutritional value.

That said, if you care about the welfare of the creatures that produce your food, free-range is the only choice – though I prefer, unless buying from a producer I know, to go organic, for the simple reason that the hens in such systems must have outdoor access all year round, and stocking levels are less dense than for other free-range birds.

Eggs sold as enriched with omega-3 have been laid by chickens fed a diet rich in these fatty acids (fish oil, flaxseed, etc.) – though I'd always prefer to get mine from some pilchards on toast.

The Lion mark you'll find on British eggs (except those from very small producers) indicates adherence to high food safety standards – including, most importantly, vaccination against salmonella. Our egg industry is now considered to be a salmonella-free zone, and where periodic outbreaks can be traced back to eggs, they tend to have been imported, which is why many health experts now see no reason that pregnant women, and other vulnerable groups, should avoid runny eggs.

Unless it's very hot, or you need to keep them for months, eggs don't need to be stored in the fridge; indeed, they're less likely to crack when put into boiling water, and will bind better with other ingredients, if they're kept at room temperature. (This is not the case in countries where salmonella is still prevalent.)

Eggs must be sold within twenty-one days of laying, though they'll remain perfectly edible for much longer.

Very fresh eggs (a day old or so) are easier to poach, as the thicker whites hold together better, making for a neater result. Conversely, the thinner whites of slightly older eggs are easier to whip up into meringues and the like. Older eggs will also be less of a pain to peel.

Egg floating test

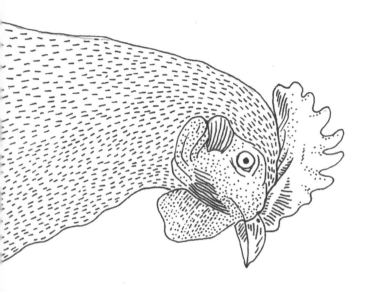

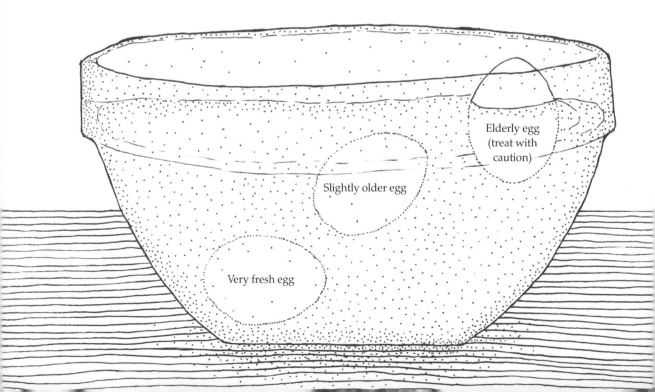

Elderly egg (treat with caution)

Slightly older egg

Very fresh egg

Cooking basics

The simplest and easiest way to cook an egg is to boil it, and unless you want a runny yolk, you'll get the best, creamiest results by cooking them from cold.

— *Soft-boiled (firmish white, runny yolk)*: lower into boiling water, turn down the heat and cook for 4 minutes
— *Medium-boiled (firm white, soft yolk)*: lower egg into cold water, bring to the boil, turn down the heat and cook for 5 minutes
— *Hard-boiled (firm white, firm yolk)*: lower egg into cold water, bring to the boil, turn down the heat and cook for 7 minutes

If you want to peel the eggs, or won't be eating them immediately, run them under cold water or drop into iced water to stop them cooking any further.

When it comes to omelettes, scrambled and fried eggs, remember that eggs are protein rich, and leaving those proteins on a high heat for too long will cause them to coil so tightly that the texture cannot be anything but tough. Thus they should be cooked briefly over a fairly high heat (an omelette) or slowly over a gentle one (scrambled eggs), but nothing in between. Which gives them something surprising in common with the creatures in Octopus and other cephalopods (page 205).

See also: Mexican chilli chocolate mousse (page 116, Hot), Spinach, ricotta and feta tart with hard-boiled eggs (page 154, Kale), Japanese carbonara (page 194, Noodles), Black risotto with eggs (page 212, Octopus), Aloo tikki Scotch eggs (page 227, Potatoes), Goat's cheese custards with honey-glazed hazelnuts and black olive toasts (page 242, Quiver), Kichri-kedgeree (page 275, Smoke), Smoky black dal with eggs (page 276, Smoke), Scrambled eggs with crab and samphire (page 330, Wild), Michaelmas mess (page 332, Wild), Pomelo sour (page 375, Zest).

Bacon devilled eggs

makes 12

6 eggs
½ teaspoon smoked paprika
A small bunch of chives, finely
    snipped

For the bacon mayonnaise:
10 slices of smoked streaky
    bacon with plenty of fat
75ml neutral oil (vegetable,
    sunflower, groundnut, etc.)
1 egg yolk
½ teaspoon Dijon mustard
1 teaspoon white wine vinegar

Devilled eggs are proper party food, and these are even better than the original thanks to the bacon-fat mayonnaise. (This is also pretty excellent in chicken sandwiches, by the way – don't try and refrigerate it, though, or it will start to set). Should you need any further convincing, note you'll be left with six slices of crisp bacon; perfect for a post-party breakfast, if your guests don't get there first.

1. Put the bacon into a dry frying pan over a medium-low heat and fry gently until browned on both sides, pressing the rashers down towards the end to squeeze out as much fat as possible. Lift out the bacon and put on kitchen paper to dry. Pour the fat into a measuring jug; you should have about 50ml. Allow to cool to warm room temperature, then pour in the other oil.
2. While it's cooling, put the 6 whole eggs into a pan and cover with cold water. Bring to the boil, then turn down the heat and cook at a bare shiver for 7 minutes. Drain and run under cold water until completely cool.
3. Whisk together the raw egg yolk, mustard and vinegar in a medium bowl and then slowly drizzle in the oil, whisking all the time, until it thickens into a mayonnaise, at which point you can start adding it slightly faster. Once the oil is all incorporated, season to taste, and add a splash of water if it seems too thick.
4. Roll the boiled eggs along the counter to crack the shells and then carefully peel. Cut them in half through both ends and gently scoop out the yolks. Finely chop these and add to the mayonnaise. Snip 4 rashers of bacon into small shards and mix three-quarters of these into the mayonnaise. Taste and season if necessary.
5. Spoon the mayonnaise into the holes left by the yolks. Arrange on a serving plate and sprinkle with the remaining bacon bits, smoked paprika and chives.

Deep-fried quail's eggs with celery salt mayonnaise

**Makes 24
(though the dip will probably take more – it's also nice on crudités, crisps, etc.)**

24 quail's eggs
50g plain flour
1 egg, beaten
50g panko breadcrumbs
Neutral oil, to fry

For the celery salt mayonnaise:
1 head of celery with leaves
    intact (lots of leaves, not a
    couple of wisps)
Flaky sea salt (about 75g)
1 egg yolk, at room temperature
1 teaspoon English mustard
    powder
250ml groundnut or sunflower oil
25ml extra virgin olive oil
1 tablespoon lemon juice

Boiled quail's eggs and celery salt seem like a canapé from a different age: if I had to position them in history, I'd go for a country house weekend some time in the 1930s.

That's all very well, of course, but if you'd like to take the same flavours and bring them kicking and screaming into the twenty-first century, the answer is simple: coat them in ultra-crunchy Japanese breadcrumbs and deep-fry the hell out of them. Soft and runny inside, hot and crisp without, dipped in a punchy homemade celery salt mayonnaise, they're even better than the original.

You can make the celery salt, and indeed the mayonnaise, and boil and peel the eggs, well ahead of time. The extra salt is very fine in Bloody Marys.

1. To make the celery salt, strip the celery leaves from the stalks and wash, then drain. Heat the oven to 200°C/fan 180°C/gas 6 while you leave them to dry, then finish the job very thoroughly with paper towels or a clean tea towel. Arrange in a single layer on one or two baking sheets and bake for 5–6 minutes, until dried out but not browned. They should feel crisp, but they will continue to dry out as they cool.
2. Once cool, crumble the leaves to a fine-ish powder with your fingers – at this point you will probably find some little bits of stalk which won't have dried out, so discard these as you don't want any moisture in the salt. Put in a jar and top up with the same volume of flaky sea salt, then shake to combine.
3. Put the yolk into a large bowl with the mustard powder and anchor the bowl by putting a damp tea towel beneath it. Whisk well until the colour lightens, then start to beat in the neutral oil, a little at a time, whisking all the while to incorporate it into the sauce. Do not be tempted to rush this stage – it will split. As it thickens, you

can add the oil a little more quickly. Switch to the extra virgin olive oil once the neutral oil is all incorporated, then lastly, whisk in the lemon juice. If it still seems a little thick, add a drop of room temperature water. Then add celery salt to taste – I use just over a teaspoon.

4. Once you're ready to cook, gently lower the quail's eggs into a small pan of boiling water and cook for 2½ minutes. Meanwhile, prepare a bowl of iced water and, once they're done, transfer the eggs quickly to this to cool down.

5. Gently roll the eggs against a hard surface to crack the shells, then very carefully peel the shells off. Set out the dishes of flour, beaten egg and breadcrumbs near the hob, prepare a plate for the eggs (with some kitchen paper nearby for once they're cooked), and put a large pan a third full of oil on a high heat.

6. Roll each egg in turn in the flour, egg, breadcrumbs, egg and breadcrumbs again. When the oil comes to about 150°C, or is hot enough that a breadcrumb sizzles and turns golden when dropped in, lower a batch of eggs in and cook for 1 minute. Scoop out on to the kitchen paper and season. Serve hot with the mayonnaise to dip.

Baked eggs, creamed corn and spinach

serves 4

4 ears of corn
2 tablespoons butter
1 tablespoon flour
2 teaspoons sugar
½–1 teaspoon salt
A whole nutmeg, to grate
200ml whole milk
250g spinach
2 tablespoons soured cream
4 eggs

I can't believe I lived so long in ignorance of the glorious existence of creamed corn – until the serendipitous day I stumbled across a video of a very jolly woman knocking some up in her Memphis kitchen. The internet is a wonderful place.

This version, using milk rather than cream, is a little less rich than hers, allowing the natural sweetness of the corn to take centre stage, ably backed up by a generous grating of nutmeg, an old friend to both spinach and eggs. It is an utterly delicious breakfast or brunch.

1. Remove the leaves from the corn if necessary, then stand one up on a chopping board and cut down its length to remove the kernels. Rotate and repeat until they're all stripped off, then tip these into a bowl and, holding the corn over the bowl, run the back of a knife down the stripped husks to squeeze out all the liquid. Repeat with the remaining ears.
2. Melt the butter in a medium saucepan and stir in the flour. Cook for a minute or so until it smells toasty, then stir in the sugar, salt, the corn and a generous grating of nutmeg. Stir to coat, cook for another minute, then stir in the milk.
3. Bring to a simmer, then turn the heat down low and cook, stirring regularly, for about 15–25 minutes, depending on how firm you like your corn. Meanwhile, heat the oven to 200°C/fan 180°C/gas 6.
4. Stir the spinach into the corn mixture and allow to wilt, then stir in the soured cream and check the seasoning. Spoon into four ovenproof dishes, or one large one. Crack an egg into a cup, make a divot in the corn and pour the egg into it. Repeat with the rest, then grate a little more nutmeg over the top and bake for 13–15 minutes, until the whites are set and the yolk is still runny inside.

Omelette farcie

serves 1, decadently

For the scrambled eggs:
3 eggs, lightly beaten
1 tablespoon butter
½ tablespoon chopped chives
2 teaspoons lumpfish or salmon
   roe (optional)

For the omelette:
A generous knob of butter
2 eggs, lightly beaten and
   seasoned

Yes, it's an omelette stuffed with eggs. What of it?

When I first read Daniel Boulud's recipe for this Gallic classic I couldn't believe my eyes – I made it for breakfast the very next day, just to see if such a thing was even possible, and was blown away by the clever contrast in textures, the ridiculously creamy, slow-cooked scramble spilling out of a firmer, fluffier jacket. When scaling it down, I reluctantly decided adding a third in the form of a rich hollandaise would be over-egging the pudding, so instead I've substituted salty little fish eggs.

1. To make the scrambled eggs, set a heatproof bowl about 4cm above a pan of gently simmering water. Add the eggs and whisk until they foam, then continue to stir until they come together into smooth, creamy scrambled eggs. Immediately take the bowl off the pan (it will be hot) and stir in the butter to stop them cooking any further, along with the chives.
2. To make the omelette, heat the butter in a small frying pan over a medium heat. Once the foam has died down, tip in the eggs and cook for about 20 seconds, until they start to set.
3. Using a spatula or fork, draw in the sides of the eggs to the centre while shaking the pan to redistribute the liquid to the edges. The omelette is done when still slightly runny in the middle.
4. Take off the heat, add the scrambled eggs and fold the two edges into the middle. Shake the pan so they roll together, then tilt it and turn your omelette on to a warm plate. Add a dollop of roe if using.

Rum flip

makes 1

300ml still cider
2 teaspoons soft brown sugar,
    or more according to taste
A grating of nutmeg
A good pinch of ground ginger
25ml rum (or more, as you see fit)
1 egg yolk

This is a very old recipe which would originally have been warmed with a red hot poker. Considerably less practical these days, the idea itself stands the test of time, a mix of fiery spices and spirits with sweet cider and brown sugar which gives mulled wine a serious run for its money. Feel free to use ale instead of cider, or whisky (or just about any other spirit) in place of the rum, as you like.

1. Warm the cider in a small pan until hot, but not simmering. Take off the heat, then stir in the sugar and spices to dissolve, followed by the rum. Taste and add more sugar or spice if necessary.
2. Whisk in the egg yolk, pour into a heatproof glass and serve (drink, obviously).

Pandan and coconut burnt creams

makes 4

4 pandan leaves
325ml coconut cream
3 egg yolks
50g caster sugar
2 tablespoons
    desiccated coconut
2 tablespoons
    demerara sugar

I first encountered the aromatic pandan leaf in Singapore, where I fell in love with its strikingly aromatic, almost soapy flavour. The pretty pale green colour the pandan essence gives these dairy-free custards is an added bonus.

You can get the leaves, either fresh or frozen, in oriental supermarkets (which should also stock various pandan-flavoured cakes and sweets to give you an idea of whether to invest), or online, but if you can't find them, or don't care for the stuff, you can replace it with any other flavour that goes with coconut: vanilla essence, for example, or lime zest would work well.

1. Heat the oven to 170°C/fan 150°C/gas 3. Cut the pandan leaves into smallish pieces, then blend with 50ml of water, using a stick or mini blender, to make a bright green liquid. Strain through a sieve and discard the solids.

2. Bring the coconut cream to a simmer in a small pan, adding the pandan liquid to taste (I like about 3 tablespoons). Whisk together the yolks and caster sugar in a heatproof bowl next to the hob.

3. Pour the hot cream on to the yolks, whisking constantly. Divide the mixture between four ramekins and bake in a bain-marie (roasting tin of water) for about 40 minutes, until set. Cool, then chill until set completely.

4. Heat the grill (unless you have a cook's blowtorch). Divide the coconut between the dishes and sprinkle the demerara sugar on top. Grill until the sugar is bubbling, then serve.

F

is for Fat

Until recently the culinary love that dared not speak its name, after several decades of self-denial we seem to finally be coming to our senses with regards to the benefits, both medical and otherwise, of a certain amount of fat in our diet. And thank God for that – the world would certainly be a poorer place without peanut butter, or duck fat roast potatoes.

But from a gastronomic point of view, fat has always been a good thing. Fat in food makes it rich and smooth, while food cooked in fat will be savoury and full of flavour. Fillet steaks and white fish have their place, of course, but think of the deeper joys of slow-cooked beef shin, braised until it melts from the bone, or oily salmon with brown bread and sweet, creamy butter.

There are few foodstuffs, however healthy, that aren't enhanced by fat, whether that's dal makhani laced with ghee and cream, or deep-fried tofu, hot and crisp, yielding to an almost panna-cotta-like softness within, or indeed a wholesome bowl of vegetable minestrone set off with a generous pour of green olive oil. Most of the flavour in meat comes from fat: try stripping all the fat from lean pieces of beef and lamb; you'll find it surprisingly hard to distinguish between them.

Humans, like all animals, have embraced fat from the get-go, and after the whole fire thing took off, it assumed an even greater importance as a cooking medium; vital if you weren't to burn that precious mammoth steak to a cinder. But in recent years, we've turned our back on millennia of pleasure, and given fat the cold shoulder. We do not seem to be any healthier for it.

Our bodies need fat to function. Somewhat amazingly, the human brain is almost 60 per cent fat. It is essential to the functioning of every cell in our bodies, from the workings of the immune system to the way our hair looks.

That said, not all fats are created equal; in fact, as anyone following a diet for the past forty years will be aware, there are a bewildering number of different fats out there, some of which are better for us than others. For the information below I am indebted to two very patient chemist friends.

The most common terms bandied about are saturated and unsaturated fats, though actually, as Jennifer McLagan points out in her excellent book *Fat*, 'there is no such thing as a completely saturated or completely unsaturated fat; every fat is a combination of both saturated and unsaturated fatty acids'.

In a very small, but rather dense nutshell, fats are made up of fatty acids, themselves chains of carbon atoms, with each carbon atom in the chain bonded to hydrogen atoms.

The difference between saturated and unsaturated fats lies in the arrangement of these atoms. In the carbon chains of unsaturated fatty acids, one or more of the carbon-carbon bonds can be a double bond. As each carbon atom can only be involved in four bonds in total, the carbon atoms involved in such a double bond can only thus be bound to one hydrogen atom, instead of two.

If there is one double bond in the fatty acid chain, the fat is monounsaturated; more than one and it's known as polyunsaturated. All the carbon-carbon bonds in saturated fatty acids, meanwhile, are single bonds, which leaves more room for hydrogen atoms along the chain.

(Omega-3 and -6 fatty acids, which are often singled out for special praise, have their double bonds as the third and sixth bonds from the end of the chain respectively. The body is unable to create these fatty acids itself, which is why they're so vital to our diet, and hence why we're always being urged to eat more oily fish and seeds.)

Fat facts

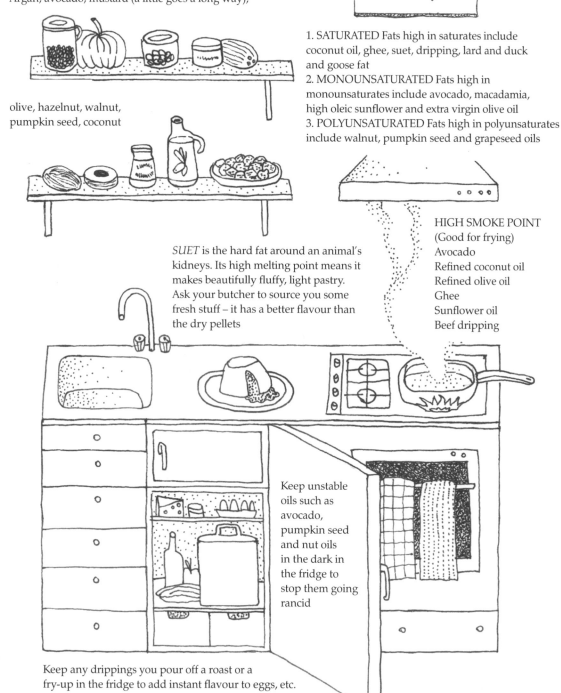

OILS THAT TASTE GREAT
Argan, avocado, mustard (a little goes a long way),

olive, hazelnut, walnut,
pumpkin seed, coconut

CHEMISTRY

1. SATURATED Fats high in saturates include coconut oil, ghee, suet, dripping, lard and duck and goose fat
2. MONOUNSATURATED Fats high in monounsaturates include avocado, macadamia, high oleic sunflower and extra virgin olive oil
3. POLYUNSATURATED Fats high in polyunsaturates include walnut, pumpkin seed and grapeseed oils

SUET is the hard fat around an animal's kidneys. Its high melting point means it makes beautifully fluffy, light pastry. Ask your butcher to source you some fresh stuff – it has a better flavour than the dry pellets

HIGH SMOKE POINT
(Good for frying)
Avocado
Refined coconut oil
Refined olive oil
Ghee
Sunflower oil
Beef dripping

Keep unstable oils such as avocado, pumpkin seed and nut oils in the dark in the fridge to stop them going rancid

Keep any drippings you pour off a roast or a fry-up in the fridge to add instant flavour to eggs, etc.

This is all important because these double bonds change the structure of the fat. Carbon-hydrogen bonds are less volatile than carbon-carbon bonds, which means that the more saturated fatty acids a fat contains, the more stable it is at room temperature, and the less likely it is to spoil.

Animal fats tend to be about half saturated fatty acids, as compared to only 15 per cent of vegetable fats, which is why lard is solid in the pantry and olive oil liquid. The more unsaturated the fat, the quicker it will go rancid on contact with air, microbes and so on; beef stays fresh for longer than white meats like chicken for the simple reason that it contains more saturated fat.

The third class of fats, which has only come to the attention of most of us relatively recently, so long have we been told that saturated fat is the enemy, is hydrogenated or trans fats. These do occur in low levels in nature, but the ones that make the headlines are vegetable fats that have been chemically altered to make them solid at room temperature, and improve their shelf life – 'hydrogenated' to turn some of the double bonds in the chain into single bonds, and add the associated missing hydrogen atoms. Unfortunately our body finds these hard to process in the normal way, and trans fats appear to raise the levels of undesirable cholesterol in the blood.

Fortunately, trans fats are not widely used in this country, but there is no obligation for manufacturers to highlight them on the label – the words hydrogenated or partially hydrogenated fats or oils should ring warning bells.

Sources of fat

The good news is that saturated fats, labelled as the enemy in the 1970s and 80s for their link to coronary heart disease, have largely been exonerated. Many people I know still cut the fat off chops, and regard the skin of a chicken with deep suspicion – goose fat may have been rehabilitated thanks to some good publicity from television cooks, but few would give house room to the more homely charms of dripping or lard.

Although studies are still inconclusive, more recent research seems to agree that the only fats associated with an increased risk of heart disease are those aforementioned trans fatty acids. Indeed, replacing fat in the diet with carbohydrates, as was once suggested by the diet lobby, seems to actually encourage weight gain. Because it takes the body a while to digest fat, it keeps us feeling fuller for longer, while carbohydrates, particularly the refined sort, like pasta and bread, prompt a short-term spike in sugar levels, followed by a crash – which is when, if you're anything like me, you reach for the snacks.

It seems that the old adage, a little of what you fancy does you good, holds true; while I'm not suggesting we all go completely Atkins, there is little evidence a low-fat regime is good for you. Instead, that boring thing, a balanced diet, with moderate amounts of both animal and vegetable fats, and without any trans fats, seems the way to go. So I hope you fancy a little of some of the recipes in this chapter.

See also: Vietnamese caramel and pork hotpot (page 42, Caramel), Duck fat garlic bread (page 98, Garlic), Salted brown butter and buttermilk ice cream (page 123, Ice), Pork rillettes with rhubarb chutney (page 258, Rhubarb).

Cultured butter

makes 1 pat (about 200g)

400ml double cream,
   at room temperature
2 tablespoons live natural
   yoghurt, at room temperature
½ teaspoon sea salt flakes
   (optional)

One of those things which shouldn't be worth making at home, but somehow is – not just for the magic of producing something so fundamental to our cooking in a quarter of an hour, but because it seems to taste better, especially if you seek out some really great cream (farmers' markets are a good source). Taking the time to culture (or ferment) it overnight is not strictly necessary, but will give the butter a more interesting, complex flavour. If you don't want to do this, omit the yoghurt and start at step 2.

Obviously once it's made you can add any extra flavourings you fancy at step 4 – herbs, chilli, sugar and spice, as you wish, but I'm not sure you can beat simple salt. The buttermilk left over is excellent in smoothies, or indeed the buckwheat pikelets on page 356.

1. Stir together the cream and yoghurt in the bowl of a stand mixer, then cover and leave in a warmish place for 8 hours. Check it at regular intervals after this – it's ready when the surface is bubbly and it smells faintly sour and tangy.
2. Whisk the mixture at a medium-low speed, scraping down the bowl as necessary, for about 8–10 minutes, until it separates into a solid, cottage-cheese-like mass (which will stick to the whisk) and a milky liquid. Alternatively you can put it into a large jar (much larger than the volume of cream) and shake it vigorously until it reaches this point, but it will take longer.
3. Drain the butter in a sieve set over a bowl to catch the buttermilk. Scoop it up and rinse it well under cold water to get rid of any remaining whey, which will cause it to spoil more quickly, then squeeze out any water.
4. If you're planning to add salt, do so now, kneading it into the butter until evenly distributed. Shape the butter into a pat, or put into a bowl, and refrigerate to firm it up a bit, or eat it immediately, toast optional.

Bacon refried beans

serves 4

200g dried pinto beans, soaked
    overnight
1½ onions
¼ teaspoon Mexican oregano
    (optional)
12 rashers of dry-cured streaky
    bacon, or 4 rashers and 50ml
    bacon drippings

Tinned refried beans are a vaguely guilty pleasure of mine, but these taste even better thanks to a goodly, and authentically Mexican, dollop of smoky pork fat. If you keep a pot by the stove for bacon drippings, as I do, you can use those instead, but cook some specially and you'll be left with a few rashers of crisp streaky to top.

1. Put the drained soaked beans into a large pan with the half onion and cover with plenty of cold water. Bring to the boil, skim off the scum, then turn down the heat and stir in the oregano if using. Simmer until very tender – about 2 hours, but the time varies wildly depending on the age of your beans, so check regularly. Don't allow the pan to boil too dry, as you'll be needing some cooking liquid later.
2. Meanwhile, if you don't have the benefit of a big pot of bacon drippings, put a large frying pan on a medium-low heat and line with a layer of bacon. Cook gently until golden brown on both sides, then tip into a sieve set over a bowl, making sure you get all the fat out of the pan. Repeat with the remaining bacon; you should have a generous amount of bacon fat in the bowl by the end. Don't bother to wash up the frying pan.
3. When the beans are very tender, drain, reserving about 250ml of the cooking liquid. Mash them well along with a splash of liquid, or use a stick blender if you'd prefer a smoother texture. Finely chop the remaining onion.
4. Melt a generous few spoonfuls of bacon fat in the frying pan over a medium-high heat and add the chopped onion. Fry until soft, then add the beans. Fry for a minute or so, stirring, then stir in the reserved cooking liquid until you have a loose-ish paste – you probably won't need it all. Season to taste.
5. Finely chop 4 of the bacon rashers and stir into the pan just before serving, along with another spoonful of bacon fat if you're feeling authentic/reckless.

Red-braised pork

serves 6 with other dishes

1kg pork belly, skin on
Groundnut oil
1½ star anise
2 cloves
1 cinnamon stick
½ teaspoon Sichuan
    peppercorns (optional)
4 garlic cloves, squashed with
    the back of a knife
A large chunk of ginger (about
    60g), squashed with the back
    of a knife
4 spring onions, cut into
    3–4 pieces each
50g soft light brown sugar
2 tablespoons dark soy sauce
4 tablespoons Shaoxing
    rice wine
1½ teaspoons salt

I first came across this idea when I was putting together
a selection of *Guardian* reader recipes for the Chinese
New Year celebrations – and was immediately struck by
its simplicity, and the joy of producing something so rich
and intensely flavoured with so little effort. OK, so it has
a fair few ingredients, but none of them are hard to find,
with the possible exception of the peculiarly tingly Sichuan
peppercorns, and there's little more to do than simply stick
them all into a pan, cover and wait for heat and time to work
their magic.

Fatty and gorgeously sticky and savoury, this is best served
with plain rice and some simply steamed greens. Like many
slow-cooked dishes, it reheats well – you'll probably need to
add a splash of hot water as you do so, but don't be tempted
to spoon off all the fat.

1. Bring a large pot of salted water to the boil, then add the pork, in
one piece if possible, and blanch for 4 minutes. Drain well and cut into
chunks approximately 4 x 4cm.
2. Heat a good splash of oil in a wide, lidded pan over a high flame until
it begins to smoke, then sauté the pork in batches for a couple of minutes
until it starts to brown.
3. Lightly bruise the spices in a pestle and mortar, then add to the
pan with the last batch of pork. Fry for 30 seconds, stirring, then add
the garlic, ginger and onions. Finally stir in 600ml of water and the
remaining ingredients, scraping the bottom of the pan to deglaze.
4. Replace the rest of the pork and bring the pan to a simmer, then
turn down the heat and cook, partially covered, for about 90 minutes
to 2 hours, until the pork is very tender and the sauce well reduced
and clinging to the meat. (Although this isn't a dish with a great deal
of sauce, keep an eye on it and stir in a little more hot water if the pork
starts to stick.)

Lamb 'porchetta' with salsa verde

serves 6

2 tablespoons black
  peppercorns
½–1 tablespoon red chilli flakes
  (I use mild *pul biber*, or
  Aleppo pepper, but if you
  use another chilli, you may
  want to err on the side
  of caution)
3 tablespoons fennel seeds
1.5kg boned lamb breast
  (probably 2 or 3)
6 garlic cloves, crushed
4 tablespoons chopped thyme
  and rosemary
½ teaspoon bicarbonate
  of soda

For the salsa verde:
1 large bunch of basil
1 large bunch of flat-leaf
  parsley
6 anchovies (rinsed if
  packed in salt)
2 tablespoons capers
  (rinsed if packed in salt)
1 garlic clove, crushed
Juice of ½ a lemon
1 teaspoon Dijon mustard
Olive oil

You don't see a lot of lamb breast around, so if you're not familiar with it, the best way to think of it is as the ruminant equivalent of pork belly – fatty, yes, but cooked right, utterly melt-in-the-mouth delicious.

As this recipe shows, pretty much anything you can do with belly you can do with breast, and actually, I think the garlicky, herbaceous flavours of a classic rolled porchetta work even better with the sweet mellow flavour of lamb, especially when offset by a zingy green sauce. It remains extraordinarily good value, and any decent butcher should be able to get you some without too much trouble.

1. Between 16 and 48 hours before you want to eat the lamb, depending on how long you have to marinate it, put the peppercorns, chilli flakes and fennel seeds into a hot dry frying pan and toast for a minute or so or until aromatic. Allow to cool slightly, then crush in a pestle and mortar.
2. Lay the lamb breast or breasts out flat on a board, fat side down, and salt generously. Spread over the crushed garlic (unfortunately, fingers are the easiest thing to use – rub them with lemon juice afterwards to help neutralize the smell), followed by the crushed spices and chopped herbs. Roll up tightly from one of the short ends and tie with string in several places. Rub the skin with bicarbonate of soda and a little more salt, then refrigerate overnight, or for up to 48 hours.
3. Take the meat out of the fridge an hour or so before you want to cook it, to bring it up to room temperature. Heat the oven to 240°C/fan 220°C/gas 9 and roast the lamb for about 30 minutes, until golden, then turn down the heat to 170°C/fan 150°C/gas 3 and roast for a further 2–2½ hours, or until the meat is very tender. Rest for at least 20 minutes in a warm place.

4. To make the salsa verde, whiz the herbs, anchovies, capers and garlic up in a food processor (or roughly chop and then pound in a pestle and mortar if you're feeling more energetic), then beat in the lemon juice and mustard, followed by enough olive oil to make a thick sauce – it doesn't need to be super smooth. Taste and season or add more lemon juice if necessary.

5. Cut the lamb into thick slices and serve with the salsa verde.

Bourbon and bacon butter

makes 125g

2 rashers of smoked streaky bacon
120g butter, at room temperature
1–2 tablespoons bourbon
1 teaspoon soft light brown sugar

It's hard to improve on good butter, but if you're going to try, you may as well go all-out: Parmesan and garlic, anchovies and chilli, or this smoky sweet all-American version, which is particularly great on barbecued corn and, I must confess, also works disgustingly well on toast.

1. Dry fry the bacon until crisp, then drain, reserving both the bacon and the liquid fat from the pan. Chop the bacon into small pieces.

2. Once the fat has cooled slightly, beat 1 teaspoon into the butter, plus the bourbon and sugar. Taste, season and add a little more booze, or indeed sugar, then once you're happy with the flavour, stir in the bacon pieces until evenly distributed.

3. Chill until ready to serve (you can roll it into a cylinder before chilling if you like the idea of neat little discs of butter, but I'm happy just to pass the bowl round at the table for people to scoop as much or as little as they want).

Coconut ice magic

serves 6

65g dark chocolate, chopped
50g coconut oil
2 tablespoons golden syrup
    (optional)
A generous pinch of salt

Anyone who grew up in 1970s and 80s Britain will have fond memories of Bird's Ice Magic, the sweet gooey sauce that set to a brittle shell on contact with cheap vanilla ice cream, just right for shattering with an aggressively wielded teaspoon.

Sadly it seems it was just too magic for the market, and it seems to have disappeared from shelves, along with its almost equally thrilling squeezy cone-shaped bottle – but never fear, because help is at hand from an unlikely source.

Extra virgin coconut oil may not have been a kitchen staple in the 1980s, but its high melting point means it hardens as it cools – which is exactly what we want here. For the sweet flavour of the original, albeit with a totally tropical coconut taste, add a little golden syrup – if you want to pretend sophistication, leave it out.

1. Melt all the ingredients together in a heatproof bowl set over a pan of simmering water, stirring to combine.
2. Pour into a jug and serve with ice cream – pour over while warm, and, within 30 seconds, it should have set to a shell.

G

is for Garlic

I feel blessed to be born in an age where it's socially acceptable to indulge in a love of garlic. I probably wouldn't risk it on a first date or just before a job interview, but at least few British people these days would claim, like the eighteenth-century Scottish writer Tobias Smollett, to be 'grievously offended' by the stuff.

How anyone, literary lion or not, could be blind to its charms is beyond me; juicy and almost sweet in its fresh green form, sharp and emphatically savoury when dried, garlic has a flavour more complex than the onion, more pungent and spicy than the chive or the leek, and somehow more addictive than the rest of the family put together – the more you eat, in my experience, the more you crave.

But garlic phobia is not a peculiarly British, or indeed even a modern complaint; though it was much eaten in the ancient world for its medicinal qualities, there seems to have been a rather aristocratic disdain for its powerful odour. The Roman poet Horace describes garlic as 'more baneful than hemlock' in his *Odes*, while Pliny warmly recommends it . . . for repelling scorpions, snakes and 'every kind of beast'.

Worse was to come: by the Middle Ages, garlic, a notably pungent bulb even in a memorably pungent age, stood accused of encouraging intemperance and lechery, and the sixteenth-century herbalist John Gerard claimed that consumption 'ingendreth naughty and sharpe bloud'.

Indeed, garlic did not find any sort of popularity in this country until the latter half of the twentieth century, with John Evelyn declaring in 1699 it was fit only for 'rustic northerns' thanks to its 'intolerable rankness . . . 'tis not for ladies palates, nor those who court them', and Mrs Beeton including it in just one recipe, for mango chutney, followed by a note describing garlic as the most 'acrimonious in its taste of the whole of the alliaceous tribe'.

It wasn't until we began to travel more widely in the 1960s, bringing the Mediterranean flavours of our holidays home with us, that garlic began to make inroads into the British kitchen. It is also, of course, a key ingredient in the Asian cookery we took to our hearts around the same time, though it tends to be used in conjunction with other spices rather than as the star attraction.

Tolerance for garlic, like chilli, is a very personal thing, and some people seem to be able to take far more of it than others. When following other people's recipes I generally add more than they suggest, and you should feel free to adjust my quantities according to your own taste.

NB: for wild garlic, a related plant with a similar flavour, see W is for Wild.

Chemistry

Interestingly, garlic does not smell until it is cut – breaking the cell membranes brings an enzyme called alliinase into contact with a sulfoxide called alliin, and the two combine to create alliicin, which is responsible for garlic's pungent scent. This explains the mysterious phenomenon by which crushed garlic smells far more strongly than its sliced or chopped counterpart; the more membranes are destroyed, the more allicin is produced.

These allicin molecules are highly volatile, and once released change readily into other organic, sulphurous compounds, including those responsible for garlic's many miraculous qualities, for example its antibacterial and anti-clotting properties. Though we rarely consume enough to think of it counting towards our daily intake of fruit and vegetables, garlic is also a good source of vitamins B1 and C.

Buying and storing

Though most of us don't imagine cultivated garlic having a season because we generally eat it dried, the milder green sort, known as 'wet garlic', appears in May, with the main crop being pulled from July.

The two are the same thing at different stages of development (wet garlic is the immature bulb, harvested before the cloves have had a chance to form completely) and can be used pretty interchangeably, but it's nice to take advantage of the former's sweeter, more delicate flavour by pairing it with easily overwhelmed ingredients like fresh cheeses, eggs and salads. The comically large elephant garlic, meanwhile, which you might sometimes see at markets, is actually a kind of leek, which explains its muted flavour.

When buying garlic, look for firm heads with plump cloves, avoiding any with green tips that suggest they have started to sprout, and store them in a cool dry place to discourage this.

Confit garlic, thyme and Parmesan tart

**makes a 22cm tart
(serves 6–8)**

240ml milk
240ml double cream
3 eggs, beaten
120g Parmesan, finely grated
2 bushy sprigs of thyme, leaves
    only, plus an extra sprig for
    garnish

For the confit garlic:
2 heads of garlic
250ml olive oil

*For the herb pastry (or use 200g
ready-made shortcrust):*
120g plain flour
60g cold butter, finely diced
¼ teaspoon fine salt
½ teaspoon herbes de
    Provence or dried thyme and
    rosemary
3 tablespoons ice-cold water

Garlic, slow cooked in oil, is a remarkable thing – the raw sharpness completely melts away, leaving a soft, caramelized, even toffeeish sweetness that needs something savoury to play off. Hopelessly wobbly and rich, this Parmesan custard is the perfect foil. It makes a lovely lunch, served with a plain green salad.

1. Peel the garlic cloves (the best way to do this in quantity is to put the separated cloves into a large bowl and invert a similarly-sized bowl over the top to make a lid, or put them in a large lidded saucepan or jar, and shake the bejesus out of them), then put them into a small pan with the oil. Bring to just below a simmer, then turn down the heat and cook gently for half an hour. Strain into a bowl so they stop cooking, then chill immediately (please don't ignore this – the refrigeration is important if you want to be sure of avoiding any botulism growth on the garlic). The leftover oil makes great salad dressing.

2. Make the pastry by whizzing together the flour and butter to make coarse crumbs, then add the salt, herbs and just enough icy water to bring it together into a dough; you'll probably need about 2 tablespoons. Wrap well and chill for at least 30 minutes.

3. Heat the oven to 200°C/fan 180°C/gas 6. Grease a 22cm tart tin, put it on a baking tray and roll out the pastry on a lightly floured surface until large enough to line the tin. Gently press it in, prick the base a few times with a fork, then line with baking paper or foil and baking beans, and blind bake for 15 minutes.

4. Remove the paper and beans and bake for another 5 minutes until golden. Take out of the oven and turn the heat down to 180°C/fan 160°C/gas 4.

5. Whisk together the filling ingredients and season lightly. Arrange half the garlic on the base of the tart, then put the baking tray with the tart on it back into the oven and pour the filling into the pastry. Bake for 20 minutes, then push the remaining garlic into the setting tart, put back into the oven and bake for 25–30 more minutes, until set but slightly wobbly, checking its progress regularly after 15 minutes. Allow to cool for at least 20 minutes before serving with a sprig of thyme snipped on top.

Hot and sour seafood soup with black garlic aïoli

serves 4

8 raw shell-on king prawns
A dash of oil
1.5 litres good fish stock,
    not too strong
1 long red dried chilli
4 stalks of lemongrass, trimmed
4 kaffir lime leaves, torn
3 thick slices of galangal
2 Thai shallots, roughly
    chopped
A small bunch of coriander,
    with roots if possible
1 tablespoon palm sugar
24 mussels, cleaned
200g cod cheeks (or other
    meaty white fish), cut
    into chunks
2 medium squid, cut into
    bite-sized pieces and lightly
    scored
2–5 red bird's-eye chillies, finely
    sliced
3 tablespoons lime juice,
    or to taste
2 tablespoons fish sauce,
    or to taste

For the black garlic aïoli:
1 egg yolk
2 cloves of black garlic
¼ teaspoon coarse salt
150ml groundnut or other
    neutral oil

A kind of south-east Asian take on the classic Provençal bouillabaisse, this zingy Thai seafood soup is paired with a sauce made with sweet, richly flavoured aged black garlic in place of the usual rouille. Defiantly spicy and sour, shot through with the funky flavour of the garlic, consider this a wake-up call to your palate. Black garlic can be found in Asian supermarkets, fancy grocers, and very easily online.

1. To make the aïoli, mash together the egg yolk, garlic and salt in a pestle and mortar until smooth, then add 2 teaspoons of tepid water and mash to incorporate.

2. Transfer to a larger bowl and very gradually whisk in the oil (you can also do this in a food processor if you prefer) until you have a smooth emulsion. Taste and adjust the seasoning if necessary.

3. Shell and devein the prawns, saving the shells, and set the meat aside. Heat the oil in a large pan on a medium heat and fry the shells until pink. Add the stock and dried chilli, bring to the boil, simmer for a couple of minutes, then strain and discard the shells, replacing the chilli.

4. Meanwhile, bruise the lemongrass, lime leaves, galangal and shallots, plus the roots of the coriander if you have them, in a pestle and mortar. Finely chop the coriander leaves.

5. Add the contents of mortar to the stock along with the sugar and simmer for a minute or so.

6. Add the mussels to the pan and cover for a couple of minutes. Once they have begun opening, add the fish and squid and cook for a minute or so, then take off the heat.

7. Add the bird's-eye chillies, plus lime juice and fish sauce to taste. Garnish with the black garlic aïoli and the coriander leaves.

Brined and slow-cooked lamb with flageolet beans, white wine and garlic

serves 6

1 large lamb shoulder,
    about 2kg
500g dried flageolet beans
1 head of garlic
1 lemon
2 rosemary sprigs, bruised with
    the back of a knife
400ml white wine
500ml chicken stock

For the brine:
350g coarse sea salt
225g sugar
4 garlic cloves, peeled and
    squashed with the back
    of a knife
2 rosemary sprigs, bruised with
    the back of a knife

Like cassoulet? Then you'll love this. Minus the duck fat and the sausage, it's a (slightly) lighter take on that south-western French classic.

You don't have to brine the lamb beforehand if you're pressed for time, but I'd recommend it for the infusion of savoury flavour it gives the dish.

1. Put the salt and sugar into a very large pan with 2 litres of cold water. Bring to a simmer, stirring to dissolve, then add the garlic and rosemary and allow to cool. Add another 2 litres of water and the lamb (or transfer to a larger container if necessary), and refrigerate for between 24 and 48 hours, turning occasionally.

2. The night before you want to cook, soak the beans in water.

3. Take the lamb out of the fridge, drain it and bring it to room temperature. Pat dry with kitchen towel. Drain the beans and put into a large pan. Cover with cold water and bring to the boil. Skim off the scum from the top, and simmer for about 30–40 minutes, until just tender – they'll cook further in the oven.

4. Meanwhile, heat the oven to 250°C/fan 230°C/gas 10 (or your oven's hottest temperature if lower). Put the lamb into a roasting tin and bake for 30 minutes, until the fat is golden.

5. Drain the beans. Take the lamb out of the oven and turn it down to 160°C/fan 140°C/gas 3. Put the lamb into a lidded, flameproof casserole dish just big enough to hold it, and cover with the beans. Cut the head of garlic in half laterally and push into the beans, cut sides down, then squeeze the lemon in and add the cut halves to the beans along with the rosemary. Pour over the wine and stock, which should come just to the top of the meat. Bring to a simmer on the hob, then cover and bake for about 3½–4 hours, until the lamb is soft enough to spoon, stirring occasionally to ensure the beans cook evenly.

6. Remove the lamb and spoon apart. Taste the seasoning of the beans and adjust if necessary, then serve the two together with a green salad.

Duck fat garlic bread

makes 1 loaf

4 garlic cloves
¼ teaspoon salt
100g duck fat, at cool room
    temperature (solid, but
    spreadable)
A small bunch of parsley, finely
    chopped
1 baguette

No groundbreaker here, but if you've got some decent duck fat left over, say, from the miso caramel roasted bird on page 41, this is an indecently delicious way to use it up.

1. Heat the oven to 200°C/fan 180°C/gas 6. Mash the garlic to a smooth paste with the salt, then blend with the fat and the parsley.
2. Put the bread on a large sheet of foil. Cut into slices, being careful not to go all the way through the bread. Carefully stuff the duck fat into the cuts – this is quite a messy job, but make sure you get it all in (if your hands stink afterwards, squeeze some lemon juice over them).
3. Wrap up and bake for 15 minutes, then open the foil a little and bake for another 5–8 minutes, until golden and crisp on top. Serve immediately.

Georgian griddled chicken on toast

serves 4 (with sides)

For the chicken:
2 plump garlic cloves, roughly
    chopped
1 teaspoon salt
½ teaspoon paprika
1 small chicken, about 1.2kg
2 large, thick (about 2cm) slices
    of robust chewy bread
25g butter

For the sauce:
4 garlic cloves, roughly
    chopped
¼ teaspoon salt
¼ teaspoon paprika
300ml chicken stock
A small bunch of coriander,
    roughly chopped

Crisp, smoky, buttery, this is a dish that demands to be eaten messily with fingers – I've stolen the brilliant idea of roasting the bird on toast, which I've never come across in a Georgian restaurant, from Stevie Parle's east London restaurant Rotorino. The combination of garlic and butter seemed too good an opportunity to pass up, and sodden with these, and the sticky, savoury chicken juices, it's a treat worth fighting over.

1. Mash the garlic, salt and paprika for the chicken to a paste in a pestle and mortar. Put the chicken, breast side up, on a board. Untie the legs and wings, and use a heavy knife to cut down the middle of the bird, through the backbone. Turn it over and use a meat mallet or some other heavy item to flatten the bird out. Rub all over with the paste, then cover and leave to marinate for at least an hour (if you want to leave it much longer, refrigerate it, but bring it back to room temperature before cooking).

2. Heat the oven to 200°C/fan 180°C/gas 6 and put a greased griddle pan or large frying pan on a medium-high heat. Find a heavy heatproof chipping board or baking tray and a couple of heavy heatproof objects (I use my pestle and mortar). Put the chicken on pestle and to the hot griddle, put the board on top and weight it down. Cook for 7 minutes, then turn over and repeat.

3. Put the bread in a roasting tin, put the chicken on top, then the butter on top of that. Roast for 10 minutes, then add the board or tray and weights and roast for about another 20 minutes, until cooked through, checking the colour of the juices after 15 minutes.

4. Set the chicken and bread aside to rest while you make the sauce. Mash the remaining garlic with the salt and paprika to make a paste. Heat the stock in a small pan along with any juices from the chicken (most will probably have gone into the bread), then whisk the garlic paste into it.

5. Carve the chicken and cut the bread into smaller pieces (unless there are just the two of you, in which case you can be greedy and have one slice each). Stir the coriander into the sauce and serve the two together.

Grand aïoli for heretics

serves 8

For the aïoli sauce:
1 head of garlic
2 egg yolks
450ml olive oil
Juice of ½ a lemon
A small bunch of basil

For the salt fish (optional):
900g thick fillet of pollack, cod
    or other firm white fish,
    skin on
Coarse salt, to cover the fish
1 bay leaf
Fronds from the top of the
    fennel (opposite)

For all their ancient reputation, many regions of France are disappointingly restrained with the garlic – I think of Michel Roux's half a clove rubbed around the gratin dish for dauphinoise – but down in the south, in Provence, they have no such qualms. This pungent sauce, which is served with everything from barbecued sausages to fish and warm salads, is also the centrepiece of the classic Provençal feast, the Grand Aïoli, flanked by an army of vegetables and seafood, simply cooked so as not to distract from its glorious garlickiness.

I love salt cod, but the other traditional accompaniments of green beans and carrots, beetroot and cauliflower have always seemed too northern to me – shaking off the yoke of tradition, I prefer more stereotypically Mediterranean vegetables, sweet fennel and peppers, even courgette and aubergine batons, plus a few big pink nutty prawns for good measure.

You, however, can use whatever you like; I've given a few ideas opposite, but the sauce is the point here. I've also taken the liberty of adding basil and a little lemon juice to it, which is definitely against the rules, but gives it a gorgeous green colour, and a slightly peppery, fresh flavour. Be warned, however, it's still very, very garlicky.

1. If you're making the salt fish, 48 hours before you want to eat, find a dish just large enough to hold it. Cover the base of the dish with 1cm of coarse salt, then lay the fish on top. Add another centimetre of salt, then cover and refrigerate for 24 hours.
2. Rinse the fish well, discarding the brine, then put into a large bowl of cold water and leave to soak for 24 hours, changing the water three times during that time. (If using bought salt cod, start by rinsing and soaking it.)

To accompany (as desired):

16 small new potatoes, boiled
 in their skins

2 red peppers, deseeded,
 brushed with a little oil and
 charred on a hot griddle until
 soft and blackened

2 heads of fennel, cut into
 wedges and chargrilled
 as above

2 courgettes, cut into strips and
 chargrilled as above

16 quail's eggs, hard-boiled
 (put into a pan of cold water,
 bring to the boil, simmer
 for 2½ minutes, then run
 under cold water)

8 large ripe tomatoes

800g large cooked prawns

1 baguette

3. To make the aïoli, peel the garlic and pound to a smooth paste in a pestle and mortar with a hefty pinch of salt. Add the egg yolks, one at a time, and pound to combine. If you're feeling energetic, you can add the oil, very gradually, in the same way, but at this point I prefer to transfer the mixture into a large clean bowl and use electric beaters, whisking in the oil little by little until you have a thick mayonnaise.

4. Add the lemon juice and enough warm water to give a thick but creamy dipping consistency. Roughly chop the basil, then add to the aïoli and use a hand-held mixer to whiz to a vibrant green. Check the seasoning.

5. Put the salt fish into a wide pan and just cover with cold water. Add the bay leaf and fennel tops, then bring gently to the boil. Cover the pan, take off the heat, and leave the fish to poach for 15 minutes before taking it out of the water, removing the skin and flaking the flesh into large chunks.

6. Serve the aïoli sauce as the centrepiece of a platter, flanked by potatoes, peppers, fennel, courgettes, quail's eggs, tomatoes, prawns and salt cod, with the baguette on the table too for everyone to tear into as desired.

H

is for Hot

You can't beat a bit of heat: English mustard spread so thickly on a bacon sandwich that the first bite makes you sneeze, the sinus-cleansing satisfaction of a Sichuan chilli chicken or the sour buzz of a pickled jalapeño with a cold beer – there's something about the sensation that reminds you you're alive. It's the reason I slosh sriracha on a hangover breakfast with such abandon, or crave tom yum when I'm feeling under the weather; heat is a sharp kick to the palate.

Of course, you can't avoid the fact that said wake-up call comes in the form of pain – childhood memories of being fed 'green beans' by my brother at the local Indian restaurant are burned deeply into my psyche. A taste for heat is not the same as a taste for sugar, or fat – heat doesn't register with our taste buds, but with pain receptors on our tongues; we're the only animal known to seek out danger or discomfort for kicks, whether that comes in the form of an insanely spicy curry or a insanely dangerous base jumping holiday.

Although I'm secretly quite proud of my tolerance for chilli (I once ate an entire bhut jolokia, at that time the world's hottest variety, and felt mildly euphoric for a full twenty minutes after I stopped crying), I'm not one of those perverts who seek out foods just for their heat; for me, the spice has to be justified by flavour.

Though capsaicin, the compound responsible for the feeling of heat, is flavourless by itself, chillies, like any fruit, do have a taste; they can be sweet or smoky, grassy or citrussy, and which variety you choose has a great bearing on the character of the final dish.

Those crazier, often American, 'hot sauces' such as Grim Reaper, 100% Pain or Ass Blaster which are pure capsaicin are, to my mind, as pointless as an artificial sweetener – there's no flavour there, just burn.

If you need any more reason to avoid products that come with a pipette and a safety warning, remember that synthetic capsaicin is often used in self-defence pepper sprays, which should be some indication that it's not a good thing to ingest, mugger or not.

Chilli immunity

It's often thought that chillies are something we can develop a tolerance for; after all, children from all cultures react badly to early experiences of them, however spicy the food around them. In fact, studies focusing on Mexicans and Americans found little correlation between either age or custom and tolerance for capsaicin – the Mexicans who ate hot food regularly didn't seem any less sensitive to the pain of the heat, they just enjoyed the sensation more. You grow to love the burn, in other words. This chapter should help.

Chilli first aid

As capsaicin isn't very soluble in water, cold drinks are only helpful if you hold them in the mouth to cool down the troubled receptors – they won't wash the stuff away. Roughly textured foods, like rice crackers or crusty bread, will distract the tongue from its predicament. And, from personal experience, I took on the bhut jolokia with a tableful of thick Turkish yoghurt and flatbreads, and came out alive.

The science of heat

Capsaicin, an irritant alkaloid, is mostly concentrated in the placental tissues of the fruit – which is a weird, if biologically accurate way of describing the soft pale stringy stuff that the seeds are attached to – though clearly it's also present in the rest of the flesh, or a carefully trimmed chilli would have no heat at all.

It's made up of at least five different chemical components that hit the tongue in different places, so what starts as a sharp burn in the throat will progress to a less intense, but lingering heat on the tongue.

Capsaicin triggers a response in receptors on the tongue similar to that of heat – so although the flesh isn't actually burning, or indeed damaged at all, the brain is tricked into thinking it is. This is why, despite the searing sensation, your mouth remains as puzzlingly cool as ever.

It's almost impossible to judge the potential heat of an individual fruit before you tuck in, though gently nibbling on the pointed end, the mildest part, will give you some idea. The heat will vary from season to season, soil to soil, and even among the fruits hanging on the same plant at the same time, depending on how ripe they are, so chillies really are a game of chance.

Hot dry weather increases capsaicin production, which begins at pollination and stops when the fruit begins to ripen, which means that, contrary to popular belief, chillies are hottest at about the time they start to change colour from green to red or yellow.

Chilli heat is traditionally measured on the Scoville scale, which is based on how far a chilli extract has to be diluted with sugar water before tasters can no longer detect it in the liquid. It has largely been replaced with less subjective methods among the scientific community, but is still commonly cited in culinary circles.

See also: Hot and sour seafood soup with black garlic aïoli (page 96, Garlic), Spicy peanut butter noodles with sprouting broccoli (page 196, Noodles), Turkey mole poblano (page 346, Xmas).

Six useful chillies

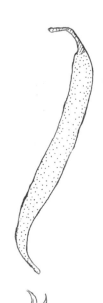

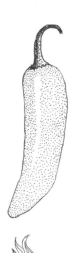

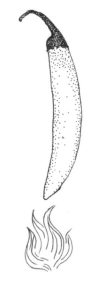

JALAPEÑO
red / green / 5–9 cm
mild / medium
(2,500–8,000 sco)
grassy flavour
good all-rounder
sturdy, suitable for stuffing

FINGER CHILLI
red / green / up to 10 cm
mild / medium
(5,000–10,000 sco)
fresh sharp flavour
used a lot in Indian cooking

SERRANO
red / green / 2.5–5 cm
medium
(5,000–20,000 sco)
sweet flavour
excellent in salsa

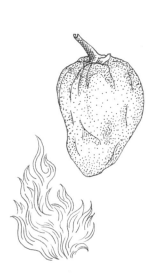

BIRD'S-EYE
red / green / 2–3 cm
hot
(100,000–225,000 sco)
fruity flavour
south-east Asian

SCOTCH BONNET
green / yellow /
orange / red / 2–5 cm
very hot
(100,000–350,000 sco)
just right for jerk

HABANERO
similar appearance and
heat to Scotch Bonnet
fruity flavour
popular in
Latin America

Blackened jalapeño and avocado slaw

serves 4–6

1 large raw beetroot, peeled
2 large carrots, peeled
3 limes
½ teaspoon salt
3–5 green jalapeño chillies
   (depending on heat
   tolerance)
3 spring onions
2 garlic cloves, unpeeled
1 ripe avocado
A small bunch of coriander

Slaw, in this case, because there's no cabbage involved – sweet beetroot and carrot just seemed a more apt pairing with the zingy, creamy avocado dressing, but really you could use any thinly sliced vegetable that takes your fancy. Toss it all together before serving if it's more convenient, but I like the contrast between the colourful vegetables and the pale green dressing.

Jalapeños vary in heat, so I'd advise cooking five, then starting off with three in the dressing and tasting before adding more, unless you like a Russian roulette element to your salads.

1. Grate the beetroot and carrots and squeeze the limes over the top, along with ¼ teaspoon of salt.
2. Heat a dry griddle pan over a high heat until smoking, then cook the chillies, spring onions and garlic until well charred on all sides. When cool enough to handle, peel the garlic, trim and roughly chop the onions and trim and deseed the chillies.
3. Put these charred vegetables into a food processor with the avocado and whiz until smooth. Add the remaining salt and 60–75ml of cold water – just enough to bring it to the consistency of a thinnish mayonnaise. Season to taste.
4. Roughly chop the coriander and toss through the vegetables. Serve with the avocado sauce on the side for people to drizzle over at the table (see above).

Sweet sriracha cakes

makes about 30 squares

35g peanut butter
15g coconut oil
1 teaspoon fine sea salt
2 teaspoons chilli flakes
300g marshmallows
180g Special K or similar
   crunchy cereal
Oil, to grease
1 tablespoon sesame seeds
   (optional)
Sriracha or other hot
   sauce, to finish

This is a mash-up of those horribly addictive little chilli crackers sold in pubs, and the sticky treats popular at children's party teas. The sweet heat of the sriracha goes strangely well with the sugary marshmallows – in my experience, people are usually thrown by the first bite, and then several squares later are begging for them to be taken away. Excellent make-ahead no-cook party food to go with some ice-cold beer.

1. Put the peanut butter into a pan over a medium heat with the coconut oil. When they've both melted, stir together, then stir in the salt and chilli flakes. Add the marshmallows and heat, stirring regularly, until melted.
2. Meanwhile, put the cereal into a large bowl and lightly grease a small baking tin.
3. When the marshmallows have melted into a bubbling mass, pour this over the cereal and stir quickly to mix before it sets. Tip into the tin and press down with a lightly greased spatula or greased hands to flatten. Top with a sprinking of sesame seeds, if using, and leave to set.
4. Just before serving, drizzle artistically with sriracha and cut into small squares.

Red lentil and tomato soup with harissa

serves 4

2 tablespoons olive oil
1 red onion, finely chopped
2 garlic cloves, finely chopped
1 teaspoon cumin seeds
½ teaspoon ground cinnamon
200g red lentils
½ a tin of plum tomatoes,
    roughly chopped
1 litre chicken or vegetable
    stock
5 teaspoons harissa, or to
    taste
4 teaspoons plain
    yoghurt (optional)
Coriander, to garnish

Comfortingly thick, with a sucker punch of spice, this is one of the best winter soups in my repertoire, and surprisingly quick to put together. If you're feeling in need of some extra bolstering, a spoonful of plain yoghurt adds richness – and is a good way of remedying a heavy hand with the harissa.

1. Heat the oil in a large pan over a medium heat and add the onion. Cook for about 7 minutes until completely softened, then stir in the garlic and cumin seeds and cook for a further couple of minutes. Stir through the cinnamon and cook for another minute.
2. Stir in the lentils, followed by the tomatoes and their juice, mashing them well, and finally the stock. Bring to a simmer, then turn down the heat and cook for about 20 minutes, until the lentils have broken down completely and the soup is thick.
3. Stir in the harissa to taste; brands vary considerably in their heat, so do this very gradually until you reach the level that suits you, then season.
4. Serve with the yoghurt swirled on top, if you're using it, and the coriander roughly snipped over it.

Green chilli, New Mexico style

serves 4

6 green jalapeño chillies
    (or more if you want it
    smokin' hot)
400g tomatillos or 200g
    gooseberries
1 tablespoon lard or
    vegetable oil
800g boneless pork
    shoulder, diced
1 large onion, finely sliced

New Mexicans are passionate about their local Hatch chillies, which are sold fresh and green, or left to ripen to a rich mellow red, and sometimes dried – according to locals, the green version has a fruitier flavour, while the red boasts an earthier heat.

Sadly it's impossible to get them outside the Southwest, but charred jalapeños make a very decent substitute, and tomatillos, a relative of the Cape gooseberry, are easily found online. Surprisingly, however, the very British gooseberry makes a decent alternative – I promise, it works.

6 garlic cloves, crushed
2 teaspoons Mexican oregano
2 teaspoons ground cumin
2 teaspoons ground coriander
800ml chicken stock
A small bunch of coriander,
    roughly chopped

Good with all the things you'd usually serve chilli con carne with – rice, cornbread, tortillas, you know the drill. A dollop of soured cream wouldn't go amiss either.

1. Char the chillies and fresh tomatillos under a hot grill for about 10 minutes, turning, until blackened (if using tinned tomatillos or gooseberries, come to them in step 3). Set aside to cool. Heat the oven to 160°C/fan 140°C/gas 3.

2. Heat the fat in an ovenproof casserole over a medium-high heat. Brown the meat in batches, making sure not to overcrowd the pan. Set the meat aside and turn the heat down to medium.

3. Add the onion to the pan (you can add a little more fat if necessary) and soften. Meanwhile, deseed the chillies and roughly chop them and the tomatillos, fresh or tinned. If using gooseberries instead, top, tail and roughly chop.

4. Once the onion is soft, stir in the garlic, chillies and tomatillos or gooseberries and cook for a minute before adding the oregano, spices and a little more fat if necessary. Stir until fragrant, then return the meat to the pan and add the stock. Scrape the bottom and bring to a simmer, then cover and put into the oven for 1½–2 hours, until the meat can be cut with a fork.

5. Season to taste and allow to rest for at least 15 minutes before stirring in the coriander.

Lemongrass and chilli tofu

serves 2

350g firm tofu
2 teaspoons salt
1 stalk of lemongrass
2 bird's-eye chillies
2 garlic cloves
Oil, to fry

I admit, I'm not a heavy user of tofu (it's so often bland and spongy with oil) but in a higgledy-piggledy hip little restaurant in a suburb of Saigon with some friends, I had an epiphany. I can't remember why we ordered so out of character – perhaps the waiter recommended it? – but my God, when it came, crisp on the outside, creamily rich and soft within, and perfectly seasoned, the whole table was momentarily silenced.

I've never had anything as good since, which, as Vietnam isn't exactly round the corner, forced me to try and recreate it at home. I'm pretty pleased with the results – and I beg fellow tofu sceptics to give it a try. (It took me a while to twig just how gentle you have to be with tofu, but if yours does stick, or break up, don't worry, it will taste good, even if it looks like scrambled eggs.)

1. Cut the tofu into roughly 4cm chunks. Dissolve the salt in 500ml of hot water, then add the tofu and leave for 15 minutes.
2. Meanwhile, finely chop the inner part of the lemongrass stalk, discarding the tough outer leaves, and deseed the chillies. Finely chop these and the garlic.
3. Carefully lift the tofu out of the water (it's fragile stuff) on to a bed of kitchen towel and gently blot dry on both sides. Heat enough oil in a large frying pan or wok to come about a third of the way up the tofu chunks.
4. When the oil is shimmering, add the tofu. Leave for a couple of minutes, then gently turn one of the pieces; if it has a golden crust, flip the others, being very careful not to break them up or disturb the crust. A thin, flexible metal spatula is the ideal tool.
5. Sprinkle with the lemongrass, chilli and garlic and fry for a couple more minutes, then scoop out and serve immediately.

Meatball curry

serves 4

For the meatballs:
1 teaspoon coriander seeds
1 teaspoon cumin seeds
60g yellow split peas, soaked in cold water for at least an hour
400g minced lamb
1–2 small green chillies (to taste), deseeded and finely chopped
4 garlic cloves, minced
½ teaspoon salt
4 shallots, chopped
2 tablespoons poppy seeds
2 tablespoons fennel seeds

For the sauce:
2 tablespoons neutral oil
1 onion, finely chopped
5 garlic cloves, crushed
5cm piece of ginger, finely grated
½ teaspoon chilli powder
½ teaspoon turmeric
A small bunch of coriander, stems finely chopped
1 x 400g tin of plum tomatoes, roughly chopped
1 tablespoon tomato purée

Beef mince I can largely take or leave (hence its absence from this book), but I get really quite excited by the lamb and pork varieties, which contain enough fat and flavour to make them worth cooking with.

Kofta curry is one of those staples of home cooking which is puzzlingly hard to find in British Indian restaurants, which is all the more reason to make it at home. Spicy, juicy little meatballs in a rich tomato gravy – it's a familiar combination, but in this instance probably better served with flatbreads or rice than spaghetti.

1. Toast the coriander and cumin seeds in a hot dry pan until fragrant, then tip into a pestle and mortar. Allow to cool, then grind to a powder.
2. Drain the split peas and put them, along with ½ teaspoon of the coriander and cumin powder, into a food processor along with the remaining ingredients for the meatballs. Whiz until well combined. Heat a little oil in a frying pan and cook a bit of the mix to test the seasoning, adjusting if required. Roll the mixture into little meatballs and refrigerate to firm up if necessary.
3. Heat the oil in a wide frying pan over a medium-high heat until smoking, and cook the meatballs until nicely browned all round. Scoop out and set aside.
4. Turn the heat down and add the onion to the same pan. Cook, stirring, until soft and golden, then stir in the garlic and ginger. Cook for a couple of minutes then stir in the spices, including the remaining coriander and cumin mixture, and the chopped coriander stems.
5. Pour in the tomatoes and purée, and stir the bottom of the pan. Bring to a simmer, then cook until the oil just begins to separate around the edge of the pan. Put the meatballs back into the pan and cook, covered, for 30 minutes. Season the sauce to taste. Top with the coriander leaves, roughly chopped.

Mexican chilli chocolate mousse

serves 4

¼ teaspoon chipotle
    chilli flakes, plus extra to
    serve
½ teaspoon ground cinnamon
½ teaspoon ground nutmeg
½ teaspoon ground ginger
40g caster sugar
A pinch of salt
175g dark chocolate, broken
    into pieces
7 egg whites (or 14 tablespoons
    egg white if you buy it in
    a carton)

Ten years on, Oaxaca's vast Mercado 20 de Noviembre remains as vivid in my mind as ever. It's that kind of place. One of the things I remember making the biggest impression, aside from the wicker baskets of deep-fried grasshoppers that I never quite plucked up the courage to try, was the hot chocolate. Thick, and at once astonishingly sweet and powerfully bitter, the spices brought out the flavour of the cocoa like a dream. This is the mousse version.

A word of caution from one who's been there; though all egg-white mousses are beautifully light, you really do have to be quick when combining the ingredients in step 4, or the chocolate will seize. I keep extra ingredients on hand in case of such disaster.

1. Grind the chipotle flakes into a fine powder, then mix with the other spices, sugar and salt.
2. Put the chocolate into a heatproof bowl set over, but not touching, a pan of simmering water, and melt, stirring to help it along.
3. Meanwhile, whisk the egg whites in a large bowl until they hold soft peaks. Whisk in the spiced sugar to stiff peak stage, being careful not to overwhisk (if they droop, you'll have to start again).
4. Once the chocolate has melted, take the bowl off the pan and, working very quickly, vigorously whisk in a third of the whites; you need to do this as fast as possible or the chocolate will seize and harden – the mixture should be thick, but not dull or grainy.
5. Gently fold in the remaining egg whites with a large metal spoon until the mixture has no white streaks, being careful to keep as much air in as possible. Divide between four glasses or bowls and chill until ready to serve. Top with a few flakes of chilli for extra drama.

I

is for Ice

However old you get, or much you eat, ice cream retains the excitement of a special treat; something you'd be allowed on a summer's afternoon if you were really, really good, or if your mum was just too exhausted to say no to the prospect of five minutes' peace courtesy of the magic singing van.

It's delicious in the sweltering heat (which calls for a citrussy ice lolly rather than a full-on clotted cream number – the classic lemonade sparkle is my usual) but a rich, barely sweet, plain milk ice cream also makes a marvellous accompaniment to steamy, stodgy wintery desserts, like crumble, sticky toffee or Christmas pudding – it's all in the contrast between the textures and temperatures. In short, there is no wrong time to indulge in good ice cream (who am I kidding, I'll eat, and enjoy, a Mr Whippy if that's all that's going).

That said, though there are many, many excellent ice creams available to buy these days, they tend to come in disappointingly tiny tubs for the enthusiastic consumer, and unless you're lucky enough to live near a good ice cream parlour, the range of flavours tends to be fairly limited. Yes, I like chocolate, but I prefer rum, or fig, or avocado and lime, and if you're going to eat a big bowl of ice cream it ought to be one that you really, really want. Plus, it's easier to make than you might imagine.

Equipment

With the exception of kulfi and granita, all sorbets and ice creams require churning before their final freezing, to incorporate air into the mixture, or they will set like a house brick. I would highly recommend, if you have any interest at all in the subject, investing in an ice cream maker, preferably one with its own refrigeration unit, so you can churn the ice cream as it freezes. They're bulky, but make life so much easier that you're almost guaranteed to get more use out of one than the simpler, churn-only sort, and working on the price per wear principle I employ when trying to justify expensive clothing purchases to myself, this makes them better value.

That said, you can make ice creams and sorbets without them thanks to a method known as still freezing, which resembles that used for granita (although if you do it right, the results should be quite different). Chill the mixture before use, then pour it into a container large enough for the liquid inside to be about 4cm deep. Cover and freeze for an hour, then check at regular intervals; once it has frozen around the edge, use electric beaters, a food processor, or a very vigorously applied hand whisk, to beat it all back into a homogeneous slush, then refreeze. Repeat every hour (or however long it takes for the mixture to start solidifying again) for the next two hours, then leave undisturbed for at least another half an hour to set firm before serving.

See also: Poached plum crumble with blue cheese ice cream (page 34, Blue Cheese), Rhubarb gin granita (page 264, Rhubarb).

What's my ice?
A field identification guide

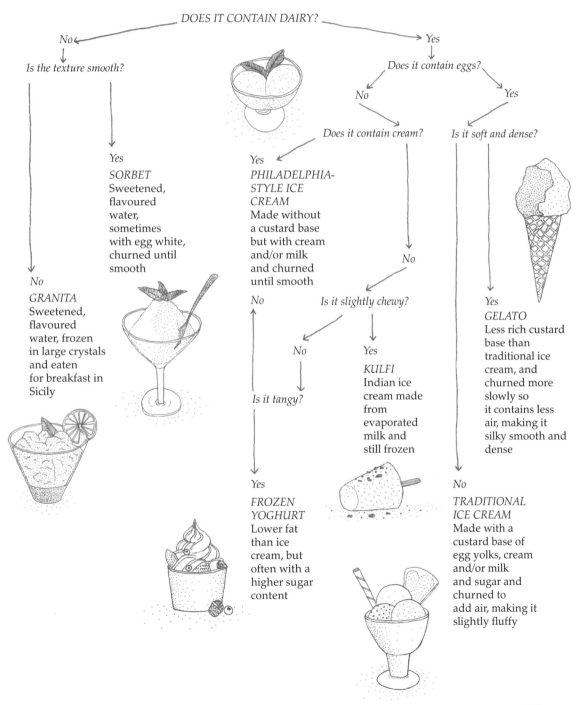

DOES IT CONTAIN DAIRY?

No

Is the texture smooth?

Yes

No

Yes
SORBET
Sweetened,
flavoured
water,
sometimes
with egg white,
churned until
smooth

No
GRANITA
Sweetened,
flavoured
water, frozen
in large crystals
and eaten
for breakfast in
Sicily

Yes

Does it contain eggs?

No

Does it contain cream?

Yes
PHILADELPHIA-
STYLE ICE
CREAM
Made without
a custard base
but with cream
and/or milk
and churned
until smooth

No

No

Is it slightly chewy?

No

Is it tangy?

Yes
FROZEN
YOGHURT
Lower fat
than ice
cream, but
often with a
higher sugar
content

Yes
KULFI
Indian ice
cream made
from
evaporated
milk and
still frozen

Yes

Is it soft and dense?

Yes
GELATO
Less rich custard
base than
traditional ice
cream, and
churned more
slowly so
it contains less
air, making it
silky smooth and
dense

No
TRADITIONAL
ICE CREAM
Made with a
custard base of
egg yolks, cream
and/or milk
and sugar and
churned to
add air, making it
slightly fluffy

Simple banana and peanut butter ice

**serves 2–4
(2 greedily, 4 more
moderately)**

4 very ripe bananas
2 tablespoons peanut butter
  (see intro)
A handful of salted roasted
  peanuts, to top (optional)

The idea is an old one, but it was such a revelation to me that I just had to share it in case anyone else was languishing in dark ignorance with regard to the miraculous properties of frozen bananas. This is so unbelievably creamy that you won't miss the dairy one bit – the peanut butter is optional, and can be left out or substituted with honey, chocolate spread or chips, nuts, spice, maple syrup . . . you get the idea. Ideal for children, and best eaten as soon as it's made rather than frozen.

NB: the bananas must be really ripe, or they won't be sweet enough.

1. Peel the bananas, chop into even slices, and freeze for at least 3 hours.
2. Put into a food processor and whiz until smooth and creamy (you'll probably need to keep sticking a spatula in to stop it clumping into large frozen balls, but it will happen, I promise).
3. Add the peanut butter, or any other flavourings, and a pinch of salt and whiz to incorporate, then serve with a few roughly chopped peanuts scattered on top, or, indeed, a generous drizzle of chocolate sauce (see the black and white shake, page 186).

Salted brown butter and buttermilk ice cream

serves 4

75g salted butter
4 egg yolks
50g soft light brown sugar
¼ teaspoon salt
200ml whole milk
200ml buttermilk

Butter ice cream may sound outrageous, but trust me, this is so, so good any scruples will fly out the window with the button on your trousers. (Although actually, unlike most ice creams, this is made with naturally low-fat buttermilk, which not only makes it not as bad as it could be, but supplies a tangy edge to cut through all that butter, almost like a frozen yoghurt. If you want to go to hell in a handbasket, however, replace it with cream.)

1. Melt the butter over a medium-low heat, then turn up the heat slightly and cook until, under the froth, the milk solids turn brown. Take off the heat immediately and pour into a bowl so it stops cooking. Set aside to cool to room temperature.
2. Once the butter is cool, whisk the egg yolks, sugar and salt together until they turn distinctly paler, and voluminous. Gradually whisk in the butter until it's all incorporated.
3. Heat the whole milk in a medium pan until it comes to a simmer, then pour, whisking all the time, into the yolk mix. Pour back into the pan and gently cook, stirring with a wooden spoon, until the mixture thickens sufficiently to coat the back of the spoon, and a finger drawn down the back leaves a distinct line.
4. Allow to cool until warm, then whisk in the buttermilk. Chill for at least 4 hours if you have time, then freeze in an ice cream maker, or according to the directions on page 120.

Avocado and double lime sorbet

serves 8

150g white sugar
12 kaffir lime leaves
2 large, ripe Hass avocados
Juice of 5 limes

The first time I tried avocado in a sweet context, I wasn't convinced. But after a Damascene moment with an avocado and chocolate mousse, I've come round to the idea – the creaminess of a really ripe example makes it the perfect base for all sorts of dairy-free desserts, and here it adds a richness to a sharp, zesty lime sorbet, aromatic with tropical lime leaves, without weighing it down. Indeed, though I love it on a hot summer's afternoon (occasionally with a shot of cold rum poured over the top), it would also make an excellent pre-pudding palate cleanser at a particularly fancy dinner party.

Lime leaves can be found in oriental supermarkets, often frozen. You can leave them out if you can't find them, but they do add a lovely perfume to the sorbet.

1. Put the sugar into a pan with 150ml of water and the lime leaves and heat gently until the sugar has dissolved. Simmer for about 5–8 minutes, until slightly thickened and syrupy. Set aside to cool completely.
2. Peel the avocados and scoop into a bowl. Add the lime juice and whiz to a smooth paste using a stick blender. Whisk in the cooled syrup, discarding the lime leaves, then churn and freeze in an ice cream maker, or according to the directions on page 120.

Rum punch ice cream

serves 8

6 egg yolks
360ml whipping cream
360ml whole milk
130g soft brown sugar
4 tablespoons rum
A whole nutmeg, to grate
A dash of bitters

On holiday a couple of years ago in Barbados, my then-boyfriend's father made it his solemn duty to sample the rum punch at every restaurant we visited – it seemed rude not to join him. The best versions were rich with the island's sweet spices, balanced with a deft dash of bitters, with a healthy helping of rum. John, this one's for you.

1. Whisk the egg yolks in a medium heatproof bowl. Pour half the cream into a larger heatproof bowl and put a sieve on top.
2. Put the milk, remaining cream and sugar into a medium pan and heat, stirring to dissolve the sugar, until it comes to a simmer. Pour the hot mixture on the egg yolks, whisking constantly, until well combined, then pour back into the pan on a medium-low heat.
3. Stir constantly until the mixture begins to thicken slightly – about 5–10 minutes – then strain through the sieve into the remaining cream. Stir in the rum, grated nutmeg, bitters and a pinch of salt, and cool, then chill for at least 4 hours if you have time.
4. Churn in an ice cream maker until frozen, then freeze until solid.

Simple persimmon, lime and ginger sorbet

serves 2–4

4 very ripe persimmons
2 tablespoons chilled
    coconut cream
3 tablespoons finely grated
    ginger
Juice of 3 limes
Honey, to taste (optional,
    see intro)

Another remarkably creamy fruity sorbet on the same lines as the classic banana version on page 122. Persimmons always remind me, oddly enough, of set custard (perhaps something to do with the contrast between the tough skin and the soft, honeyed, almost jellied flesh beneath), so it's unsurprising they make great ice cream.

Because they're so sweet, they can handle the zing of the lime juice and the heat of the ginger, which gives the whole thing a refreshing, south-east Asian feel – but do make sure your fruit is properly ripe; it should be really squashy, almost bursting from its skin.

(Such very sweet fruit shouldn't need any extra help in the form of honey, but as it's impossible to know until you've made the sorbet, it's wise to keep it at hand, just in case.)

1. Freeze the persimmons until solid (this will take a good few hours). Make sure the coconut cream is chilled.
2. Prepare the remaining ingredients and put them near the food processor. Holding each persimmon with a tea towel to save your fingers, peel it. Rinse the peeler in warm water every now and then to help.
3. Stand each fruit on its flatter, stalk end and cut it in half with a stout knife (I use a cleaver), then trim off the stalk and cut into large chunks.
4. Put the persimmon into a food processor and whiz until almost smooth, then add the coconut cream and ginger and whiz again.
5. Add two-thirds of the lime juice and taste; depending on the sweetness of your fruit, you may want to add more, or honey to taste. Once you're happy with the results, serve immediately.

Frangelico and espresso granita shots

serves 10

100g sugar
300ml strongish coffee
120ml Frangelico
Cold milk, to top

A friend of mine, who shall remain nameless, introduced me to an exciting new digestif in an Italian ski resort. It consisted of a shot of Jägermeister, the herbal liqueur favoured by ancient Austrian hunters and drunk stags, deposited in a glass of milk rather than the usual noxious energy drink. The bemused barman obligingly made up a round for us, but once they were down the hatch, he brought over his own version, which replaced the Jäger with a considerably less challenging shot of hazelnut liqueur. Only one of them inspired a recipe in this book, Gemma.

1. Put the sugar into a small pan with 300ml of water and bring to a simmer, stirring to dissolve the sugar. Simmer for about 5 minutes, until slightly syrupy, then take off the heat, stir in the coffee and Frangelico and allow to cool completely.
2. Pour the granita into a tray – it should be about 2cm deep. Unless you have very steady hands, you may find it easier to pour it out again into a jug once you're chosen the right tray, put the tray into the freezer, then pour the mixture in once it's in there.
3. Freeze for about an hour, then check – once it's started to solidify around the edges, scrape into the middle with a fork. Repeat roughly every 30 minutes for the next 2½ hours, until you have a dish full of large crunchy crystals.
4. To serve, scoop some into a small glass and pour over milk to top. Consume immediately.

Ricotta ice cream terrine with fig molasses

serves 8

*For the fig molasses
(or use about 75ml honey
and 6 semi-dried figs
for the finished ice):*
1kg dried figs

For the ice cream:
550ml whole milk
140g caster sugar
3 egg yolks
250g ricotta, drained

Ricotta and figs, drizzled with honey, are a match made in Mediterranean breakfast heaven – and one of the best ways to use any really ripe figs you're lucky enough to come across in this country, or indeed on your travels. But at that almost indecent stage of ripeness, when the syrupy juice runs from their thin skins, they don't travel well, so my consumption is largely of the dried sort. Here these are simmered into submission, creating a rich kind of figgy molasses in the process, which makes the perfect pairing with the mild, creamy cheese.

1. To make the molasses, put the figs into a large pan and cover with 2 litres of water. Bring to a simmer, then turn down the heat and simmer gently for 2 hours, keeping an eye on the water situation – it should reduce by about half, but if your figs are particularly parched, you may need to add more to stop them boiling dry.
2. After 2 hours the figs should be very soft. Place a sieve over a large bowl and drain, reserving the cooking liquid. Press as much liquid through as possible (alternatively you can use a piece of cheesecloth suspended over a bowl and squeeze them dry when they're cool enough).
3. Once you're content there's no more moisture left in the fruit, set the figs aside and pour the liquid into a pan. Bring to the boil, then turn down the heat slightly and reduce until syrupy but still liquid, the consistency of warm honey.
4. Meanwhile, make the custard base. Put the milk and half the sugar into a medium saucepan and bring to a simmer, stirring to dissolve the sugar. Whisk together the remaining sugar with the yolks in a heatproof bowl.

5. Pour the simmering milk on to the yolks, whisking all the time, then pour back into the pan and heat very gently, stirring with a wooden spoon, until it has thickened enough to thinly coat the back of the spoon (a line drawn with your finger should hold its shape).

6. Take off the heat and beat in the ricotta until smooth (I find a stick blender useful here) along with a pinch of salt. Allow to cool, chill for at least 4 hours if you have time, then churn in an ice cream maker until thick but not solid (or see the still freezing method on page 120).

7. Grease a small loaf tin roughly 16 x 9cm and line with clingfilm. Spoon a quarter of the ice cream into the base, then drizzle a layer of molasses over the top. Add another quarter of the ice cream, then stud a line of figs down the centre, remembering to snip off the hard little stalks if necessary. Add another quarter, drizzle with molasses, then add the rest and smooth the top. Drizzle with molasses and swirl with a skewer or toothpick.

8. Freeze for an hour to set the top, then wrap the clingfilm over the top and freeze for at least another 2 hours until solid. Turn out and remove the clingfilm to serve.

J

is for Junk

Not an entirely fair term, I've always thought, suggesting as it does food that's no better than rubbish – but one with a certain undeniable allure. Bombarded as we are by healthy eating messages, by the unwelcome certainty that we'd be doing ourselves a favour by opting for fruit salad instead of an ice cream, it's all the more wonderful sometimes to throw wisdom to the wind and choose the wrong thing.

Some of my favourite vices contain so many ingredients not found in nature that it would be pointless to try and recreate them at home – the kind of cheap, aggressively cheesy corn snacks that coat your fingers with orange powder, for example, or the frozen potato waffle (best appreciated topped with baked beans and cheese, should you be lost for a serving suggestion).

I'm not ashamed to admit I prefer Bird's custard to the egg yolk sort, and would always choose tinned tomato soup over the lumpy, oven-roasted, heirloom variety strewn with fresh basil, for all its Italian virtues.

Some of these tastes can be attributed to nostalgia, no doubt, though very few of these things were part of my diet growing up – the potato waffle, for example, retains the attraction of forbidden fruit, consumed only at other people's houses, where the distinctions between 'proper food' and rubbish were less closely observed. But largely I like them because they appeal to the basest of human tastes, that primitive part of us that craves salt and fat and sugar, an instant addictive calorie hit to keep us warm in the cold of the cave, and something interesting to break the monotony of chewy roots and stringy meat. I am by no means suggesting you should incorporate any of these recipes into your daily diet. They're for special occasions only. And nothing says special like Angel Delight, right?

See also: Salted almond toffee (page 21, Almond), Banoffee split (page 42, Caramel), Pecan, bourbon and salted caramel cookies (page 45, Caramel), Salted peanut caramel crispy cakes (page 46, Caramel), Walnut caramel cream pie (page 47, Caramel), Bacon refried beans (page 83, Fat), Coconut ice magic (page 89, Fat), Duck fat garlic bread (page 98, Garlic), Sweet sriracha cakes (page 111, Hot), Malted milk creams (page 183, Malt), Triple chocolate malt cake (page 185, Malt), Black and white shake (page 186, Malt), Coconut squid (page 210, Octopus), Maryland-style octopus sandwich (page 217, Octopus), Aloo tikki Scotch eggs (page 227, Potatoes), Caribbean milk punch jelly (page 248, Quiver), Crunchy soy-braised pig's tails (page 304, Umami), Marzipan violets (page 316, Violets), Wild garlic bread (page 331, Wild), Georgian cheesebread (khachapuri) (page 354, Yeast), Pissaladière (page 357, Yeast), Marmite and cheese mini doughnuts (page 359, Yeast), Chocolate orange cheesecake (page 374, Zest).

Sweet paprika cheesy chips

serves 4

700g sweet potato
(roughly 2 medium ones)
Sunflower or other neutral oil,
to grease
2 tablespoons cornflour
2 teaspoons smoked paprika
50g Parmesan or other hard
cheese, finely grated

If I learnt anything of lasting value at university, it was the beauty of chips and cheese. But these are a cut above those served at my favourite kebab van (sorry, Hassan) – sweet potato makes excellent fries, dense and fudgey, with crisp edges, and the perfect foil for salty savoury Parmesan and smoky paprika. Don't be tempted to skip the soaking process, or you'll end up with soggy fries.

1. Peel the sweet potatoes and cut into chips of your desired width. Put into a large bowl as you cut them and cover with plenty of cold water, then leave to soak for at least 30 minutes.
2. Heat the oven to 240°C/fan 220°C/gas 9. Once it has come to temperature, put two baking trays, well greased with oil, in there to heat. Meanwhile, drain the chips and dry thoroughly with a tea towel or kitchen roll. Dry the bowl too.
3. Put the dry chips back into the dry bowl and toss with the cornflour, paprika and a generous shake of salt until well coated. Divide between the trays, spreading them well out and tossing them as you add them, to coat with oil.
4. Bake for about 20–25 minutes, until crisp and beginning to blacken – keep an eye on them, as the exact time depends on both your oven and the thickness of your chips.
5. When they look almost ready, whip them out of the oven and transfer to an ovenproof serving dish. Sprinkle over the cheese and put back into the oven for 3–5 minutes, until melted, then serve immediately, while they're still finger-burningly hot.

Buttermilk onion rings

serves 4 (as a side)

1 large onion
280ml buttermilk
100ml milk
About 1.5 litres sunflower,
    vegetable or groundnut
    oil, to cook
80g flour
20g cornmeal (or use 100g
    flour)
1 teaspoon black onion seeds
1 teaspoon smoked paprika
½ teaspoon salt

Who doesn't love onion rings? Even when they're bad they're good, which makes these ones out of this world. The buttermilk tames some of the fire of the onion – ordinary milk will give much the same result, though with less tang – while the cornmeal brings crunch to the trashy party in your mouth.

1. Slice the onion into thickish rings (½–1cm) and separate them. Put them into a bowl with the buttermilk and milk and leave to soak for at least 30 minutes.
2. Heat a deep pan a third full of oil on a medium-high heat. While you're waiting for it to come to the right temperature (180°C, when a breadcrumb dropped in should sizzle), mix together the flour, cornmeal, onion seeds, paprika and salt in a wide bowl and put the oven on to warm. Remove the onions from the buttermilk and shake off any excess, then drop into the bowl in batches and toss to coat.
3. Once the oil has come to sizzling temperature, drop in a handful of onion rings (don't overcrowd the pan) and stir once, then cook until golden. Scoop out with a slotted spoon, season and put into the oven to keep warm while you repeat the process.

Vietnamese crispy pork and prawn pancakes (bánh xèo)

serves 4–6

Coconut or vegetable
  oil, to cook
300g cooked pork, diced
  (I use 3 thin shoulder steaks,
  thinly sliced and poached,
  but any leftovers will be fine,
  especially pork belly)
150g cooked prawns
8 spring onions, finely sliced
120g beansprouts
2 little gem lettuces, separated
  into leaves
A small bunch of coriander and
  mint, stalks trimmed
Hot sauce, to serve

For the batter:
60g moong dal
120ml coconut milk
225g rice flour
A generous pinch of turmeric
1 teaspoon fine salt

These were my absolute favourite breakfast discovery in Vietnam; with that addictive crunch that only comes from hot fat (the 'xèo' imitates the sizzle the batter makes as it hits the pan), they seemed like the Vietnamese equivalent of our own fried egg sandwich, only served with rather more in the way of fresh herbs on the side.

1. Soak the dal in hot water for 30 minutes, then drain and put into a large bowl with the coconut milk. Whiz to a paste with a stick blender, then stir in the flour, turmeric, salt and 570ml of water. Whisk well to combine, then leave to stand for at least 30 minutes (though you can keep it overnight if you like).
2. Grease a non-stick frying pan well and put it over a medium heat. Leave it to get nice and hot, so a drop of batter sizzles as it hits the surface. Arrange the pork, prawns, onions and beansprouts near the stove.
3. Once the pan is good and hot, whisk the batter to bring it back together, then pour a ladleful into the pan, quickly swirling it to spread it out; it should be very thin, and, if the pan is hot enough, full of little holes. Pour a little more round the sides, swirling again. (This may take a few practice goes to get right.)
4. Drop some pork, prawns, spring onion and beansprouts over one side of the pancake and cook until the edges start to curl and come away from the sides of the pan, then very gently check the base. Once it's golden, and the top of the pancake is dry and cooked through, fold in half and slide on to a plate.
5. Serve with plenty of lettuce, herbs and a good squiggle of hot sauce.

Texan queso dip

**makes as much as 4 of
you should probably eat at
one time, but easily doubled
for a party**

175g grated mature Cheddar
85g grated Gouda
   (the young, rubbery sort)
   or Monterey Jack
2 tablespoons cornflour
60ml whole milk
½ a white onion, finely minced
   (yellow onion will do at a
   pinch, but make sure it's very
   finely chopped)
1 tablespoon pickled jalapeño
   rings, chopped, plus
   2 tablespoons of their
   pickling juice

That gloopy yolk-yellow nacho dip served in cinemas promises so much; after all, isn't all cheese just processed milk, so what's not to love about a molten bowl of the stuff? The answer, sadly, is the taste: cloying, artificial and actually just plain nasty.

This is closer to the original version, ubiquitous in the great state of Texas, though without that suspicious 'cheese product' orange colouring. Monterey Jack would be used stateside, but a young Gouda is easier to get hold of in my neck of the woods, and melts just as well. Eat with loads of nachos. Obviously.

1. Toss the grated cheeses with the cornflour, and put into a medium pan over a low heat. Add the milk and allow the cheeses to melt, stirring regularly, until smooth.
2. Mix in the onion, chilli and pickle juice and serve immediately if possible; you can keep it warm over a low heat, or in a bain-marie (a heatproof bowl set over a pan of simmering water) if necessary for about half an hour, but it will start to solidify, so keep stirring.

Homemade butterscotch 'Angel Delight'

serves 6–8

75g butter
100g soft light brown sugar
¼ teaspoon salt
600ml whipping cream
2 egg whites
2 tablespoons caster sugar

Angel Delight is one of my basest pleasures – a dollop of this unpromisingly beige wobbly stuff takes me straight back to school days, only this time around, I can eat the whole packet on my own (they claim they serve two, but I've never found this to be the case). It is a guilty pleasure though, whereas this version, heavier on the cream and lighter on the old tetrasodium diphosphate, is just pure unadulterated joy, especially with some stewed apple.

1. Put the butter, brown sugar, salt and 50ml of the cream into a small pan over a medium heat, stirring until the sugar has dissolved and you have a smooth sauce. Allow to cool to warm room temperature, stirring occasionally to keep it liquid.
2. Whisk the egg whites to soft peaks, then whisk in the caster sugar. In a new, larger bowl, whisk the remaining cream to soft peaks, then fold in the caramel sauce.
3. Fold a spoonful of egg white into the cream mixture to loosen it, then gently fold the remainder in until well combined.
4. Spoon into serving dishes and chill until required.

Marathon pie

serves 8–10

*For the base (makes about
28 digestive-sized biscuits):*
195g butter, at room
    temperature, plus a little
    extra to grease
200g granulated sugar
110g cocoa powder, sifted
1 egg, beaten
200g plain flour

For the caramel layer:
100g salted roasted peanuts,
    roughly chopped
165g white granulated sugar
    (golden stuff is fine, but will
    make life harder)
50g butter, at room
    temperature, diced
110ml double cream,
    at room temperature
½ teaspoon salt flakes

For the nougat mousse:
5 egg yolks
150g honey
3 gelatine leaves
375ml whipping cream

To top:
5 tablespoons white sugar
1 Snickers bar, chilled

I'll admit, this is some serious self-indulgence – when I put the picture online, someone asked if the name came from the fact you have to run a marathon to justify it; I suspect an ultra event might be the bare minimum. That said, I've done neither, and I'm still alive, and the combination of a crunchy, cocoa-rich base, salty peanut caramel and light honey mousse is surely worth the sacrifice of a few hours of life at the other end.

The different stages make this a little bit of a project (you could use ready-made bitter chocolate biscuits for the base if you want to speed up the process – something like Oreos would do, though because of the filling you won't need as much butter to stick it together), but there's nothing particularly complicated here, and most of it is chilling time. (Which you could always use for that thirty-mile run, of course.)

1. Start by making the biscuit base. Cream together 165g of the butter with the sugar until fluffy, then beat in the cocoa and a pinch of salt. Scrape down the sides of the bowl, then beat in the egg, followed by the flour. Once it comes together into a dough, form into a ball and flatten. Wrap well and chill for at least an hour, until firm.
2. Heat the oven to 200°C/fan 180°C/gas 6. Roll out the dough to about 3mm thick and cut out circles about 7cm in diameter. Arrange on a lined baking tray and bake for 9 minutes. Allow to cool.
3. Melt the remaining 30g of butter. Blitz 350g of the biscuits (about 12 digestive-sized ones) to coarse crumbs, add the melted butter, whiz until finely ground, then press the crumbs into a roughly 22cm loose-based pie dish, making sure they reach up the sides. (If you don't have enough, whiz a couple more biscuits with a little more melted butter.) Chill in the fridge for at least 30 minutes before making the caramel.
4. Scatter the peanuts evenly over the crust. To make the caramel, put all the ingredients close to the hob, including the dish. Pour the sugar into a large heavy-based pan over a medium-high heat and allow to melt. Once it's done so, leave it until it turns amber, then whisk in the

butter and continue whisking until this has melted. Take off the heat and whisk in the cream (careful, it will bubble up), followed by the salt, pour into the dish and allow to cool, then chill until set.

5. To make the nougat mousse, whisk the egg yolks in a heatproof bowl until thickened and pale. Put the honey into a pan with 75ml of water and bring to a simmer. Cook until it reaches 115°C. Meanwhile, soak the gelatine in cold water, then squeeze out. Whip the cream to soft peaks, keeping an eye on the syrup all the time.

6. Working quickly, whisk all but a couple of tablespoons of hot syrup into the egg yolks. Dissolve the gelatine in the remaining syrup, then whisk this into the yolk mixture too. Continue to whisk until cool, then fold in the cream, spoon on to the caramel, and allow to set in the fridge, which will take at least 3 hours.

7. Put the remaining sugar into a light-coloured pan with a splash of water over a medium heat until toffee-coloured, then use to decorate the top of the cake, along with thin slivers of Snickers.

K

*is for Kale
and other greens*

Whoever does the PR for kale, I want in. This is a tough vegetable to warm to, quite literally – chewy and woody, with a distinctive bitter flavour, it's an unlikely candidate for hipness, but in the last five years it's somehow gone from cattle fodder to the culinary catwalk.

Take this quote from the *New York Times*, which I had to read twice to be sure it wasn't an April Fool: '"For some reason when you go to a restaurant and they have a kale salad on the menu, you automatically accept that it's a cool spot," said Chelsea Leyland, a D.J. and downtown fixture. "It's like playing the right music of the moment. It gives it that stamp of coolness."'

Yet so unpopular was kale as human food until relatively recently that Jane Grigson's excellent *Vegetable Book*, first published in 1978, devotes a whole chapter to wild seakale, but makes no mention of the cultivated sort, while Nigel Slater's *Tender*, published just over thirty years later, gives it a twelve-page hagiography. In a single generation, kale has been reborn. And hurrah for that – for all that I've said, like coffee or Campari, once you've developed a taste for the stuff, it's hard to remember what your problem was in the first place.

As hardy as its texture suggests, it thrives in climes other species find challenging (it was common in wartime kitchen gardens), so it's perhaps no surprise that our modern word comes from the Scottish name; in English, kale was known as cole (see also coleslaw, which comes to us from the German, and cole-flower, or cauliflower). The flavour, like that of traditional Brussels sprouts, actually improves after a frost, which is why it was so very prized in the depths of winter, when vitamins and variety were thin on the frozen ground.

As the selection in this chapter suggests, I like greens that, like kale, demand a bit of effort. Give me adult spinach over the boring baby stuff any day; crinkly Savoy cabbage over the smooth white variety – if we're going to eat leaves, let's at least go for those with some personality.

So often relegated to the role of a warm side salad; obligatory for a balanced meal, but not deemed worthy of anything more than the most basic preparation (steamed then dropped damply on to the plate), at the risk of coming over all sincere, they're capable of so much more if we let them shine. Greens can easily be the centrepiece of a dish, like the chard gratin and spinach tart in this chapter, but they're so quick to cook that they can also be stirred into almost any soup, stew or noodle dish at the last minute.

In short, eat your greens. They're good for the soul.

Health benefits

I tend to treat anything labelled as a superfood with a certain amount of suspicion, but leafy greens like kale, spinach and chard at least have some claim to the title; they're a great source of vitamins K, A and C, and contain good amounts of folate, calcium and other minerals too.

Kale

Unsurprisingly, just like the latest denim, trendy kale comes in a range of styles. The most common in this country is curly kale, the green variety of which is (rather annoyingly to my mind) often sold ready chopped in bags in the supermarket. This looks like a labour-saving boon, but seems generally to mean you purchase a dispiriting assortment of older leaves and thick chunks of browning stalk along with the good bits – much better to go somewhere where they sell it in pretty frilly bunches for you to trim as you see fit. If you want to use it in a salad, make sure the leaves are young and relatively tender, or you'll still be chewing come doomsday.

The other variety you'll often see is cavolo nero, or black kale (sometimes excitingly known, especially in the States, as dinosaur kale). This has broad, spear-shaped purple-green leaves with the same crinkly texture as a Savoy cabbage, and is one of the most beautiful vegetables I know. Despite the Italian name, it works well with all sorts of different flavours, though it does seem particularly suited to chucking into a minestrone with a healthy glug of olive oil. Look for proud, firm leaves rather than limp, slug-nibbled ones. (The less common flat-leaf, or Russian, kale is like a cross between the two – frilly at the edges, flat in the middle.)

Kale is harvested from midsummer onwards, but as mentioned it's at its best in midwinter, after a frost (and when there's not much else going on, perhaps more importantly).

Spinach

Spinach is another vegetable that's badly served by the supermarkets, who have collectively decided to sell only the tender baby leaves. These are fine in a salad, but are far too delicate for cooking with, and, to my mind, have a less interesting, more strongly iron-tinged flavour of the kind likely to leave you with oddly furry teeth. Mature spinach is still sold at street markets and grocers (and, near me at least, in little Turkish corner shops), and though the washing can be a pain, the flavour makes it well worth the effort, not to mention the reduced cost.

Whatever sort of spinach you use, however, it is remarkable both for the speed at which it collapses down to nothing (you'll need sinkfuls to make a decent portion for more than a couple of people) and, perhaps thankfully in that case, the speed at which it cooks. You barely need to show it the heat, so be very careful not to leave it too long, and if you think you may have done so, rinse it under cold water before any further damage is wreaked.

Homegrown spinach is in season from spring to midsummer.

Chard

Finally, as far as this chapter is concerned (though most of the recipes below would work equally well with Savoy or green cabbage leaves and spring greens), we come to chard, close cousin of spinach, a member of the beetroot family, and perhaps the blingiest green vegetable of them all.

It takes its name from its wide ridged stems, known as chards, which come in a gorgeous rainbow of colours, from sunshine yellow to vivid pink; even the workaday white-stemmed Swiss chard has a certain handsome quality. Only perhaps the candy-striped beetroot can rival it for sheer Liberace-style exuberance.

Chard has an earthy, slightly minerally sweetness, but the width of those stems, and the delicate, spinach-like quality of the leaves, means that all but the youngest examples should be divided between stems and leaves, and the two cooked separately if you're to avoid boiling the latter to death while waiting for the former to soften (though even the toughest stalks are unlikely to take more than three minutes). If this sounds like too much work, look for the smallest leaves, which, at the farmers' market, can generally be found lurking at the bottom of the box. Chard is in season from June to November.

All these vegetables are best stored in the salad drawer in the fridge, and consumed as soon as possible after purchase, though kale in particular does keep fairly well.

What they go with

A simple dressing of olive oil, lemon juice and salt suits all three just fine, but they also have a great affinity with umami flavours like bacon, anchovies and Parmesan, and creamy sauces too. I find orange and nuts surprisingly good pairings and they can also take a certain amount of chilli heat, especially if you're generous with the garlic.

See also: Blue cheese creamed spinach (page 34, Blue Cheese), Black kale salad with anchovy dressing (page 172, Leaves), Potato, black kale and anchovy pie (page 229, Potatoes).

Spinach soup with spiced anchovy butter toasts

serves 4

2 tablespoons butter
2 shallots, roughly chopped
A whole nutmeg, to grate
600g spinach
1 litre chicken stock
2 tablespoons double
    cream (optional)
1 baguette

For the anchovy butter:
125g unsalted butter, softened
½ teaspoon cayenne pepper
¼ teaspoon finely ground
    black pepper
¼ teaspoon finely ground
    nutmeg
¼ teaspoon finely ground mace
¼ teaspoon finely ground
    cinnamon
¼ teaspoon ground ginger
50g anchovy fillets in olive oil,
    drained and roughly chopped
2 teaspoons lemon juice

The almost nutty sweetness of spinach works particularly well with this emphatically savoury anchovy relish.

1. Start by making the anchovy butter. Melt about a quarter of the butter in a small pan over a medium heat, then add the spices. Cook for a minute or so, stirring, then add the anchovies and cook for another couple of minutes, mashing them up with a spatula or wooden spoon as they begin to soften. Take off the heat and allow to cool to warm.

2. Put the anchovy mixture into a pestle and mortar and mash until fairly smooth, then stir in the lemon juice and gradually work in the remaining butter. Taste and add more lemon juice or cayenne pepper if you think it needs it, then shape into a sausage, wrap in clingfilm and chill until sliceable.

3. To make the soup, melt the butter in a large pan over a medium-low heat and soften the shallots with a pinch of salt and a good grating of nutmeg. Meanwhile, wash the spinach well.

4. When the shallots are soft and golden, add the washed spinach to the pan with a pinch of salt, turn up the heat slightly and cover. Cook until wilted, shaking the pan occasionally to make sure it cooks evenly.

5. Add the stock to the pan, bring to a simmer, then take off the heat and allow to cool slightly. Purée, then stir in the cream, if using, and taste; you can add a little more if you like, but bear in mind that the more you add, the less vibrant the colour. Season.

6. Cut the baguette into thin rounds and toast under the grill until golden and crisp. Serve the soup with a couple of baguette croutons per bowl, topped with a disc of anchovy butter.

Spicy cashew kale crisps

makes 1 large bowl

200g cavolo nero
60g cashew butter
1 teaspoon nam pla (fish sauce)
1 teaspoon keçap manis (see
    page 15)
2 teaspoons soft light
    brown sugar
2 tablespoons crispy fried
    shallots (optional, see
    intro), crumbled
1 teaspoon togarashi or other
    chilli powder, or to taste

Let's get one thing straight: kale crisps are not the same as potato crisps, whatever those health bloggers might claim. Just as addictive, sure, but not the same – thinner and more friable, they shatter in your mouth like savoury honeycomb, flooding it with a rich green, earthy and very savoury flavour.

The trick here is the low, slow cooking – kale crisps baked hot and fast tend to dissolve into scorched dust – and the use of robust black kale, which stands up better to cooking than the more delicate curly variety, though you can substitute that if you prefer; just keep an eye on it during cooking.

NB: I use the crispy dry shallots sold in Asian supermarkets as a topping, but they're entirely optional.

1. Wash the kale and dry very well – I like to do this an hour or so ahead and spread it out on paper towels to dry. (Water is the enemy of crispness.) Roughly chop into large pieces, cutting out the central stems if the leaves are very large, or you don't like chewing, and bearing in mind it will shrink significantly during cooking. Grease two large baking sheets.
2. Heat the oven to 120°C/fan 100°C/gas ½. Whisk the cashew butter with 1 tablespoon of warmish water to loosen, then whisk in the fish sauce, keçap manis and sugar.
3. Put the kale into a large bowl and add the dressing. Massage it into the leaves, then spread them out over the baking sheets in a single layer and dust with the crumbled shallots, if using, and chilli powder.
4. Bake for about 1 hour 45 minutes, until the leaves are crisp and dry, turning the sheets round every half hour or so, then run a thin fish slice under them to detach them from the sheets and leave to cool before transferring to an airtight container, or better still eating immediately while they're still lovely and crisp.

Fava e cavolo nero

serves 4

500g dried, split broad
    beans (see intro)
700ml chicken
    or vegetable stock
2 tablespoons extra
    virgin olive oil

For the kale:
1kg cavolo nero
4 tablespoons olive oil
8 garlic cloves, thinly sliced
1 teaspoon chilli flakes

Dried fava (or broad) beans are a starchy staple in Puglia, in Italy's heel, where I first came across them, though I was later to find they're a key ingredient in falafel as well (which means they can be found in Middle Eastern grocers). I remember eating a vast plate of this creamy, nutty, slightly bitter purée, as comforting in its own way as a bowl of mash, with a pile of wilted chicory, slick with olive oil, in a tiny stuffy restaurant in the ancient city of Lecce one baking hot lunchtime. As a fan of all things starchy, I was an instant convert, though I must say I think it works better on a cold British afternoon.

Unless you grow it yourself, it's well nigh impossible to buy Italian dandelion, or cutting chicory, here, but kale makes a decently bitter substitute, and you could also use spinach, chard, or indeed any kind of greens. Be aware that the purée sets quite solid when cool, so if you want to reheat it, add a little more liquid.

1. Soak the beans in cold water for at least 6 hours, or overnight. Drain, rinse, and put into a pan with the stock. Bring to the boil, then skim, turn down the heat to medium, and simmer for about an hour until they begin to dissolve into a mush.
2. Meanwhile, blanch the kale for a minute in a large pan of boiling salted water, then drain and roughly chop.
3. Heat the 4 tablespoons of oil in a frying pan over a medium heat, then add the garlic. Fry until golden, then scoop out and set aside. Replace with the chopped kale and fry, stirring occasionally, until dark and beginning to crisp around the edges. Return the garlic to the pan along with the chilli and season to taste.
4. Mash the beans into a sloppy purée, or use a stick blender if you'd prefer a smoother texture (careful, they'll spit like angry snakes). Season to taste and stir in 1 tablespoon of the extra virgin olive oil. Divide between shallow bowls and plonk the kale on top. Drizzle with the remaining extra virgin olive oil and serve.

Spinach, ricotta and feta tart with hard-boiled eggs

serves 6–8

3 eggs
1.3kg mature spinach, trimmed
    and well washed, or 900g
    frozen whole leaf spinach,
    defrosted
2 tablespoons olive oil,
    plus extra to glaze
1 large red onion, finely sliced
6 garlic cloves, finely sliced
A whole nutmeg, to grate
250g ricotta
100g feta, crumbled
Zest of 1 lemon
A dash of olive oil
3 tablespoons pine nuts

For the polenta pastry:
190g cornmeal
190g plain flour
½ teaspoon salt
120ml olive oil

A pleasingly substantial, and incidentally vegetarian main course which plays merry havoc with the flavours of southern Europe – it's a little bit Greek, a little bit Italian, with a ridiculously easy pastry that's rich with olive oil and crunchy with polenta, and some sunny eggs on top for colour.

You really need mature spinach for this one – see the introduction on page 147 for advice on sourcing. The whole leaf frozen sort is fine.

1. Put the cornmeal and flour into a large mixing bowl and whisk together with the salt. Whisk the olive oil with 120ml of cold water, then make a hollow in the middle of the flour, pour in the liquid and stir to make a soft dough that comes cleanly away from the sides of the bowl (if it doesn't, add a tiny bit more flour). Wrap well and put into the fridge while you prepare the filling.
2. Put the eggs into a pan of cold water, cover, bring to the boil, then simmer for 5 minutes. Run under cold water to cool, then set aside.
3. If using fresh spinach, bring a very large pan of salted water to the boil and blanch the spinach for a minute until wilted, working in batches for ease. Drain in a colander and, when cool enough to handle, squeeze very well until no more water comes out; you'll be amazed at how much is in there. If using defrosted frozen spinach, skip straight to the squeezing stage.
4. Heat the oil in a large frying pan over a medium-low heat and cook the onion until pink and soft. Stir in the garlic and cook for another couple of minutes, then add the spinach. Turn the heat up slightly and cook until dry. Grate in a generous amount of nutmeg and season well. Heat the oven to 220°C/fan 200°C/gas 7.
5. Grease a 26cm tart tin with oil. Roll out the pastry on a generously floured surface – it will be soft, but elastic – then use to line the tin. Line with foil or baking paper and baking beans and bake for 20 minutes.

6. Meanwhile, mix the ricotta with the feta, lemon zest and a dash of olive oil. Season to taste.

7. Remove the beans and paper and bake the tart for a further 7 minutes, then spread the base with the ricotta mixture, followed by the spinach. Bake for 15 minutes, then sprinkle the top with pine nuts and put back into the oven for another 5–10 minutes, until the nuts are golden. Meanwhile, peel the eggs and slice in half.

8. When the tart is ready, poke little hollows in the spinach and arrange the eggs in them. Serve hot or cold.

Homemade orecchiette with sausage and kale

serves 4

For the orecchiette:
155g '00' pasta flour
300g semolina flour (available from Italian delis or online)
1 teaspoon salt
About 255ml warm water

For the topping:
500g cavolo nero
2 tablespoons olive oil, plus extra to grease
4 meaty Italian pork sausages, preferably with chilli or fennel seeds
4 garlic cloves, thinly sliced
120ml white wine
Zest of 1 lemon

Much as I love eating homemade pasta, it cannot be denied that the making part can be a bit of a faff – all that rolling and cutting and hanging of floury noodles over chairbacks means it's definitely a weekend project rather than a run-of-the-mill kitchen task as far as I'm concerned.

Orecchiette, or little ears, are an honourable exception – no rolling required, just a satisfying squidging of pasta into tiny mouse-sized hats, they may not be the ideal quick after-work dinner, but they are a nice way to spend an hour or so on a more leisurely evening, and a task that everyone can pitch in with.

I remember seeing black-clad women sitting on kitchen chairs on the pavement outside their houses in Puglia, gossiping as they shaped their orecchiette; throw in a glass of wine, and that's an ideal scenario here.

1. Put the flours into a large bowl with the salt and whisk. Make a well in the middle and pour in most of the water, then mix together. Add just enough water to bring the mixture into a coherent dough.

2. Lightly oil a work surface and turn the dough out. Knead for about 8–10 minutes until smooth and elastic, then wrap in clingfilm and leave at room temperature for about an hour before shaping.

3. To shape the orecchiette, put the dough under a damp cloth and prepare a couple of lightly floured trays.

4. Pinch off a piece roughly the size of a shelled hazelnut, then use your thumb to squash and drag it towards you, flattening it in the process, to form a thin disc with a slightly thicker rim. Shape this over the top of your thumb to make a little hat. Put on the lightly floured tray and repeat. You can leave them at this point to dry for a couple of hours, or cook immediately.

5. Wash and roughly shred the cavolo nero, then steam for a couple of minutes until just wilted. Prepare a large pot of boiling well-salted water for the pasta (you can use the steaming water as a start).

6. Heat the oil in a frying pan over a medium-high heat and slit the sausages down the middle, scooping the meat from the inside into the pan. Fry, breaking it up with a spatula, until beginning to brown and crisp. Meanwhile, add the pasta to the boiling water, stirring vigorously as you do so to stop it sticking together. Cook for 5 minutes, then begin checking it at regular intervals until it's done to your liking (the exact time will depend on how thick your orecchiette are, and how chewy you like them).

7. Add the garlic to the pan with the sausage and fry for a couple of minutes, stirring, then add the cavolo nero and stir to coat. Turn up the heat, then pour in the wine and stir to deglaze the pan.

8. Once the pasta is done, drain well and add to the pan. Toss together, season with salt, pepper and lemon zest, and serve immediately.

Chard gratin with a Gruyère crumb

serves 4

275ml double cream
1 fat clove of garlic
A whole nutmeg, to grate
200g chard
Butter, to grease
50g hazelnuts
A little oil
20g breadcrumbs
50g Gruyère, grated

Luxuriously, creamily rich, with a crunchy, nutty crumb, this is a killer side dish for something plain – a roast chicken, perhaps, or even just a dollop of mash or polenta.

1. Pour the cream into a small pan, crush in the garlic and add a good grating of nutmeg. Bring to a bare simmer, then turn off the heat and leave to infuse.
2. Heat the oven to 180°C/fan 160°C/gas 4. Bring a large pan of salted water to the boil. Separate the chard leaves and stalks. Add the stalks to the pan and blanch for 2–4 minutes, depending on thickness, then add the leaves and blanch for a further minute. Drain and rinse under cold water, then squeeze dry.
3. Butter a small oven dish. Stir the chard into the cream, season and spoon into the dish. Bake for 30 minutes.
4. Meanwhile, toast the hazelnuts in a dry frying pan until fragrant, then tip out and set aside to cool. Put a little oil into the pan, allow to heat up, then toast the breadcrumbs until pale golden and crisp. Roughly grind the hazelnuts in a food processor (or finely chop), add the cheese and pulse briefly. Stir this into the breadcrumbs, then tip on to the gratin and bake for 15 minutes more, until golden.

L

is for Leaves

Having gone into rhapsodies over cooked leaves in the previous chapter, here I'd like to sing the praises of the raw variety, in the form of salad. That once sad side dish has become a seriously slick operation, bursting with fresh zesty herbs, crunchy stems and peppery stalks; all micro greens and maximum flavour – and the epitome of culinary cool.

Since the health food revolution, you can serve a salad as the main event at a lunch or dinner party and no one will bat an eyelid. But, though they're always healthy, salads don't have to be dull diet fodder; fresh green leaves provide the ideal foil for rich dressings like the zesty lemon butter on page 171 or the savoury bacon vinaigrette on page 174, and, of course, they can make quite a substantial meal – just think of the classic salade Niçoise (or my version on page 167).

Even the most jaded of palates will perk up at a simple, well-dressed plate of judiciously chosen leaves, and it's one of the things the French still do so well. A modest steak frites, nothing to write home about, at a service station cafeteria will come flanked by a bowl of greenery tossed with just the right amount of piquant mustardy vinaigrette – and there's no better accompaniment. Making good salad isn't difficult, it just takes a little care.

How to build a salad

1.

Choose your base

CHICORY & RADICCHIO
Compact, torpedo-shaped heads in pale
green or ruby red, with a satisfying crunch
and bitter flavour. Sturdy boat-shaped
leaves which are perfect for topping

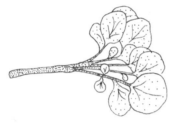

WATERCRESS
Sharp, peppery flavour, excellent with
creamy cheese and oily fish

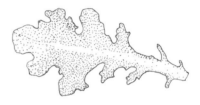

FRISÉE/CURLY ENDIVE
Frilly with a robust, spiky texture, this
member of the chicory family has
a slightly bitter flavour – ideal for a
salade Lyonnaise

ROUND LETTUCE
Underrated traditional favourite,
and the best option for a plain green salad

OAK LEAF LETTUCE
Pretty, frilly, decorative

ROCKET
Grows wild in the
Mediterranean: strongly flavoured, hot and
peppery, and best simply dressed

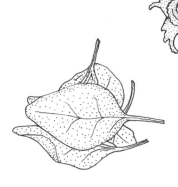

BABY SPINACH, KALE
& BEET LEAVES
Milder, more tender versions
of the more familiar large varieties

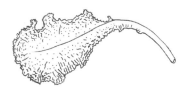

MUSTARD LEAVES (Mizuna/tatsoi)
Distinct mustardy flavour –
great with cheese, smoked meat, etc.

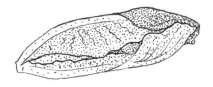

COS/ROMAINE
Long and oval with crisp leaves, the base
for a classic Caesar salad and a very
versatile all-rounder. Good cooked.
Little gem is a smaller, sweeter version

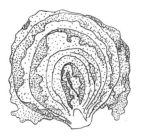

ICEBERG
Bland, but its unbeatable crunch
makes it a great choice in recipes like the
wedge salad on page 33.

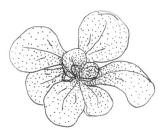

LAMB'S LETTUCE
Mild, sweet flavour, a good
all-rounder

2.

Match this to a dressing

SIMPLE
Oil + salt, best for pungent, peppery leaves. Change the flavour by changing the oil

VINAIGRETTE
Acid (citrus juice / vinegar) + oil + salt, sometimes with mustard or other condiments added. Great with sweeter, milder leaves

CREAMY
Thicker and richer than vinaigrette, this is best suited to a sturdier leaf. Dairy or egg based or an emulsion of oils and flavourings whisked together until thickened, e.g. salad creams, Caesar dressing, mayonnaise, thousand island, blue cheese

3.

Balance your toppings

RICH
Ripe avocado, oily fish,
shredded meat,
boiled eggs, cheese

CRUNCHY
Toasted nuts, croutons,
deep-fried onions, seeds,
toasted flatbreads,
baked cheese crisps

BULKERS
Beans, pasta, rice,
quinoa, couscous, chickpeas,
lentils, stale bread,
potatoes, other starchy
vegetables

FRESH
Radishes, tomatoes,
cucumber, celery,
grated carrot or
raw beetroot, spring onions,
peppers, fennel, etc.

SWEET
Fruit, roasted vegetables,
boiled beetroot,
candied nuts, sweetcorn

AROMATICS
Fresh herbs, chillies,
onions, flowers

SOUR AND SALTY
Pickles, anchovies,
capers, crumbled bacon,
feta, halloumi, sun-dried
tomatoes

On washing

Salad leaves make great hiding places for small creatures, so they do need washing unless the packaging states otherwise. The easiest way to do this is to fill a sink, or large bowl, with cold water and submerge the leaves, swishing them gently about so the dirt falls to the bottom, then scooping them out.

Bear in mind, however, that leaves are very delicate and need careful handling. They should be dried thoroughly before dressing, or you'll end up with a soggy heap of mulch; if you have the space for such a gadget, a salad spinner is a good tool, but if not, some tender patting with kitchen towel will do the trick.

Nice salad

serves 4

8 quail's eggs
8 small new potatoes, scrubbed
8 asparagus spears
2 fillets of hot-smoked trout
1 small ridged cucumber
    (or ½ a larger cucumber)
100g watercress
100g pea shoots
A small bunch of mint, leaves
    picked

For the dressing:
1 egg
1 egg yolk
¼ teaspoon honey
½ teaspoon mustard powder
1 teaspoon water
2 tablespoons cider vinegar
150ml single cream
A small bunch of chives, finely
    chopped

My take on the classic salade Niçoise, using the best ingredients the British summer can offer. Packed with asparagus, pea shoots, watercress and cucumber, and topped with creamy new potatoes and blushing pink flakes of fish, the flavours are subtler and more delicate than the original, but just as delicious. The dressing is based on Eliza Acton's 1845 recipe for English salad sauce (as opposed to 'French salad dressing') – and has very little in common with salad cream, I promise.

1. Put the whole egg for the dressing into a small pan, barely cover with cold water, cover the pan and bring to the boil. Uncover, turn down the heat, cook for 7 minutes, then scoop out with a slotted spoon and run under cold water. Add the quail's eggs to the pan and cook for 2 minutes, then drain and run under cold water.

2. When the eggs are cool enough to handle, peel them all and cut in half. Set the quail's eggs aside. Scoop out the yolk of the hen's egg, crumble it into a small bowl with the raw yolk, honey, mustard powder and water, and whisk together. Whisk in the vinegar, then the cream, then add the chives and season to taste. (The egg white can be finely chopped and added to the salad if you like, or fed to the dog.)

3. Bring a medium pan of well-salted water to the boil. Add the potatoes and cook until tender (how long will depend on size), then scoop out with a slotted spoon. Prepare a large bowl or sink of iced water, then add the asparagus to the pan, leaving the tips sticking out of the water, cover and cook for about 3–4 minutes, until just tender. Drain and cool in the iced water.

4. Cut the potatoes in half, and chop the asparagus into shortish lengths. Flake the trout and thinly slice the cucumber. Put the watercress and pea shoots into a large salad bowl and toss with enough dressing to lightly coat. Scatter over the potatoes, asparagus, trout and quail's eggs and top with a few mint leaves. Serve immediately.

Green herb cauliflower 'tabbouleh'

serves 2–4

1 smallish cauliflower
3 tablespoons butter
3 tablespoons sultanas
1 tablespoon barberries
    (or dried sour cherries or
    cranberries if unavailable)
3 tablespoons pine nuts
4 slim spring onions
20g chives
25g tarragon, leaves picked
25g dill
25g coriander
25g mint, leaves picked
25g flat-leaf parsley
A squeeze of lemon juice

Those ridiculously flavourful leaves we single out as herbs are the star of this dish. Inspired by both the Persian *sabzi*, or herb 'salad', and Middle Eastern tabbouleh, the bland, creamy sweetness of cauliflower makes it the ideal base for a plethora of zesty green flavours and sweet dried fruits. This is an incredibly moreish addition to a selection of mezze, or a side dish for lamb or chicken, and looks even lovelier scattered with pomegranate seeds.

1. Cut the cauliflower in half and cut out the core. Discard the woody base from the core and roughly chop the rest, then break the head of the cauliflower into florets. Put it all into a food processor and pulse briefly until chopped into couscous-size pieces.
2. Melt 1 tablespoon of butter in a large frying pan over a medium-high heat and fry the cauliflower with a little salt for a couple of minutes until just tender. Scoop into a large salad bowl.
3. Melt another tablespoon of butter in the pan and fry the sultanas and barberries for a minute until plump, then tip into the bowl and toast the pine nuts in the remaining butter. Tip into the bowl.
4. Trim and roughly chop the spring onions, then put into the food processor and whiz until more finely chopped. Add the herbs and whiz again until it's all fairly finely chopped, then tip in with the cauliflower and toss everything together with a squeeze of lemon juice, and salt and pepper to taste.

Three pea salad with lemon butter dressing

serves 4

200g mangetout
160g shelled peas (frozen
are fine)
120g pea shoots

For the butter dressing:
4 tablespoons butter
3 tablespoons lemon juice

Three peas are better than one, and this fresh, sweet salad of sharply dressed, delicate little pea shoots is the proof – as well as an elegant starter, it makes a lovely accompaniment to fish or chicken.

1. Melt the butter in a small, preferably light-coloured pan over a medium-low heat. Skim the froth from the surface, then carefully pour off the clear yellow liquid beneath, leaving the milky solids in the pan. Allow the liquid to cool slightly, then whisk with the lemon juice and season generously with salt and black pepper.
2. Heat a large pan of well-salted water. Prepare a large bowl or sink of iced water. Blanch the mangetout for 90 seconds, then scoop out with a slotted spoon and put into the iced water. Blanch the peas for about a minute, depending on size, until tender but not mushy, then drain and add to the mangetout.
3. Put the pea shoots into a large salad bowl and add the drained mangetout and peas. Toss together with just enough dressing to coat, and serve immediately.

Black kale salad with anchovy dressing

serves 4

350g young cavolo nero,
　　well washed
150ml olive oil
Juice of ½ a lemon
1 small garlic clove
4 anchovy fillets in oil
1 egg yolk
A handful of finely grated
　　Parmesan

This recipe was inspired by a vast and addictively savoury salad I enjoyed in the bar of the Soho Grand Hotel, New York, washed down by a couple of equally generous martinis. They know how to make both a great salad and a great cocktail over there: healthy, but by no means health food (the salad, I mean. The martini is obviously both).

1. Rip or cut the central stem from the kale, discard, and tear the leaves into shreds. Massage vigorously with your fingers for a couple of minutes with a drizzle of oil, a squeeze of lemon and some salt, until softened.
2. Mash the garlic and anchovies together in a pestle and mortar, then pound in the egg yolk until well combined.
3. Transfer to a larger bowl (unless your pestle and mortar is vast) and slowly whisk in the olive oil, a little at a time, followed by the lemon juice, until you have a thick salad dressing. Season to taste with salt and black pepper; depending on the saltiness of your anchovies, and your tolerance, you may not need any extra salt, though I usually do.
4. Toss through the kale along with the Parmesan just before serving.

Chicory with beetroot, goat's cheese and walnuts

makes about 18

3 beetroots
50g walnut pieces
2 tablespoons cider vinegar
2 heads of chicory

For the whipped goat's cheese:
250g soft goat's cheese
2 tablespoons walnut oil
1 teaspoon coarsely cracked
    black pepper, or to taste

Great canapés, not only do they look rather gorgeous, the hot pink of the beetroot against the cool green of the leaves, but the refreshing crunch of the chicory makes a nice change from starchy crisps or breads. You can use ready-cooked beetroot if you like, but baking your own will give a more intense flavour (they can be done several days ahead, when you've got the oven on for something else, then refrigerated until use).

1. Heat the oven to 220°C/200°C fan/gas 7. Trim the beetroots, wrap in foil and bake for about 50 minutes to an hour, until tender all the way through. Allow to cool, then peel (the skin should just rub off, though it is a messy business – so wear rubber gloves or wash your hands immediately afterwards) and roughly chop.
2. While the beetroots are cooling, toast the walnuts in a dry pan until fragrant, and set aside.
3. Put the beetroot into a bowl, add the vinegar and purée with a stick blender (or use a food processor). Add salt to taste.
4. Put the goat's cheese into a bowl and whisk to loosen, then whisk in the walnut oil until well incorporated. Add pepper to taste.
5. Separate the leaves of the chicory and top each with a spoon of beetroot, followed by a blob of cheese, and finally a piece of walnut.

Mustard leaves and little gem with bacon vinaigrette and toasted walnuts

serves 2

2 spring onions, finely sliced
8 walnut halves
50g mustard leaves
   (see intro)
1 little gem lettuce

For the bacon vinaigrette:
75g smoked pancetta or diced
   streaky bacon
1 tablespoon red wine vinegar
½ teaspoon Dijon mustard
1 tablespoon vegetable oil
2 tablespoons walnut oil

Spicy mustard leaves are something you'll either have to grow yourself (they're pretty hardy), or seek out at a farmers' market, but I think they're well worth the effort – their distinctive heat adds interest to any salad, and cuts through the richness of the salty bacon and creamy nuts beautifully.

1. Heat a frying pan over a medium heat and add the pancetta. Cook until it has browned and the fat has rendered, then pour off the fat into a small bowl and set the pancetta aside.
2. Put the pan back on the heat and add the spring onions. Cook for a couple of minutes until just softened, then scoop out and add to the pancetta. Turn up the heat slightly and toast the walnuts for a minute or so until fragrant.
3. Whisk the vinegar and mustard into the bacon fat, then whisk in the remaining oils until emulsified and season to taste.
4. Put the mustard leaves into a salad bowl and separate the leaves from the little gem and add them too. Toss with the dressing, then divide between plates and top with the pancetta, spring onions and walnuts.

M

is for Malt

I'd describe malt as the sweet equivalent of umami – a flavour that brings out the best in others. For all its recent popularity, it still tends to play a supporting role, rather than hogging the limelight, bringing an attractive complexity and depth to everything from milkshakes to beef and ale pie. The taste itself is hard to describe; toasty is probably the first word that springs to mind, with a certain earthy sweetness and a lingering nuttiness.

Malt is a broad church, the base of many great things, from beer to whisky, as well as that wonderfully savoury vinegar that so many heretics like to drown their chips in. It's a key ingredient in bagels and the criminally underrated rich tea biscuit. And, of course, it plays the lead in malt loaf and Horlicks; two of the most comforting things I can possibly imagine in a crisis.

The science bit

Malting is a process familiar to anyone who has ever been on a tour of a brewery or a whisky distillery, in which cereal grains, usually barley or wheat, are soaked in water to encourage them to sprout. As the seeds germinate, their starches turn into sugars and other digestive enzymes, at which point the grains are heated to halt the germination process and dry them out.

The dried grain, or malt, can then be ground to make malt powder, which may be used to make beer or whisky, or mixed with dried milk, salt and sugar to produce malted milk powder. Malt powder can also be turned into the malt syrup I use in the malt loaf recipe in this chapter.

Health benefits

Those of a certain age will remember malt syrup being proffered during childhood as something 'good for you', though as it was often mixed with cod liver oil, those memories may not be entirely fond ones.

Nowadays, the high sugar content means malt is unlikely to win on its nutritional value alone (though it does contain protein, vitamins and minerals), but you can't argue with the flavour – look for it in whole and health food shops and chemists, in a large, dark brown jar.

Malted milk powder also has a medicinal history. It was launched in the States by a British pharmacist, James Horlick, and his brother William in the late nineteenth century as a 'granulated food for infants'. Light and easy to transport, it found favour with explorers, and made its way on to expeditions to both the North and South Poles in the early twentieth century.

Taken to all corners of the empire by the British, Horlicks (made from buffalo rather than cow's milk) remains incredibly popular in India to this day, where it's the best-selling packaged drink after bottled water, outselling Pepsi two to one.

Other brands of malted milk powder are available of course: chocolaty Ovaltine, for example (a homely, old-fashioned name that, somewhat to my surprise, turns out to be Swiss) and even more chocolaty Milo, but my loyalty lies with Horlicks, which is the next best thing to a single malt nightcap as far as I'm concerned. Use whichever sort you have to hand in recipes that call for malted milk powder, but avoid the light versions, which won't work as well (and often contain artificial sweeteners).

And once it's installed on your shelf, try adding it to biscuits, cakes and other puddings as takes your fancy – it goes brilliantly with chocolate, coffee and dairy flavours in particular, and adds a certain old-fashioned *je ne sais quoi* to most sweet things.

Moules marinières écossaises

serves 2

1kg mussels
A knob of butter
2 shallots, finely chopped
1 garlic clove, finely chopped
2 sprigs of thyme, leaves picked
50ml whisky
120ml double cream
A small bunch of parsley,
    roughly chopped

A dish that started off life as a Burns Night starter, but which stands proudly alone as a milder, richer, fruitier version of the classic wine-based dish. It's also lovely tossed through cooked linguine or spaghetti as a kind of northern take on an Italian favourite usually made with tomatoes.

Note, if you'd prefer to have it as a starter or light lunch, the amount here should serve four. Hot crisp fries are optional, but bread to mop up the sauce is not.

1. Rinse the mussels well under cold water and scrub if necessary, discarding any with broken shells. If any are open, give them a sharp tap – live mussels will slowly close. Any that remain open should be discarded. Pull out the little beards hanging from the shells by tugging them sharply towards the hinge end of the mollusc. You can leave them in cold water for a couple of hours if you like, though most mussels these days tend to be grit free, rendering this step unnecessary.
2. Heat the butter in a large pan over a medium heat and sauté the shallots until soft. Add the garlic and thyme and sauté for a further minute, then add the whisky, turn the heat up and cook for a minute or so before tipping in the drained mussels.
3. Cover and cook until most have opened: 3–5 minutes. Take off the heat and stir in the cream, season well with both salt and black pepper, sprinkle over the parsley and divide between two bowls, discarding any closed mussels and making sure each has a good helping of whisky cream.

Single malt loaf

makes 1 small loaf

9 tablespoons malt extract
2 tablespoons treacle
100ml strong warm tea
50ml whisky
75g dried prunes
75g dried figs
75g soft light brown sugar
150g spelt or wholemeal flour
100g plain flour
3 teaspoons baking powder
½ teaspoon salt
½ teaspoon ground ginger
50g flaked almonds

OK, so you don't actually need to use a single malt whisky for this (although a really salty, peaty one does work surprisingly well with the fruit), but I couldn't resist the name. Any cheap old blend will work, giving this teatime classic a bit of a kick – it keeps very well (indeed, it's even stickier a day or two after baking) and reaches its apotheosis with the addition of cold salty butter.

1. Whisk together the malt extract, treacle, tea and whisky. Finely chop the prunes and figs, add to the bowl and leave to soak for 30 minutes. Heat the oven to 200°C/fan 180°C/gas 6.
2. Stir the sugar into the tea mixture, then whisk together the rest of the ingredients and fold them in too.
3. Grease a 1lb loaf tin (about 20 x 10cm) and spoon in the mixture. Level the top and bake for an hour, turning halfway through so it bakes evenly. Leave to cool in the tin.

Rye and porter porridge with bacon, leeks and cheese

serves 4

300g rolled rye flakes
50g butter
6 rashers of streaky bacon,
    finely chopped
2 large leeks, finely chopped
700ml porter or other
    dark beer
500ml chicken stock
2 teaspoons honey
100g Gruyère or similar Alpine
    cheese, grated

A kind of northern European version of polenta, inspired by the Danish rye bread and beer porridge usually eaten sweet with milk for breakfast. The malty, savoury flavour of beer marries particularly well with nutty cheeses, like Gruyère, though you could use any sweetish, hard variety with good melting properties. Be warned, this isn't a pretty dish, or a light one, but once you taste it, you won't care – it's a great wintery lunch or supper.

1. Toast the rye in a large dry frying pan until it smells nutty, then set aside.

2. Melt a good knob of the butter in a large saucepan over a medium heat and soften the bacon and leeks until they begin to caramelize. Scoop out of the pan and set aside, then add a little of the beer and scrape the bottom of the pan to deglaze. Pour in the remaining beer and the stock, stir in the rye, then bring to a simmer.

3. Turn down the heat and cook, stirring very regularly, until the rye has broken down and absorbed the liquid to produce a thick, porridgy consistency. Stir in the honey and cheese until melted, then add the leeks and bacon, and season to taste.

Malted milk creams

makes about 16

125g plain flour
75g cocoa powder
1 teaspoon bicarbonate
   of soda
¼ teaspoon baking powder
½ teaspoon salt
200g caster sugar
140g butter, softened and diced
1 egg, beaten

For the filling:
100g butter, softened
100g icing sugar
25g malted milk powder (e.g.
   Horlicks or Ovaltine)
A splash of milk

This is a homemade take on the famous American Oreo cookie, but with added malt – because bitter chocolate and sweet milky malt go together like Mickey and Minnie, or Homer and Marge. They are utterly, utterly gorgeous with a large glass of cold milk, for extra wholesome American goodness.

1. Heat the oven to 200°C/fan 180°C/gas 6 and line two baking trays.
2. Sift the dry ingredients into a food processor, then add the butter and egg and pulse until the mixture comes together into a dough.
3. Pinch the mixture into balls about 15g in weight, and flatten them with your hand. Spread out on the trays and bake for 9 minutes, turning the trays round halfway so they bake evenly. Leave to cool for 5 minutes on the trays, then lift on to wire racks to cool completely.
4. Beat together the first three filling ingredients with a pinch of salt and add a splash of milk to loosen to a spreadable consistency, then use to sandwich the cooled biscuits together.

Triple chocolate malt cake

serves 8

50g dark chocolate
250g butter, softened
250g soft light brown sugar
½ teaspoon salt
100g cocoa powder
150g malted milk powder (plain
    Horlicks does nicely)
100g plain flour
3 teaspoons baking powder
3 eggs, beaten
250ml milk

For the decoration:
140g butter, softened
50g malted milk powder
200g icing sugar
4 tablespoons milk
10 Oreo biscuits
A handful of Maltesers

This, if I say so myself, is a real stunner of a cake – and remarkably easy to make. If you can't find, or don't want to buy Oreos (or can't risk keeping the rest of the packet in the house), then the biscuit recipe on the previous page makes an excellent homemade substitute.

1. Heat the oven to 200°C/fan 180°C/gas 6 and grease and base-line two 20cm sandwich tins. Melt the chocolate in a heatproof bowl set over, but not touching, a pan of simmering water.
2. Cream together the butter, sugar and salt until fluffy. Meanwhile, sift the cocoa, malted milk powder, flour and baking powder together.
3. With the mixer still running, add the eggs to the butter and sugar mixture, then, once well combined, fold in half the sifted dry ingredients, followed by the melted chocolate, then the rest. Finally, add enough milk to give a soft dropping consistency – i.e. it drops easily from a spoon, but doesn't run off.
4. Divide the mixture between the tins (I weigh them to make sure they're even) and smooth the tops. Bake for 25–30 minutes, until just firm in the middle. Allow to cool for 10 minutes in the tins, then turn out on to a wire rack to cool completely.
5. Meanwhile, make the icing by beating the butter until very soft, then beating in the malted milk powder, sugar and a pinch of salt, followed by a little milk to loosen the mixture.
6. Once the cakes are completely cool, put the less flat or attractive one on a serving plate and spread with a third of the icing, banking it up round the edge a little. Top with the other cake, and spread the remaining icing on top. Crush the biscuits by putting them into a clean plastic bag and whacking repeatedly with a rolling pin, then sprinkle these on top. Finish with the Maltesers, lightly crushed.

Black and white shake

**serves 2, very generously
(plus extra syrup)**

500g plain or vanilla ice cream,
    slightly softened
250ml cold milk
2 tablespoons malted milk
    powder (e.g. Horlicks)
6 Maltesers, crushed

For the chocolate syrup:
165g soft light brown sugar
65g cocoa powder
A dash of vanilla extract

An old-fashioned diner classic with a certain wow factor thanks to the contrasting layers of creamy shake and dark syrup. The syrup recipe makes more than you will need for two drinks, but keeps well in the fridge for next time life throws you some lemons. For really bad days, add a splash of bourbon.

1. To make the syrup, whisk together the sugar and cocoa in a small saucepan with 180ml of cold water to make a smooth paste. Bring to the boil, then turn down the heat and simmer for about 5 minutes, until slightly thickened and syrupy with a glossy sheen. Stir in a dash of vanilla extract and salt to taste, then set aside to cool.
2. Put the ice cream and milk into a blender with half the malted milk powder and whiz until well combined, adding a little more milk if you'd prefer it thinner. Taste and add more powder as you see fit.
3. Pour the syrup down the side of a glass, rotating it so it coats the inside, then carefully pour the shake into the middle so it doesn't disturb the syrup. Top with the crushed Maltesers and serve immediately.

N

is for Noodles

Such a pleasingly onomatopoeic word, noodles – instantly conjuring up hundreds of happy, slurpy memories.

In Britain, the term has come to refer to almost all strips of unleavened dough, from Germanic spätzle to Japanese soba – except for the most famous noodle of them all, Italian pasta. This distinction seems to me both puzzling and arbitrary, and as I love pasta with a burning passion, and P is rightly occupied by the mighty potato, I'm going to invite it to this particular party instead. *Vi do il benvenuto, Signora Pasta.*

In reality, the difference between Eastern and Western noodles is not great. The wheat versions eaten in northern China have more in common with the Italian variety than the rice noodles of the south.

But while almost all European noodles are wheat-based (though ancient buckwheat and chestnut flour varieties linger on in odd corners), in Asia they can be made from everything from rice to mung beans, all of which, of course, offer yet more choice for the lucky consumer.

In addition, pasta is almost always cooked to the same al dente consistency, whatever the dish or shape, but further east, noodles can be bouncy and firm or doughy and soft, slippery or crunchy, boiled, sautéd, deep-fried or even eaten cold.

Yet all noodles, whether spaghetti or soba, have the same allure; a pleasure more textural than tasty. There's something fundamentally satisfying about a big bowl of noodles, steaming in a delicately spiced meaty phở broth in Saigon, peeping out from underneath a rich goulash in Szeged, or doused in butter and Marmite and eaten in front of the television on a Monday evening in Salford. There's a noodle for every occasion, and they always seem to hit the spot.

Pasta

As with many basic foods, pasta has a fuzzy history – though ancient Greeks, Romans and Etruscans all made unleavened doughs that sound as if they may have been a bit like the stuff we know and love today, there is little evidence as to what they looked like, or indeed how they were cooked.

More conclusive early mentions come from the Middle East, but the first definite European pasta sighting was in twelfth-century Sicily, where strings of dough were reported a full century before Marco Polo is said to have brought the idea back from China. Macaroni pops up in England surprisingly soon afterwards, often paired with cheese – yet more proof of the astonishingly cosmopolitan nature of the (aristocratic) medieval diet.

At its simplest, pasta is made from durum wheat (a very hard variety also used for semolina and couscous) and water, though eggs can be added to enrich the dough, and other ingredients like spinach juice or squid ink deployed for colour and flavour. When making it at home, you can swap in fine white flour, as they do in northern Italy, which gives a softer, silkier result.

Contrary to popular belief, fresh pasta is not better than the dried variety; they're simply used for different things. Fresh pasta, which is lighter and more delicate, and will absorb more of whatever sauce you're adding to it, is best paired with subtle flavours, usually dairy based – Marcella Hazan reckons that olive oil 'obliterates its fine texture . . . and strong flavours deaden it'. More robust dry pasta, meanwhile, can take the weight of oil, tomato and hearty meat-based sauces.

The right shape, of course, depends on the dish: the thicker the sauce, the chunkier the pasta required. Ragù works best with hollow rigatoni or large conchiglie shells, while smoother, thinner sauces suggest spaghetti, or even the very thin spaghettini. (For more information on this subject, I'd recommend consulting Caz Hildebrand and Jacob Kenedy's comprehensive and beautiful book *The Geometry of Pasta*.)

Don't be tempted to scrimp on dried pasta; as it should form the bulk of the dish, it's worth spending an extra pound for the good stuff. This will have a slightly rough surface, which enables it to trap the sauce; cheaper varieties are slippery and wormlike, and the sauce will run off them like oil on a non-stick pan. Although it's sometimes hard to judge the texture from the packet, look for clues like 'bronze die' (the mould through which the dough is formed to shape it).

Cooking pasta is simple. You need a large pan of boiling water, larger than you might think necessary (crowding the pan will encourage the pasta to stick together), generously salted. It should taste like the sea (don't worry, your pasta won't).

Once it comes to the boil, add the pasta, stir once, and cover until it comes back to the boil. Uncover and cook for a couple of minutes shy of the time recommended on the label, then begin checking it – only you will know when it's done to your taste,* but err on the side of underdone, as it will cook a little more in the sauce.

Scoop out a cupful of cooking water, drain the pasta well and stir it into the sauce while it's still hot, adding any extra cooking water as necessary. That's it; no rinsing, and no oil until the end. (Then you can add as much as you like.)

---

* Interestingly Italians always seem to have had a taste for al dente pasta; a collection of recipes from 1475 directs the reader to cook pasta for just as long as it takes to say three paternosters (AKA the Lord's Prayer), which isn't very long at all, even for the fresh variety.

Asian noodles

An even more dauntingly broad topic than pasta, and one which deserves far more space than I can give it here. As well as the usual suspects, I'd recommend MiMi Aye's *Noodle!*, to which I am heavily indebted for the following information, as an excellent overview of noodle cuisine from Japan to Jakarta.

Although noodles in general are thought to have originated in the Arab world, where they are little eaten today, they have a long history in the Far East. A decade or so ago, archaeologists found a 4,000-year-old bowl of millet noodles buried under three metres of earth in northern China.

These days, wheat noodles are more popular in the north and Japan, while rice noodles predominate in southern China and south-east Asia, and mung and soya bean, buckwheat, tapioca and yam noodles are found scattered throughout the region too. Here's a very brief guide to a few of the most common types in this country, though a quick browse of the noodle aisle at any oriental supermarket is likely to tempt you into more exotic territory almost immediately.

Some commonly available noodles

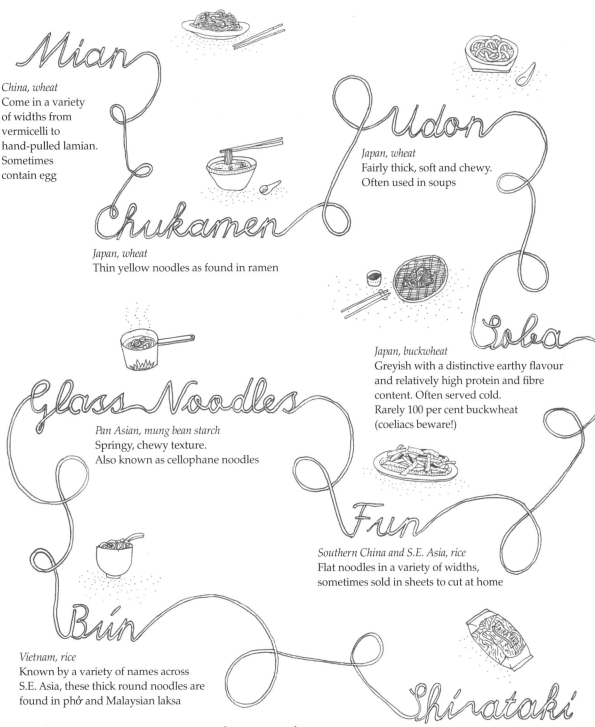

Mian

China, wheat
Come in a variety of widths from vermicelli to hand-pulled lamian. Sometimes contain egg

Udon

Japan, wheat
Fairly thick, soft and chewy. Often used in soups

Chukamen

Japan, wheat
Thin yellow noodles as found in ramen

Soba

Japan, buckwheat
Greyish with a distinctive earthy flavour and relatively high protein and fibre content. Often served cold. Rarely 100 per cent buckwheat (coeliacs beware!)

Glass Noodles

Pan Asian, mung bean starch
Springy, chewy texture. Also known as cellophane noodles

Fun

Southern China and S.E. Asia, rice
Flat noodles in a variety of widths, sometimes sold in sheets to cut at home

Bún

Vietnam, rice
Known by a variety of names across S.E. Asia, these thick round noodles are found in phở and Malaysian laksa

Shirataki

Japan, yam starch
Rubbery, translucent, impossible to digest and therefore almost calorie free. Also virtually flavour free, so use in strongly flavoured hotpots, stir-fries, etc.

Japanese carbonara

serves 2

200g dried udon noodles
1 tablespoon vegetable oil
4 spring onions, roughly
    chopped
2 eggs, plus 1 yolk
2 tablespoons bonito flakes
    (see intro), plus a little extra
    to serve
Togarashi seasoning, to serve
    (optional, see intro)

For the dashi soy sauce:
100ml light soy sauce
5g kombu (dried kelp)
3 teaspoons mirin rice wine
3g bonito flakes

Inspired by the traditional kamatama udon, which is served with a raw egg cracked into it, this version has the same rich, umami flavour as the Italian variety, and is just as satisfying to eat, though the dashi soy sauce requires a little more in the way of advance preparation.

You can easily order things like the dried tuna flakes (bonito) and kombu seaweed online if you don't happen to live near an oriental supermarket – they're super light and keep for ages, so they're good things to have in the cupboard. Togarashi seasoning is a spicy mix of chilli, peppers, seaweed, roasted orange zest and sesame seeds, and is increasingly widely available, but a pinch of chilli flakes would also do nicely.

1. Put the soy sauce, kombu and mirin into a small pan and bring to the boil. Stir in the bonito flakes, then leave to cool and infuse for at least a couple of hours before straining.
2. Cook the udon in boiling salted water until just al dente. Meanwhile, heat the oil in a medium saucepan on a medium heat and cook the spring onions until soft. Whisk together the eggs, yolk and remaining bonito flakes in a bowl and place next to the hob.
3. Drain the noodles. Pour 4 tablespoons of the infused soy sauce into the hot pan with the spring onions and stir in the noodles to coat. Take off the heat and immediately tip the eggs into the pan, stirring furiously so they don't scramble. Once the sauce has begun to thicken, divide between bowls and sprinkle with a little more bonito, if you like, and some togarashi if using.

Baked ziti with sausage and kale

serves 4–6

6 Italian sausages
Olive oil, to fry
1 large red onion
400g large tubular pasta,
  preferably ziti if you can
  find it, but large penne or
  tortiglioni will do
200g kale, trimmed and
  roughly chopped
250g firm mozzarella
  (of the sort sold for pizza)
4 tablespoons extra virgin
  olive oil
200g ricotta

For the sauce:
8 garlic cloves, crushed
3 tablespoons olive oil
1 teaspoon chilli flakes
4 x 400g tins of plum tomatoes
2 teaspoons sugar
A generous dash of red
  wine vinegar

This Italian-American classic is dedicated to the memory of Carmela Soprano, whose cooking fascinated me for six seasons of mob violence and family feuding. With big, strong flavours worthy of Tony himself, this 'zee-tee' is great food to feed a crowd, and can be made well in advance up to the end of step 5, then baked to finish.

1. For the sauce, fry the garlic gently in the oil in a wide pan for a couple of minutes, then stir in the chilli and fry for 30 seconds. Add the tomatoes, rinsing out the tins with a dash of water, the sugar and vinegar. Bring to a simmer, turn down the heat and cook for 30 minutes, until thickened. Season to taste.
2. Meanwhile, strip the sausages of their casings and roll the meat into little balls. Fry in a little oil over a medium-high heat until well browned.
3. While the meatballs are cooking, finely slice the onion. Scoop out the meatballs and fry the onion in their fat until well softened. Turn off the heat and tip the meatballs back in.
4. Bring a large pan of salted water to the boil and heat the oven to 200°C/fan 180°C/gas 6 if baking immediately. Cook the pasta for 6½ minutes, then scoop out with a slotted spoon and add to the pan with the meatballs and onion. Cook the kale in the pasta water for a minute or so until softened, then drain thoroughly and add to the pasta. Toss together until it's all well coated with oil.
5. Finely dice the mozzarella and add three-quarters to the pan. Pour in the sauce and stir it all together, then pour it into a large baking dish.
6. Cover with foil and bake for 20 minutes (or 30 if from cold). Whisk the extra virgin olive oil into the ricotta and season well. Once the timer goes off, uncover the dish and sprinkle the remaining mozzarella on top, then dot spoonfuls of ricotta on top of that. Return to the oven for 15–20 minutes, until melted and bubbling. Allow to cool slightly before serving.

Spicy peanut butter noodles with sprouting broccoli

serves 2

140g soba noodles
2 tablespoons crunchy
      peanut butter
2 tablespoons gochujang
      (see intro)
2 tablespoons Chinkiang
      vinegar
1 teaspoon sugar
1 teaspoon soy sauce
90g purple sprouting broccoli,
      stalks chopped and
      separated from the heads
      (see note)
2 spring onions, sliced
      on the diagonal
2 tablespoons roughly
      chopped peanuts

Though I wish I could take the credit for the genius idea of putting peanut butter and noodles together, I've appropriated it from the wonderful Fuchsia Dunlop, tweaked it a little bit, and added the rich, sweet heat of Korean gochujang fermented chilli paste. This is available from oriental grocers and online, but feel free to substitute rival chilli condiments as preferred – you may need to add more or less, and more sugar or soy sauce, depending on their heat and flavour profile.

Note: most other quick-cooking vegetables will work if you don't happen to have any broccoli, and feel free to chuck in whatever prawns, cooked chicken, omelette or tofu you have to hand; this is a very easy-going dish.

1. Bring a large pan of salted water to the boil and add the noodles. Set the timer for 2 minutes before they ought to be done (which will depend on the noodles: usually about 3–5 minutes, but check the packaging).
2. Meanwhile, whisk together the peanut butter, gochujang, vinegar, sugar and soy sauce, and add a few tablespoons of the cooking water to loosen to a pouring consistency.
3. Once the timer goes off, add the broccoli stalks to the pan of noodles and cook for 1 minute, then add the broccoli heads, cook for a further minute, then drain and rinse briefly under cold running water.
4. Return the noodles and broccoli to the pan, still on the heat, add the sauce and toss through until heated. Divide between bowls and sprinkle over the spring onions and peanuts. Serve immediately.

Beetroot noodles with goat's cheese, toasted walnuts and baby kale

serves 2

200g spaghetti or other pasta of
    your choice
50g walnuts
300ml beetroot juice
4 big handfuls of baby kale or
    other young greens
100g soft goat's cheese

Again, I must confess the clever notion of cooking pasta in vegetable juice is not my own; I read about it in an American food magazine on the tube one evening and could hardly wait to get home and try it. As well as turning the noodles a shockingly lovely pink, the reduced juice lends them a sticky vegetable sweetness which works particularly well with creamy, lactic goat's cheese and bitter toasted walnuts, though that first evening I used a tiny hunk of salty pecorino that had been falling from the fridge door with irritating regularity for some weeks, and that worked just fine too.

1. Bring a large pan of well-salted water to a rolling boil, then add the pasta. Cook for 5 minutes.
2. Meanwhile, toast the walnuts in a dry pan until aromatic, then roughly chop and set aside. Bring the beetroot juice to a simmer in a medium pan.
3. Drain the pasta and add to the pan with the beetroot juice. Cook for about another 5 minutes, until the noodles are al dente (exactly how long will depend on your pasta and your preferences) and the juice is thick – be careful they don't stick. If it does look a little dry before they're done, stir in a splash more juice.
4. Stir in the kale to wilt, then season well to taste; the juice will be quite sweet, so it will be able to take a generous amount of salt and black pepper.
5. Divide between bowls and scatter with chopped nuts and blobs of cheese – the cheese can be stirred in by the eater, but it looks prettier pristine and white against the pink pasta. Serve immediately.

Spätzle with cheese and onion

serves 4

A knob of butter
5 rashers of pancetta, chopped
(or a further 1 tablespoon
butter if you'd prefer to make
it vegetarian)
1 large onion, finely sliced
75ml chicken stock (or
vegetable if preferred)
A large handful of grated
Gruyère

For the noodles:
150g plain flour
85g semolina flour (or the same
weight of plain flour if you
can't find this)
1 teaspoon salt
A whole nutmeg, to grate
2 eggs, beaten
120ml milk

Hearty mountain food, these chunky central European noodles whose name, rather charmingly, means 'little sparrows' are more forgiving than most pastas. The technique for shaping them takes a bit of practice, and you'll probably end up with a few monsters to begin with (which will still taste pretty great), but as you work through the dough, you'll get the hang of it.

Spätzle are also very good served with sautéd cabbage and caraway seeds, or butter and herbs, or just about anything you might put with gnocchi.

1. To make the spätzle, put the flours into a large bowl with the salt and a pinch of nutmeg and stir in the eggs, followed by just enough milk to make a softish dough. Cover and leave for about half an hour.
2. Meanwhile, melt the butter in a frying pan and add the pancetta if using (if not, add the extra butter and skip straight to the onion). Cook until most of the fat has been released, then add the onion. Sprinkle with salt, and cook gently, stirring regularly, until soft, golden and beginning to caramelize, which will take at least 25 minutes.
3. Bring a large pan of salted water to the boil. Meanwhile, shape your spätzle dough into a long rectangle on a damp chopping board (nothing too heavy) and prepare a large bowl of iced water.
4. When the water comes to the boil, hold the board over the pan and use a palette knife or similar to cut and then flick tiny nuggets of the dough into the water – bear in mind they'll expand as they cook, so make them much smaller than you might think you need to. Once they start rising to the top, stop; you'll need to do this in several batches. Cook for a couple of minutes until the texture is firm but chewy, and they taste cooked, then scoop out with a slotted spoon and deposit in the iced water. Repeat until all the dough is used up.
5. Add the chicken stock to the onion and pancetta and bring to a simmer. Drain the spätzle well, then toss in along with the cheese and a little seasoning. Stir until the cheese begins to melt, then divide between bowls and serve.

Spaghetti with courgette noodles and Parmesan

serves 2, easily doubled

300g courgette (1 large one)
3 tablespoons extra
    virgin olive oil
2 garlic cloves, finely chopped
200g linguine or spaghetti
40g pecorino or Parmesan
A small bunch of basil
A whole nutmeg, to grate

One of the best pasta dishes I have ever eaten is also one of the simplest, the second act of a dinner in a tatty old palazzo somewhere north of Rome where they took in paying guests with an air of politely aristocratic resignation.

After a glorious fortnight of ripe red tomato sauces and sweet Neapolitan seafood, a bowl of penne with some yellowing, mushy-looking courgettes seemed a bit of a let-down. Yet we could not stop eating it: the mild, sweet courgettes, slowly cooked in olive oil until they melted on the tongue, the perfectly bouncy pasta and salty clouds of pecorino – utter bliss.

1. Bring a large pan of well-salted water to the boil. Cut the courgette into long thin strips with a spiralizer, mandoline, or the coarse side of a box grater (lay the last on its side and grate the courgette lengthways for longer strips).
2. Heat the oil in a frying pan over a medium-low flame and add the garlic. Cook for a minute or so, then add the courgette strips and 2 tablespoons of water, turn down the heat low and cook for about 15 minutes, until the water has evaporated and the courgettes are very soft, adding more water if necessary.
3. Meanwhile, cook the pasta in the boiling water until al dente (check the packet), finely grate the cheese and pick the basil leaves, tearing any large ones up.
4. Drain the pasta, reserving a little of the cooking water, and toss with the courgettes, a pinch of freshly grated nutmeg and half the cheese, then add a splash of the cooking water to loosen it. Divide between plates, top with the basil and a little more cheese and serve with the remaining cheese on the side.

Vietnamese bún chả

serves 4

400g thin rice noodles
1 soft lettuce, shredded
A small bunch of mint,
  leaves only
A small bunch of coriander,
  leaves only

For the meatballs:
2 tablespoons white sugar
450g pork mince (not too lean)
1 large shallot, finely chopped
2 garlic cloves, finely chopped
3 tablespoons fish sauce
½ teaspoon ground
  black pepper
½ teaspoon salt

For the sauce:
3 tablespoons rice vinegar
2 tablespoons palm
  or soft light brown sugar
3 tablespoons fish sauce
2 garlic cloves, finely chopped
Juice of 1 lime
1 red bird's-eye chilli, finely
  chopped

Crouched on tiny plastic stalls at the edge of a dusty, noisy road, straight off the plane, this dish, a Hanoi speciality of grilled pork, cold noodles and forests of fresh herbs, proved well worth the twelve-hour flight.

1. Start with the meatballs. Put the sugar into a small pan with 3 tablespoons of water and heat until it turns a rich brown colour. Have 2 tablespoons of water handy by the hob, then once it's ready, take off the heat and add this water to the pan, swirling quickly to combine. Set aside.

2. Put the remaining meatball ingredients into a bowl, mix well, then stir in the caramel sauce from the pan. Chill for at least an hour, then form into small balls.

3. Meanwhile, make the dipping sauce by bringing the vinegar, sugar, fish sauce and 120ml of water to a simmer in a small pan, stirring to dissolve the sugar. Allow to cool, then add the garlic, lime juice and chilli. Taste and adjust the seasoning if necessary.

4. Put the noodles into a large pan of boiling water, turn off the heat and leave for 15 minutes, then drain and rinse under cold water. Drain well.

5. Heat a griddle pan until smoking hot. Fry the meatballs until slightly charred on the outside and cooked through.

6. Divide the noodles between bowls and top with the meatballs. Put the lettuce and herbs into a bowl, and serve separately with the sauce, allowing diners to help themselves to both.

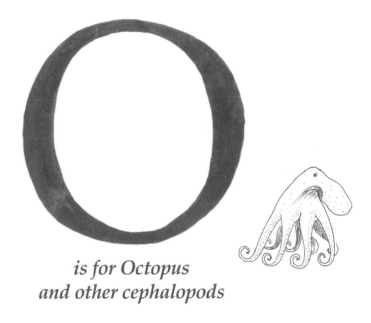

*is for Octopus
and other cephalopods*

I have a soft spot for a tentacle or two. Though I wouldn't take it quite as far as the Japanese and their erotic octopus anime, there's a strange beauty in those long, sinuous arms with their polka-dot suckers.

Strange because, as the late Alan Davidson put it, the octopus, squid and cuttlefish 'look like bags with heads on top and eight or ten arms or tentacles sprouting therefrom . . . this construction, which is entirely logical for the life they lead, appears strange, even repugnant to human eyes, and accounts for the widespread reluctance to eat them'. Appearances be damned – they taste great.

All three are on the mild side, with a certain sweetness about them – the cuttlefish more than the squid, while the octopus has an earthier, more savoury flavour, though still a surprisingly delicate one for something that looks so monstrous. This subtlety means they're best prepared simply, rather than overwhelmed with rich or spicy sauces.

I suspect that mostly, however, we relish the cephalopod family for its texture, rather than its taste – an unusual thing in the Western world, but one which may go some way to explain why the Japanese are so fond of the things. Cooked correctly, they should be tender, but with a slight springiness to the flesh, while the ends of the tentacles, and the octopus's suckers, will crisp up beautifully over a high heat.

There are two ways to cook these lovely creatures: low and slow, or hot and fast; anything in between and you'll be left with the rubber bands beloved of bad Mediterranean restaurants. (The first, of course, does not mean you can't finish them off on the heat – a gently braised octopus or squid chucked on to a smoking hot barbecue until it's charred and smoky, then bathed in olive oil and lemon juice, is a seaside dream come true.)

Sourcing

Though squid is easy to find (choose whole, rather than rings), octopus and cuttlefish will probably require a trip to a fishmonger, who ought to be able to order you some in – if you don't have one nearby, the freezers in oriental supermarkets are a surprisingly fertile hunting ground. (In this case, freezing actually benefits the cook, because it helps to tenderize the creature, so, in the case of the octopus at least, I prefer to buy them frozen.)

Squid

Found in oceans and seas throughout the world – *Loligo forbesi*, which can grow up to 90cm long, is the most common species in British waters, though the slightly smaller Mediterranean *Loligo vulgaris* is also found in the English Channel.

Anatomically, they're fairly simple: the body is a tube with two rear fins, while the head boasts two long tentacles to drag in prey, eight arms, and unnervingly large eyes (the biggest relative to their body size in the animal kingdom). These formidable predators live fast and die young.

To clean them (though many squid are sold ready to eat, and a fishmonger should happily do it for you), pull the head apart from the tube-like body and reach into the body and remove the hard quill, the last vestiges of the squid's skeleton, from inside if it's still there.

Pull or cut off the wings (the flaps at the side) if large. Trim the tough bit that attaches them to the body and set aside. Peel or rub off any membrane from the outside using a sharp knife, then turn the body inside out to give it a really good rinse with cold water.

Decisively cut the tentacles off just below the eyes. If there is a pale blueish pouch still attached to the head, carefully remove it – it will be full of ink, which you can use in a sauce or risotto if you like. Discard the rest of the head and rinse the tentacles well.

Cuttlefish

Like squid, cuttlefish are highly efficient predators, with a razor-sharp beak and one of the largest brain to body size ratios of any invertebrates (though I wouldn't let that put you off eating them).

Sepia officinalis, which can grow up to 25cm long, is the species most often found in British waters, and can be cleaned in much the same way as the squid, but with extra care given to avoid coating the entire kitchen in ink, as they have far more of the stuff.

Octopus

The southern *Octopus vulgaris* is generally considered better eating than the tougher Lesser Octopus more reliably found in British waters. (If you're not sure, have a look at the tentacles: the common octopus has two rows of suckers – hurrah! – while the lesser version has to make do with just the one.)

As anyone who remembers the late lamented Paul the Psychic Octopus from the 2010 World Cup will be aware, they are very intelligent creatures, and, like the squid and the cuttlefish, keen hunters.

The common octopus is generally found ready cleaned and frozen in this country, which is a great boon to cooks, as it takes much of the hard work out of the equation.

Note: only the smallest baby octopuses are suitable for the quick-cook treatment – larger ones will need to be braised to tenderness.

Cambodian stuffed frog-style squid

serves 2

6 stalks of lemongrass, chopped
35g galangal, chopped
5 shallots, roughly chopped
5 garlic cloves, roughly chopped
5g kaffir lime leaves, shredded
2 teaspoons ground turmeric
60g roasted peanuts, roughly chopped
250g pork mince
1 tablespoon neutral oil, plus extra to brush
4 medium squid, cleaned
4 cocktail sticks

For the sauce:
2 tablespoons oil
4 shallots, chopped
5 garlic cloves, finely chopped
1 teaspoon ground turmeric
4 tablespoons ground roasted peanuts
2 tablespoons sugar
1 tablespoon fish sauce
1 teaspoon salt
250ml coconut cream

The best meal I had in Cambodia was in a curious little place sitting on its own on a main road, on a jungly evening so wet that the power kept cutting out. I ordered the frog to entertain my companions, and then was glad none of them wanted to share its fragrant pork and peanut stuffing.

Big meaty frogs aren't so easy to come by here, but squid are, and they taste better too.

1. To make the stuffing, combine the lemongrass, galangal, shallots, garlic and lime leaves in a food processor and whiz until finely chopped. Add the turmeric and half the peanuts, and pulse until the peanuts are ground. Add the pork mince and the remaining nuts and pulse to combine. You can make this several hours ahead if you like.
2. To make the dipping sauce, heat the oil in a frying pan over a medium heat and fry the shallots until soft. Add the garlic and fry for another minute or so, then stir in the turmeric and cook for a further 30 seconds. Add the peanuts, sugar, fish sauce and salt, stir for a minute, then stir in the coconut cream to give a thickish sauce.
3. Heat the oil for the stuffing in a large frying pan and, when hot, fry the pork mince until just cooked through. Divide between the squid, stuffing them tightly but leaving enough room at the end to secure with a cocktail stick.
4. Heat a griddle pan until smoking hot. Brush the squid with a little oil, then cook for a couple of minutes on each side until charred (you can do the tentacles as well). Serve immediately with the sauce for dipping.

Coconut squid

serves 4

400g small squid
200ml coconut milk
50g sweetened desiccated
  coconut
50g panko breadcrumbs
1 teaspoon fine salt
50g plain flour
2 eggs
Neutral oil, to cook
2 teaspoons chilli flakes
Lime wedges, to serve

Inspired by the sweet, juicy coconut prawns of the Caribbean, I think squid, a creature whose anatomy lends itself perfectly to deep-frying, works even better, as well as being considerably easier on the wallet in this country.

This makes an excellent starter with a few rum punches.

1. Separate the tentacles from the bodies of the squid. Cut the bodies into triangles and score one side lightly with a knife (or cut into thick rings if you prefer). Put into a bowl with the tentacles and cover with the coconut milk. Leave to soak for up to 12 hours (though even half an hour is better than nothing).

2. Mix together the desiccated coconut, breadcrumbs and salt in a shallow bowl. Put the flour into a second shallow bowl, and lightly beat the eggs in a third. Heat a large saucepan a third full of oil on a medium-high heat.

3. While the oil heats, coat the squid. Take a piece from the marinade, shaking off any excess, and blot in the flour. Dunk in the egg, shaking off any excess, then roll in the coconut mixture. Repeat with the rest.

4. When the oil is hot enough that a breadcrumb sizzles immediately (170°C), add the squid in batches, frying until golden and turning over once during cooking, then scoop out with a slotted spoon, drain on kitchen paper and sprinkle with a few chilli flakes.

5. Make sure the oil comes back up to heat before adding any more – too cool and the squid will be pale and oily, too hot and the coconut will burn. Serve with the lime wedges.

Black risotto with eggs

serves 2, easily doubled

75g butter, diced
2 shallots, finely chopped
1.5 litres hot fish stock
    (extra dilute if using stock
    cubes, as they can be very
    salty)
250g risotto rice (arborio or
    carnaroli)
150ml dry white wine
4 x 4g sachets of cuttlefish or
    squid ink
A little oil, to grease
2 quail's eggs
100g octopus or squid pieces in
    olive oil
2 teaspoons salmon roe
    or other colourful fish roe
    (optional)
2 tablespoons flat-leaf parsley,
    roughly chopped

This is one of those dishes that's as big on visual appeal as it is on taste – inky black rice, vivid orange eggs and green parsley make for a striking dinner. Sachets of squid or cuttlefish ink can be found in fishmongers and some delicatessens, as can squid or octopus pieces in oil, but you could always cook the latter from fresh if you prefer. Do be careful about the fish stock you use; too much salt, and you'll ruin the whole dish, so taste and dilute if necessary before starting.

1. Heat a third of the butter in a wide pan over a medium heat and soften the shallots. Meanwhile, keep the stock warm on a gentle simmer on another ring of the hob.

2. Add the rice to the shallots and stir to coat with butter. Once most of the grains start to look translucent, turn up the heat and add a little wine; if it sizzles, the pan is hot enough and you can pour in the rest. Stir until it has been absorbed, then stir in half of the squid ink.

3. Turn down the heat slightly and add a ladleful of stock. Cook, stirring, until most of it has been absorbed, then add another. Continue in this way until the rice is just tender – you may not need all the stock, so start checking the texture after about 20 minutes.

4. Once the rice is done, add the rest of the butter, cover the pan and leave for 5 minutes. Meanwhile, crack the quail's eggs and fry in a little oil.

5. Stir the by-now melted butter into the risotto with the remaining squid ink, divide between shallow dishes and put a quail's egg in the centre of each. Dot with the octopus or squid pieces, the roe if using, and the parsley, and serve.

Braised octopus with chickpeas and coriander

serves 6

1 octopus, about 1.5kg, cleaned
    and defrosted if necessary
2 large onions, sliced
10 garlic cloves, sliced
2 x 400g tins of chickpeas,
    drained
150ml olive oil
800g new potatoes
Juice of 3 lemons
A large bunch of coriander

Cooking a whole octopus can be a daunting business, however much you love them – imprisoned within their icy packets, tentacles coiled up against the shrink-wrap, the frozen sort always remind me of something out of a particularly nightmarish manga tale. Once you get over that, however, they're simplicity itself to deal with, needing little more than time to soften into sweet submission.

One word of caution: octopus can be pretty salty, so the potatoes make a good, bland foil – don't be tempted to season the water.

1. Line the base of a pan large enough to hold the octopus with the onions and garlic, and add the chickpeas and olive oil. Sit the octopus on top, then cover and cook gently until very tender – this will probably take at least 2½ hours, but the longer you cook it, the better it will get.
2. About 20 minutes before you want to eat, cook the potatoes in their skins in unsalted water until tender.
3. When your octopus is done, lift it out of the pan and cut into chunks. Spoon the chickpea base into a large shallow serving dish with a slotted spoon and squeeze over lemon juice to taste; it will probably be quite salty, so you shouldn't need to season it. Roughly chop the coriander and potatoes and stir both through the chickpeas, adding a little of the cooking liquid if they seem dry, then arrange the octopus chunks on top to serve.

Maryland-style octopus sandwich

makes 2

35g plain flour
35g cornflour
½ teaspoon celery salt
    (see recipe on page 70 or
    use ready-made stuff)
½ teaspoon hot chilli powder
1 tablespoon butter
2 tablespoons oil
4 baby octopuses or 8 small
    cuttlefish or squid, cleaned
2 soft white rolls
2 ripe tomatoes, sliced
    (see intro)
4 little gem lettuce leaves

For the mayonnaise:
100g mayonnaise
1 teaspoon mustard powder
½ teaspoon paprika
½ teaspoon celery salt
½ teaspoon hot chilli powder
¼ teaspoon ground black
    pepper
¼ teaspoon ground allspice
2 pinches of ground nutmeg
2 pinches of ground cinnamon

Inspired by the simple, but compulsively tasty soft shell crab sandwiches served on the shore of Maryland's Chesapeake Bay, a beautiful place with a sadly familiar story of declining stocks – but octopus, cuttlefish or squid make a surprisingly good substitute. If ripe tomatoes are but a distant dream, the baked ones on page 365 work very well indeed here.

1. Start by mixing all the mayonnaise ingredients together and adjusting to taste.
2. Whisk together the flours, celery salt and chilli in a wide bowl. Heat the butter and oil together in a frying pan over a medium-high heat and dredge the octopus or squid in the flour mixture, shaking off the excess.
3. Once the oil is hot enough that a pinch of flour sizzles when it hits it, add the octopus or squid, in batches if the pan is too small to hold them comfortably in one layer, and fry until golden and crusted on both sides.
4. Meanwhile, split the rolls and spread the bottom halves with mayonnaise. Top with tomato and lettuce. Once the octopus or squid is ready, drain briefly on kitchen paper and divide between the rolls, making sure the tentacles hang from the sides for best effect. Add the top halves and serve immediately.

P

is for Potatoes

There was never any doubt in my mind that potatoes deserved a place in this alphabet. No other foodstuff is quite so supremely satisfying, or quietly comforting – I don't know whether it's nostalgia or just the soporific effect of all that starch, but I'd be quite happy to be buried under a big mound of mash for all eternity.

They're so wonderfully versatile, for a start, as at home in a light, summery salad as they are in a big cheesy winter gratin. A baked potato can be a meal in itself, or sit elegantly alongside the main attraction in the form of a boulangère or dauphinoise; it can be fluffy, like a tattie scone, or dense and firm like a tartiflette; crunchy, like a crisp, or gooey like a pomme purée.

You can roast potatoes to deep golden perfection, or whip them to silky smoothness, and, perhaps most importantly for many people, you can deep-fry the hell out of them in the quest for the perfect chip.

In short, with potatoes in the house, you will never go to bed hungry. Or, perhaps, entirely unhappy.

History

The homely spud is about as foreign as you can get – native to the Andes, they didn't arrive here until the end of the sixteenth century and, in Britain at least, were treated with suspicion for at least another hundred years after that, though they found favour in Ireland almost immediately.

Once they'd caught on, however, they quickly went native, as all of those mourning the decline of fish and chips as our national dish (first seen on these streets in the 1860s, some centuries after the curry) attest. Perfectly suited to our damp climate, economic and easy to grow in small spaces, with a long season and good storing potential, it was no wonder that they became a staple food for the poor.

The Victorian social reformer Henry Mayhew writes fascinatingly of the baked potato sellers who did a brisk trade on London's streets from August to April, reporting that one vendor at Smithfield, still a bustling meat market at that time, could hope to sell up to 1,000 spuds on market day, 'and to take upwards of £2' for his trouble.

Though consumption has dropped sharply in recent years in favour of quicker-cooking starchy rivals like rice and pasta, we still put away 90kg each annually, giving us quite a respectable showing in the world rankings of devoted spud munchers.

Nutrition

Nutrition-wise, potatoes are not as bad as their starchy reputation has us believe – they're a decent source of vitamin C, and not too bad on the fibre front either, especially if you leave the skins on. (And why wouldn't you, given that's where most of the flavour lies?)

Plus, of course, they're a good source of energy; indeed, it's possible to survive for a surprisingly long time eating nothing but potatoes.

It's a sad truth, however, that potatoes only come into their own when you add fat and salt; we love them more for their soothing, satiating properties than any particular nutritional benefits.

Varieties, storage and preparation

For a country apparently so enamoured by the potato, we pay surprisingly little attention to what kind we're eating. The most important distinction between the different varieties is waxy versus floury. Floury potatoes have higher levels of dry starch in their cells, which swell up and separate when cooked, resulting in a looser, fluffier texture better for mashed, roast and baked potatoes.

The cells in waxy potatoes, meanwhile, remain stuck together after cooking, which gives them the firmer, denser consistency required for potato salads and other dishes where you'd like them to keep their shape, such as sautéd potatoes, or pommes dauphinoise.

Because supermarkets often don't tell you what their potatoes are good for, here are a few of the most common names that appear on our shelves. Farmers' markets and farm shops are a handy source of more unusual varieties:

— Floury (good for mashing, roast potatoes with a fluffy texture, baked potatoes): Fianna, Golden Wonder, Kerr's Pink, King Edward, Maris Piper, Purple Majesty (dark purple skin, vivid purple flesh, very striking on the plate), Rooster, Shetland Black (dark purple outer skin, white flesh)
— Waxy (good for salads, boiling and gratins): Anya (good for salads), Charlotte (good for salads), Desiree (red-skinned), Estima, Lady Balfour, Maris Peer, Nicola, Pink Fir Apple, Vivaldi

Potatoes should be removed from any plastic wrapping as soon as you get them home, and stored in a cool, dark place. Not only are the unwashed sort cheaper, but they keep longer too.

When it comes to preparing them, always leave the skins on if possible; not just because they're the best bit of the potato, nutritionally speaking, they're also where most of the flavour lies, which is why I usually parboil my roast potatoes in a pan with their peelings. It sounds mad, but, as with so many ideas from Heston Blumenthal, there is method in it – taste the cooking water if you don't believe me.

Potatoes in the kitchen

The potato's bland starchiness makes them a good match for almost anything you can throw at them, but my absolute favourite pairing is probably potatoes and cheese, be that mild goat's curd, fresh from the market, or a chunk of dry Cheddar from the back of the fridge.

As any Scandinavian will tell you, this affinity with savoury ingredients also makes them a very good partner to cured and smoked fish and seafood, as well as, of course, its meaty equivalent. Crisp little potato and bacon cakes, fried in bacon fat, are a joy indeed on a brisk morning, especially if you add another of their natural pairings: an allium of some kind.

The creamy foil they offer for strong flavours also makes them the ideal blank canvas for spice (as the extensive repertoire of potato curries and dry-fried potato dishes from the Indian subcontinent will attest) and, of course, a very good date for a richly flavoured stew, whether that's a spicy Mexican mole or a Lancashire hotpot.

Fats like butter, olive oil and crème fraîche are vital for bringing the best out in them, and a good pinch of salt is important too. Treat them in the same way as pasta, and salt the cooking water liberally; some of the best new potatoes I have ever eaten were simmered in sea water.

I hope all this inspires you to play around a bit with your potatoes, rather than relegating them to the role of best supporting carb. Why eat them boiled when you could have aloo tikki Scotch eggs instead?

See also: Braised octopus with chickpeas and coriander (page 215, Octopus), Roast new potatoes with wild garlic dressing (page 328, Wild).

Baked potato soup

**serves 2 but easily
scaled up (or down)**

2 medium baking potatoes
20g butter
4 rashers of smoked
    streaky bacon (optional)
4 spring onions
750ml chicken stock (or
    vegetable if you'd prefer a
    meat-free dish)
1 tablespoon soured cream or
    crème fraîche
1 tablespoon chopped chives

This magnificently warming, velvety-textured soup combines the starchy creaminess of the spud with the savouriness of bacon and onions, enriched with a dollop of dairy. It's also a great way to use up leftover baked potatoes; just start from step 3.

1. Heat the oven to 220°C/fan 200°C/gas 7 (I usually bake my potatoes slightly hotter than this, but in this case we're not after a crisp skin). Wash and dry the potatoes well and prick in several places with a fork (this is insurance against them exploding in the oven and coating it in something with the properties of quick-drying cement), then wrap them in foil and bake for an hour.

2. Remove the foil and bake the potatoes for 15 minutes more, then take out of the oven and leave to cool slightly.

3. Meanwhile, melt the butter in a medium pan over a medium-low heat and finely chop the bacon if using. Add it to the pan and cook until beginning to brown. Roughly chop the spring onions. Scoop out about a quarter of the bacon with a slotted spoon and set aside as a garnish, then add the spring onions to the pan and soften for a couple of minutes. Roughly chop the potatoes, skins and all.

4. Add a little of the stock to the pan and scrape to deglaze, then tip in the potato and stir to coat with butter. Add the rest of the stock, bring to a simmer, then turn down the heat and cook gently for about 15 minutes.

5. Allow to cool slightly, then whiz with a hand blender until smoothish (don't overdo it or you'll end up with a gluey texture). Taste for seasoning (it probably won't need any further salt).

6. To serve, divide between bowls. Dribble a swirl of soured cream in the centre of each, and top with the chives and reserved bacon.

Chorizo baked potatoes with avocado crema

serves 4

4 large baking potatoes
Coarse salt
Olive oil
200g cooking chorizo, cut into
  small dice
5 spring onions, finely sliced
1 ripe avocado
2 tablespoons soured cream
Juice of 1 lime
A small bunch of coriander,
  roughly chopped

Simple, but effective – the lovely paprika-spiked oil from the sausages seasoning the creamy flesh of the potato, and setting off the zingy green avocado crema a treat. (NB: if you'd prefer to keep it dairy free, you could leave out the soured cream; the sauce will just be slightly thicker, more like guacamole.)

1. Heat the oven to 240°C/fan 220°C/gas 9. Wash the potatoes and half dry, so they're still a bit damp, then prick each one a few times with a fork to stop it exploding in the oven. Shake a layer of coarse salt on to a small plate, then roll each potato in it so it sticks in patches, and put them on a baking tray. Bake for about an hour to an hour and a quarter, depending on size, until the skin is crisp and the insides tender, then take out of the oven, turning it down to 200°C/fan 180°C/gas 6, cut a large cross in the top of each and leave to cool a little.
2. While they're cooling, heat a small frying pan with a dash of olive oil over a medium heat and add the chorizo. Cook until the pieces have released their own orange oil, then turn up the heat slightly and fry until beginning to crisp. Add the spring onions and fry for a minute until softened, then set aside.
3. When the potatoes are cool enough to handle, scoop the flesh into a bowl, being careful to leave the skins intact, and mash until smooth. Tip in the chorizo and onion mixture, making sure you get all the oil, and mix well. Season to taste, then put back into the skins and bake for 10–15 minutes, until hot all the way through.
4. Meanwhile, cut the avocado in half and scoop out the flesh. Mash with a fork into a rough purée, then add the soured cream and half the lime juice and use a stick blender to whiz until smooth. Stir in the coriander, season to taste, adding more lime juice if necessary, and then serve the jacket potatoes with a dollop of crema on top, with the rest on the table for people to help themselves to.

Aloo tikki Scotch eggs

**makes 10
(or 18 smaller versions)**

12 eggs (or 18 quail's eggs and
    2 hen's eggs)
800g floury potatoes
50g root ginger, peeled
2–3 small green chillies,
    deseeded, depending on
    taste
5 round shallots (or 1 large red
    onion)
Neutral oil, to fry
1 teaspoon cumin seeds
2 teaspoons mustard seeds
1 teaspoon garam masala
½ teaspoon ground turmeric
150g peas, defrosted
1 teaspoon salt
A small bunch of coriander,
    finely chopped
100g flour
200g panko breadcrumbs

A mash-up (forgive me) of two picnic classics from very different parts of the world, these are rich with spice, but only mildly hot, with a lovely fresh sweetness from the peas.

The hen's egg versions are quite hefty propositions, a satisfying lunch on their own, so if you'd prefer to make them just one part of a picnic, or as party food, try them with quail's eggs instead. They are good hot or at room temperature, and pair well with mango chutney, sweet and sour date and tamarind chutney or a coriander and mint raita.

1. Gently lower 10 of the eggs (or all of the quail's eggs) into a pan of boiling water and cook for 4½ minutes (2½ minutes for quail's eggs). Meanwhile, prepare a large bowl or sink of iced water and, once they're done, transfer the eggs quickly to this to cool down.
2. Cut the potatoes into large, roughly equal chunks and put into a large pan. Cover with cold water, salt liberally, put a lid on the pan and bring to the boil, then uncover, turn down the heat and simmer until tender. Drain and allow to cool, then peel off the skins and discard (doing it this way may be more fiddly, but the flavour is far better).
3. Meanwhile, use a pestle and mortar to mash the ginger and chillies to a paste and finely chop the shallots. Heat 2 tablespoons of oil over a medium heat in a medium frying pan and fry the shallots until soft, then add the ginger chilli paste and fry for a minute. Turn up the heat slightly and add the cumin and mustard seeds. Fry for 30 seconds, then stir in the other spices, adding a splash more oil if they start sticking, and fry for another minute or so, stirring. Take off the heat.
4. Mash the potatoes until smooth, then add three-quarters of the peas and mash roughly. Stir in the spice mixture and salt and, once well combined, add the remaining peas and the coriander and distribute evenly. Taste for seasoning.
5. Carefully peel the eggs. Take a roughly 125g lump (or about 60g for quail's eggs) of aloo tikki mixture and form into a ball, then poke a hole in the middle. Put the egg in it and seal up, then repeat with the rest.

6. Put three bowls – of flour, lightly seasoned, the remaining hen's eggs, lightly beaten, and breadcrumbs – next to the hob. Fill a large pan a third full of oil, and set over a medium heat until it comes to 190°C. Meanwhile, roll each egg in turn in flour, egg and breadcrumbs and then (for hen's eggs only) a second time in egg and breadcrumbs. Put a plate lined with kitchen paper next to the hob and get ready a slotted spoon.

7. Once the oil has come to temperature, lower the eggs in with the slotted spoon, two or three at a time (be careful not to overcrowd the pan or they won't crisp up) and fry for about 2–3 minutes until golden. Lift them out with the slotted spoon, salt lightly and drain on kitchen paper while you cook the rest, making sure the oil comes back up to temperature first.

Northern potato salad

serves 4

600g small, waxy
    potatoes (Jersey Royals
    or Charlottes are ideal)
1½ tablespoons cider vinegar
3 tablespoons neutral oil
4 teaspoons grated horseradish
A small bunch of dill, chopped
3 smoked mackerel fillets
A jar of cornichons or gherkins
4 tablespoons soured cream or
    crème fraîche

*For the quick-pickled
red onions:*
1 small red onion
90ml cider vinegar
¼ teaspoon salt
¼ teaspoon sugar
1 teaspoon black peppercorns,
    bruised

I'm not a big fan of bland, gloopy, mayonnaise-based potato salads, but I do love the creamy flavour and texture of cold waxy potatoes with strong smoked fish and acidic pickles, and such fashionably Scandinavian ingredients are just crying out for a little peppery horseradish heat. This is an excellent, and very satisfying weekend lunch. Note that you'll need to make the onions at least an hour in advance.

1. Very finely slice the onion and put into a colander. Pour half a kettle of boiling water over it and leave to drain. Whisk together the vinegar, salt and sugar, then put the drained onions into a jar with the peppercorns, cover with the vinegar and allow to sit for at least an hour (though you can make this days in advance if you like).

2. Cut the potatoes into equally sized pieces without peeling, then put into a pan and cover with cold water and a generous amount of salt. Bring to the boil, then turn down the heat and simmer until tender.

3. Meanwhile, whisk together the vinegar and oil with a generous pinch of salt, then stir in the horseradish. When the potatoes are done, drain well, then put into a bowl and toss with the dressing. Leave to sit for at least 30 minutes.

4. Toss the potatoes with the dill, then flake in the mackerel. Roughly chop a few cornichons or gherkins (how many depends on their size, so use your own judgement) and scatter over the top along with some of the pickled onion. Either dollop the soured cream in the middle, or divide between plates and then add it to each – or leave people to spoon on their own if you prefer.

Potato, black kale and anchovy pie

serves 6

750g large-ish waxy potatoes
A knob of butter, plus extra to grease
8–12 anchovies, rinsed well if packed in salt, and finely chopped
4 small garlic cloves, crushed
300ml double cream
150ml milk
200g trimmed black kale (cavolo nero), shredded

For the pastry:
150g butter
400g plain flour
½ teaspoon salt
1½ tablespoons mustard powder
1 egg, beaten with a little milk or water, to glaze (optional but handsome)

A cross between a French dauphinoise and a very British potato pie, with some salty little fish thrown in to add a touch of Scandi-chic, this is the kind of straightforward cold-weather food I love; creamy, rich with umami and comfortingly carby, it's an ideal lunch or dinner after a wintery walk, though you may need to go for a snooze afterwards. The kale makes it a complete meal in itself, but I usually serve a green salad too, just to balance things up a bit. It also cuts well for transportation, and makes for a nice, if rather decadent packed lunch in colder months.

The hot water crust pastry is soft, but very forgiving, almost like working with play-dough, but you can substitute shortcrust if you prefer, or, indeed dispense with the pastry altogether and bake it like a gratin – 30 minutes covered with foil at 180°C/fan 160°C/gas 4, then a further 10–15 minutes uncovered, until browned on top.

1. Use a food processor or mandoline to thinly slice the potatoes.
2. Melt a knob of butter or some oil from the anchovies in a very large saucepan (you're going to have to get the potatoes in there eventually) over a medium-low heat and add 8 of the anchovies. Cook, stirring, until they dissolve into the fat, then add the garlic, cook for about 30 seconds, then stir in the cream and milk and bring slowly to the boil. Taste, and add more finely chopped anchovies if you'd prefer a stronger flavour.

229

3. Put the potatoes into the pan, cover and simmer gently for 10 minutes, turning occasionally to redistribute, or until they are softened but not cooked through. Meanwhile, bring a large pan of well-salted water to the boil and cook the kale until just tender (about 1–1½ minutes), then drain well.

4. Heat the oven to 200°C/fan 180°C/gas 6 and grease a medium pie dish (I use one about 20 x 26cm) with butter.

5. To make the pastry, put the butter in a small pan with 110ml of water and heat until melted. Bring to a simmer. Meanwhile, put the flour in a mixing bowl with the salt and mustard powder and whisk together well. Pour in the hot butter and water mixture and stir until it comes together into a dough.

6. Set a third of the pastry aside and roll out the rest to about double the size of the pie dish, then carefully lift it into place (it will be very soft, so if you end up doing it in scraps, don't worry!), pressing it into the corners.

7. Spoon half the potatoes into the dish, followed by the kale, followed by the remaining potatoes. Roll out the rest of the pastry and place over the top, then crimp together the edges to seal. Brush with the egg wash, poke a couple of holes in the top for the steam to escape, then bake for about 45 minutes, until golden. Allow to cool a little before serving.

Aligot

serves 2–4 depending on accompaniments and greed

500g waxy potatoes
125g butter
110ml double cream
1 small garlic clove
200g Lancashire cheese,
    very finely chopped
A whole nutmeg, to grate

Potatoes, butter, cream, garlic, and vast amounts of cheese – really, there is no way you can go wrong with this classic recipe from south-west France. It's very hard to come by the fresh Tomme cheese traditionally used to make it outside its home region, but a creamy Lancashire is a fairly close match for flavour, and gives a delicious, if not entirely authentic result.

This would generally be served with meat, but I find it so rich that I serve it with nothing more than some steamed greens, or even a sharp salad.

1. Cut the potatoes into evenly sized pieces but do not peel. Put them into a pan with a good shake of salt. Barely cover with cold water and bring to the boil, then turn down the heat and simmer until tender all the way through. Drain.

2. Melt the butter and the double cream together in a small pan with the crushed garlic clove. When the potatoes are just cool enough to handle (don't wait too long), peel and mash or put through a ricer and put back over a low heat. Use a stick blender, if you have one, to whiz them, along with a splash of the melted butter and cream, to a smooth, gluey purée.

3. Beat in the remaining cream and butter mixture vigorously with a wooden spoon or the stick blender – at this point you will be moved to check you've got the amounts right, as they will seem outrageous, but don't worry, it will all be absorbed.

4. Beat in the cheese until smooth and very gluey, followed by a good grating of nutmeg. This will take a lot of elbow grease, but when it's ready the aligot should have a stringy, elastic texture. Serve immediately.

Tattie scones à la Arnold Bennett

serves 2

250g floury potatoes, e.g. Maris Pipers or King Edwards
150g smoked haddock, or other smoked firm white fish
200ml milk
50g plain flour
3 spring onions, finely sliced
A whole nutmeg, to grate
200g spinach

For the hollandaise:
2 egg yolks
125g butter, diced
A dash of white wine vinegar or lemon juice

This dish is loosely based on the outrageously rich omelette created for, or at least enjoyed by the Edwardian novelist Arnold Bennett at the Savoy Hotel.

It's lighter than the original, but if you really want to push the boat out you could also add a poached egg.

1. Put the potatoes, unpeeled but cut into equally sized pieces, into a pan, cover with cold water, salt liberally and bring to the boil. Turn down the heat and simmer until tender all the way through.
2. Meanwhile, put the haddock into a smallish pan just big enough to hold it in one layer with the milk, over a medium heat. Bring to a simmer, then turn down the heat and cook gently for 5 minutes, turning the fish over halfway through. Remove the fish from the milk and set aside.
3. Drain the cooked potatoes. Mash until smooth, then beat in just enough of the haddock-infused milk that the mixture grudgingly drops off the spoon – you certainly won't need it all. Stir in the flour to make a soft dough, then season and mix in the spring onions and a good grating of nutmeg until evenly distributed.
4. Roll the dough out on a well-floured surface to about ½cm thick. Cut round a side plate to make circles, then flour the tops and prick all over with a fork.
5. To make the hollandaise, put the egg yolks into a small pan with the diced butter and 1 teaspoon of cold water. Heat very gently, stirring constantly, until they melt together and the sauce thickens to your liking. Stir in a dash of white wine vinegar or lemon juice and keep warm.

6. Wash the spinach and put, still wet, into a large pan. Cover and heat gently for a couple of minutes, until wilted. Drain, squeeze out any excess water and keep warm.

7. Heat a well-greased griddle or heavy-based frying pan on a medium heat and fry the scones for about 3 minutes on each side, until golden. Cut into quarters and keep warm while you fry the rest. While they're cooking, flake the haddock.

8. To serve, put a tattie scone on a plate and top with spinach, followed by haddock, followed by a generous dollop of hollandaise. Season with a little black pepper for colour and serve immediately.

Potato and cauliflower curry with coconut and cashew cream

serves 2 as a main dish, 4–6 as a side

For the aloo gobi:
400g waxy potatoes
1 tablespoon vegetable oil
½ teaspoon chilli powder
½ teaspoon ground turmeric
½ teaspoon mustard seeds
½ teaspoon salt
1 small cauliflower

This is my Keralan-inspired take on the classic northern Indian aloo gobi, with a rich, thick sauce of coconut cream and cashew nuts. It's hefty enough to make a meal on its own with some plain rice and a punchy pickle of some sort, but you could also serve it as part of a curry feast if you prefer – and it would be great with sautéd greens or grilled fish.

1. Heat the oven to 200°C/fan 180°C/gas 6 and cut the potatoes into halves or quarters depending on their size. Mix together the oil, spices and salt and toss half of this together with the potatoes, then spread out on a baking tray and bake for 15 minutes. Meanwhile, cut the cauliflower into florets and then, after 15 minutes, toss together with the remaining spice mix and add to the baking tray. Bake for another 15–20 minutes, until the potatoes are about cooked through.

For the curry:
50g cashew nuts
100g creamed coconut (the
   solid stuff that comes in
   blocks)
2 tablespoons neutral oil
1 large onion, thinly sliced
2 small green chillies, 1 finely
   chopped and 1 slit down
   its length but left whole
3 garlic cloves, crushed
1 tablespoon ginger, finely
   grated
2 teaspoons ground coriander
$\frac{1}{2}$ teaspoon ground turmeric
$\frac{1}{2}$ teaspoon ground fennel
   seeds
$\frac{1}{4}$ teaspoon garam masala
A handful of coriander

2. Meanwhile, soak the cashew nuts in a generous amount of hot water for 15 minutes and dissolve the coconut in 250ml of hot water. Drain the cashews, retaining the soaking water, and whiz them up to a purée along with 5 tablespoons of the soaking water to make a loose-ish paste.

3. Heat the oil in a frying pan and add the onion. Cook until soft and golden, then stir in the chopped chilli, garlic and ginger. Cook for another couple of minutes, then stir in the dry spices and a pinch of salt and cook for a further 2 or 3 minutes.

4. Stir in the coconut cream and cashew purée, scraping the bottom of the pan, followed by the potatoes, cauliflower and remaining chilli. Simmer until the sauce thickly coats the vegetables, then serve with plenty of chopped coriander.

is for Quiver

I defy anyone to watch a jelly wobble with a straight face. It's like fireworks, or the first sunny day of spring – a joy that never gets old.

Not only are jellies mobile in a way rare in foods not actively trying to escape their fate, but they're incredibly biddable; it's possible to set almost anything that takes your fancy – the amorphous jelly can take on just about any shape, hue, flavour and texture that the heart desires. It also has the benefit, as far as visual effects are concerned, of being, at its most basic, completely transparent; something almost unique in the culinary world, and strangely alluring. A clear wine jelly, studded with jewel-like fruits, with the sun shining through it, is a vision fit for a Dutch still life.

Jellies, panna cottas and their ilk are also a great way to impress guests: quick and easy to produce, happy to sit in the fridge for several days, and, most importantly, stunning to look at – there's something quite wonderful about the way they seem to defy the ordinary laws of physics.

Science

Sadly for vegetarians, gelatine is by far the best setting agent for jellies; vegetarian alternatives such as the seaweed-based agar agar tend to lack the smooth texture, and clarity, of their animal-based counterpart.

Gelatine is extracted from a tough fibrous protein called collagen, found in the connective tissues of an animal's skin, bones and muscles; the richest sources are those cuts which require long slow cooking: feet, ears, tails and other good things. It's made up of a sequence of tightly wound chains of amino acids – when these are heated above body temperature they relax and disperse, and will not begin to reassemble until the temperature falls again.

As the mixture cools, surrounded by a stiffening mesh of gelatine molecules, the liquid in your jelly mix can no longer flow freely, and thus becomes a shaky kind of solid. This sensitivity to temperature helps explain why gelatine must not be heated to boiling point – above a certain temperature, its amino acids start to break down, and your jelly will not set.

Interestingly, jellies set firmer if allowed to cool slowly, rather than having their temperature brought down more rapidly in the fridge.

Jelly basics

If the idea of ditching the familiar fruity cubes leaves you feeling quivery, it's helpful to remember the very simple principle behind all types of jellies, blancmanges and panna cottas:

Liquid + setting agent = jelly

There's no more mystery to it than that.

The only even vaguely tricky business is working out how much setting agent you need to achieve the consistency you're after; too little and your jelly won't hold together, too much and though it will look impressive, it's likely to be unpalatably firm and rubbery on the spoon.

Helpfully, however, *one leaf of gelatine will set about 100ml liquid* firm enough to turn out on to a plate – if you'd prefer a softer consistency, and plan to serve it in whatever you've set it in (generally a glass dish, for best effect), then you can get away with less.

Dairy-based jellies will also require less, thanks to the proteins in the milk, as will jellies made with thicker liquids, such as fruit purées. Conversely, it's wise to use more gelatine than specified if the jelly is to be served in a very warm environment, or you're attempting an ambitiously large edifice, or one containing large amounts of alcohol.

I find leaf gelatine much easier to work with than the powdered stuff (which has an off-putting whiff of hoof about it); you'll find it in the baking section of most supermarkets. It requires soaking in water before use – make sure you use enough that the sheets don't stick together, and don't leave them soaking for much longer than they take to soften, or they may disintegrate. Squeeze out well before adding to your liquid, which must be above 37°C (body temperature) for the gelatine to melt, but below a simmer for it to work effectively.

If using vegetarian alternatives, follow the directions on the packet for setting the appropriate amount of liquid.

See also: Pandan and coconut burnt creams (page 74, Eggs).

For how to unmould a jelly see page 250.

Tricolore jellies

makes 6

For the tomato jelly:
600g ripe tomatoes, halved or
    quartered
1 small garlic clove, crushed
100ml tomato juice
¼ teaspoon sugar
2½ gelatine leaves
Neutral oil, to grease

For the mozzarella
panna cotta:
1 burrata (you won't need
    all of it)
100ml whole milk
1 gelatine leaf

For the basil jelly:
1 lemon
40g fresh basil leaves, plus a
    few extra
1½ gelatine leaves

Familiar flavours – the tang of tomato, the creaminess of mozzarella, the sweet pepperiness of basil – cast in a new and unexpected form: miniature jellies.

You can make them a couple of days before if you like, which is always handy – and though it looks like you've gone to great effort, the work involved is both minimal and basic.

1. For the tomato jelly, whiz up the tomatoes and garlic with the juice, the sugar and a pinch of salt and pepper in a food processor until coarsely chopped. Line a sieve with muslin or a clean tea towel, set it over a large bowl and pour in the tomatoes, then gather up the sides of the material over the tomatoes and secure the top of the bundle with an elastic band. Suspend this above the bowl (I do this from the arm of my stand mixer, but any hook or cupboard handle will do) and leave to drain for at least 3 hours, squeezing the bag occasionally to help it along.

2. Once you've drained off most of the tomato liquid (you should have about 300ml – if it's significantly less, top up with tomato juice; if more, make the excess into a Bloody Mary shot), soak the gelatine leaves in a bowl of cold water until soft and scrunchable. Meanwhile, bring the juice to a simmer in a small pan. Squeeze out the gelatine and stir into the warm juice until dissolved.

3. Grease six small dariole moulds, or small glass dishes if you don't want to turn them out, and divide the tomato mixture between them. Chill until set.

4. When the tomato jelly is beginning to set, measure out 75g of the burrata, making sure you get a good lot of the cream inside. Finely chop the solid skin. Put into a small pan with the milk and a generous pinch of salt and heat gently, stirring once warm to encourage the cheese to melt. Meanwhile, soak the gelatine in cold water until soft. Once the dairy mixture is smoothish, squeeze out the gelatine and stir into the milk, then allow to cool to warm room temperature, stirring occasionally. Pour over the back of a spoon on top of the set tomato jelly (to stop them merging) and refrigerate.

5. For the basil jelly, bring a small pan of salted water to the boil and prepare a large bowl of iced water with the juice of the lemon squeezed into it. Blanch the basil for 15 seconds, then scoop out into the iced water. Reserve 180ml of the blanching water, and allow it to cool slightly. Meanwhile, soak the gelatine as before. Stir it into the warm blanching water and allow to cool, stirring occasionally, then drain and roughly chop or coarsely purée the basil and stir it into the gelatine mixture with a pinch of salt. Pour on top of the panna cotta and refrigerate until set.

6. Turn out on to plates if you're feeling brave, or serve in the dishes, with a basil leaf on top, a drizzle of extra virgin olive oil and some toasted ciabatta.

Goat's cheese custards with honey-glazed hazelnuts and black olive toasts

makes 4

150ml single cream
150ml whole milk
1 sprig of rosemary, bruised
    with the back of a knife
85g strong hard goat's cheese,
    finely grated
2 egg yolks
Butter, to grease

For the honey-glazed hazelnuts:
15g butter
1 tablespoon hot water
1 tablespoon honey
100g hazelnuts
½ teaspoon salt
¼ teaspoon sugar
Leaves from 3 sprigs of
    rosemary

Not strictly a jelly, but wobbly enough that they qualify for this chapter anyway. Inspired by Rowley Leigh's dreamy Parmesan custards, but with a southern French twist, they pair piquant goat's cheese with sweet, honeyed nuts. The tapenade toasts aren't essential, but as with Leigh's anchovy variety, the two salty flavours work surprisingly well together.

An ideal dinner starter, all the elements can be prepared well in advance, and the custards, which are lovely both warm and cold, grilled just before serving.

1. Heat the cream, milk and rosemary together in a small pan and whisk in 75g (or all but a tablespoon) of the finely grated cheese until melted and smooth. Take off the heat and allow to cool.

2. Meanwhile, turn your attention to the hazelnuts. Melt the butter in a small pan over a medium-high heat, and whisk the hot water and honey together. Add the nuts and cook until they start to colour, then add the salt and sugar. Cook until the liquid has mostly evaporated. Meanwhile, line a baking tray with foil or greaseproof paper. Stir the

For the black olive toasts:
150g stoned black olives
2 tablespoons capers, rinsed if
  salted
4 anchovies, roughly chopped
Juice of ½ a lemon
3 tablespoons extra virgin
  olive oil
4 thin slices of bread

rosemary leaves into the glazed nuts and spoon the nuts on to the tray, spreading them out well. Cool.

3. Heat the oven to 150°C/fan 130°C/gas 2 and boil a kettle. Fish out the rosemary from the cheese mixture and discard, then pass through a fine sieve into a jug and whisk in the egg yolks. Grease four small ramekins and put them into a baking tin. Divide the mixture between them and put the tin into the oven. Pour in the boiling water to come halfway up the ramekins. Bake for 20–30 minutes, until set on top, but still wobbly in the middle. Allow to cool to warm, or completely if you prefer.

4. Meanwhile, whiz the olives, capers and anchovies together until smoothish, then whisk in the lemon juice and oil. Taste and adjust as necessary.

5. When ready to serve, heat the grill. Scatter the remaining cheese over the top of the custards and grill until golden and bubbling (you could also use a blowtorch).

6. Toast the bread until crisp. Serve the custards with a few roughly chopped hazelnuts and rosemary needles scattered on top, and the toast, thinly spread with the olive paste and cut into soldiers.

Jelly cherry jubilee

serves a large party (10–12)

For the cherry jelly:
1 litre unsweetened cherry
    juice (see intro)
8 gelatine leaves
Neutral oil, to grease
200g cherries, stoned and
    halved

For the kirsch cream:
275ml double cream
850ml whole milk
8 tablespoons white sugar
8 gelatine leaves
150ml kirsch

Should you ever have had your fill of cherries straight from the paper bag (competitive pit-spitting entirely optional), try this impressive stripy jelly, based on the flavours of a flambéd cherry pudding created by the great French chef Escoffier for Queen Victoria's Diamond Jubilee in 1897, but far easier to make.

Unsweetened cherry juice can be found at health food shops; if you can't lay your hands on any *kirschwasser*, substitute any other clear, unsweetened brandy instead. (Cherry brandy, despite the name, is a sugary liqueur which won't do at all.)

1. Heat the cherry juice in a pan until quite warm, but not hot. Meanwhile, soak the gelatine leaves for the cherry jelly in cold water. Once the juice is warm, take off the heat, squeeze out the gelatine thoroughly and whisk into the pan, then set aside to cool.
2. Heat the cream and milk in a new pan until quite warm, but not hot, whisking in the sugar until dissolved. Meanwhile, soak the remaining gelatine leaves in cold water. Once the milk is warm, take off the heat, stir in the kirsch, squeeze out the gelatine thoroughly and whisk into the pan, then set aside to cool, whisking each jelly mixture regularly as it cools.
3. Grease a 2 litre mould (a bundt tin makes for an impressive shape), then arrange a ring of cherries around the base. Gently pour in a layer of the cooled cherry jelly (you're aiming for three layers of each, but it will depend on the shape of your mould), then put into the fridge to set.
4. Once set, top with a layer of the milk jelly, pouring it on to a spoon angled just above the set jelly so the pressure doesn't disturb the surface, followed by a layer of the cherries and cherry jelly and so on. Cover and chill until completely set; I like to leave mine overnight if possible.
5. Dip the mould briefly into hand-hot water, then invert on to a plate.

Gooseberry and buttermilk pots

makes 6

For the gooseberry jelly:
225g gooseberries
55g caster sugar
2 gelatine leaves
2 tablespoons elderflower
   cordial

For the panna cotta:
100ml double cream
40g caster sugar
1½ gelatine leaves
250ml buttermilk

The sadly under-appreciated gooseberry is one of my favourite summer flavours – so wonderfully green and tart, it's a shame we seem to have fallen out of love with them as a nation, because we grow the finest examples in the world, particularly in the northern wilds of Scotland, where these prickly, gnarled bushes are one of the few things to withstand the punishing wind.

Their natural acidity makes them the perfect candidate for rich creamy flavours – gooseberry fool is the most obvious example. This is but a slightly more elegant take on that most excellent of desserts, perfect for when you'd like to impress. If your gooseberries are very sweet and ripe, the kind you can just about eat raw, then you may want to cook them for slightly less time, so they keep more of their shape and colour.

1. Make the jelly first. Top and tail the gooseberries and put into a small pan with the sugar. Cover and heat gently for about 15 minutes, until the fruit is soft, but still mostly retains its shape.
2. Allow to cool slightly. Meanwhile, soak the gelatine for the gooseberry jelly in cold water for a few minutes until soft, then wring out and stir into the slightly cooled fruit, along with the cordial and 175ml of water. Mix well and pour into six glass ramekins or small glasses. Put into the fridge for a couple of hours to set.
3. Once the jellies are beginning to firm up, put the cream into a small pan with the sugar over a low heat and stir to dissolve. Bring to a simmer, then take off the heat and allow to cool slightly. Meanwhile, soak the remaining gelatine in cold water for a few minutes until soft, then wring out and stir into the cooling cream.
4. Pour in the buttermilk and stir well, then divide between the glasses and chill until set.

Caribbean milk punch jelly

serves 8–10

150ml condensed milk
150ml whole milk
9 gelatine leaves
100g soft light brown sugar
600ml stout or porter, preferably
    chocolate or milk stout
1½ tablespoons cocoa powder
Neutral oil, to grease
A whole nutmeg, to grate

A rich brown, almost black underneath, with a creamy white top, this is a lovely thing to bring in, gently wobbling, at the end of a meal, and a killer choice for St Patrick's Day.

1. Put the condensed milk and whole milk into a small pan and heat until quite warm, but not hot. Meanwhile, soak two of the gelatine leaves in cold water. Once the milks are warm, take off the heat, squeeze out the gelatine thoroughly and whisk into the pan, then set aside to cool.

2. Meanwhile, dissolve the sugar in 100ml of water in a medium pan, then bring to the boil. Simmer for about 5 minutes, until syrupy, then take off the heat and add the beer and cocoa powder, stirring to dissolve the cocoa. Put back on the heat and warm through. Soak the remaining gelatine as before and whisk in when the beer is warm. Take off the heat and leave to cool, stirring both pans regularly.

3. Lightly grease a 1 litre jelly mould. Pour the cooled condensed milk jelly into it and put into the fridge to set, remembering to keep stirring the beer jelly.

4. Once the milk jelly has set, gently pour the beer jelly on to a spoon held just over its surface (this helps to stop the two merging), then cover and chill for at least 8 hours, until set. Turn out and top with freshly grated nutmeg.

How to unmould a jelly

Metal or plastic moulds are easier to work with than glass ones, but I still like to coat them with a thin film of neutral oil before filling them to make unmoulding easier. If you do this, make sure the jelly is cool before pouring it into the mould, or this layer of fat will be melted.

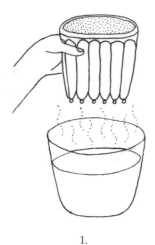

1.
Dip the outside of the mould briefly in hot water.

2.
Slightly wet the plate you're planning to turn the jelly out on to, and the surface of the jelly.

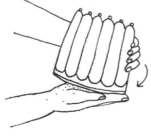

3.
Hold the mould flat in one hand and tilt the jelly slightly to one side while using the fingers of the other hand to loosen it all the way round.

4.
Tilt the mould further towards the horizontal while rotating it, holding the jelly in place with your free hand until you feel its full weight on your hand.

5.
Slide a plate underneath to replace your hand and let the jelly sit for a minute before removing the mould.

Almond and rosewater blancmange

serves 8–10

1 litre unsweetened almond
   milk
175g–200g white sugar
   (depending on sweetness
   of tooth)
3 tablespoons rice flour
8 gelatine leaves
¼ teaspoon rosewater, or to
   taste
¼ teaspoon almond essence,
   or to taste
Neutral oil, to grease
Blanched almonds, crystallized
   rose petals, edible fresh
   flowers or coloured sugar, to
   decorate

Blancmange, still a trembly feature of children's birthday parties in the 1980s, has disappeared entirely from our diet, unmarked and unmourned, which seems a shame after nearly a millennium. To be fair, those stout floury rabbits of my youth, their lurid colours making a mockery of the 'white food' name, were but a distant relation of the original, delicately spiced courtly dish, which was made from rice, almonds and finely minced chicken.

This version takes it back to its dairy-free medieval roots, using almond milk and rice flour as a thickener. If you'd like to keep it vegan, replace the gelatine with agar agar or carragheen according to packet instructions for setting a litre of liquid.

1. Put the almond milk and sugar into a medium pan and bring to a simmer, stirring to dissolve the sugar. As it heats, put the rice flour into a large heatproof bowl and whisk in a little of the warm milk to make a smooth paste, then pour the simmering milk on to it, whisking to combine well.
2. Pour back into the pan and stir until just thickened sufficiently that a finger down the back of a wooden spoon leaves a clear line. Take off the heat and allow to cool until warm, rather than hot.
3. Meanwhile, soak the gelatine leaves in cold water until soft, then squeeze out any excess liquid. Once the mixture has cooled a little, add the rosewater and almond essence to taste (brands vary greatly in strength, so this is a minimum amount), followed by the squeezed-out gelatine, stirring vigorously to dissolve.
4. Grease a 1 litre mould and pour in the blancmange mixture. Cover and chill until set – this will take several hours. Once you're sure it's solid, dip the mould briefly into a bowl of hot water, then upend on a plate. Decorate with your choice of garnish, then serve.

R

is for Rhubarb

A taste for rhubarb has always seemed a peculiarly British peccadillo – eye-wateringly tart and uncompromisingly stringy, with the look of overgrown celery, it should be a hard one to love, and yet love it we do.

We're not alone – though it still baffles the French, rhubarb is a popular addition to Norwegian baking, the key ingredient in one of Italy's beloved bittersweet aperitifs, rabarbaro, and is made into cold soup in Poland, while in Afghanistan they dip it in salt and eat it raw.

And this plant, forever associated for me with damp hockey boots and curdled custard, has a surprisingly interesting history. A native of north and central Asia, it's been valued for its medicinal qualities for millennia, and was imported into ancient Greece as a laxative (though don't worry – you have to eat quite a bit to feel the effects).

The seventeenth-century English herbalist Nicholas Culpeper claimed, somewhat hopefully perhaps, that it 'heals jaundice . . . provokes urine . . . is very effective for reins [gonorrhoea] and helps gout, sciatica . . . toothache . . . [kidney] stones and . . . dimness of sight' – little wonder that rhubarb powder was once worth more than opium. It wasn't to become popular as a foodstuff for another century, and it's no coincidence that its fortunes changed around the same time as Britain's burgeoning empire made sugar an affordable luxury for the first time.

The green stalks the girth of a terrier's leg typically found in British gardens bear little resemblance to the slender pink stems that you'll spot in greengrocers from Christmas to Easter. Forced rhubarb, a practice that always sounds faintly cruel, is grown in darkness, so the plants shoot straight up in their desperate quest for light, giving them a tender texture and delicate flavour.

Visiting one of the handful of growers still operating in the once mighty Rhubarb Triangle between Wakefield, Leeds and Bradford, I found stepping into the warm, dark sheds a distinctly unsettling experience – the plants, with their sickly yellow leaves and neon stalks thrusting vainly towards the ceiling, can put on five centimetres a day, a rate of growth that had a whiff of the triffids to me.

The summer stuff may not be as pretty, but it's criminally easy to grow – even a plant neglected at the bottom of the garden will provide you with more puddings than you can probably handle.

Season: forced indoor rhubarb, December to March; outdoor, April to September.

Cooking

That said, older rhubarb does need a little more care taken with its preparation, as those sturdy stalks can be stringy. Like celery, however, this is a problem easily solved with a peeler.

Rhubarb's high water content means it needs little in the way of liquid to cook – indeed, you're more likely to be troubled by the excess of pale pink juice that has a tendency to leave the most robust pastry soggy at the knees, and curdle your carefully made custard – so it's a great candidate for roasting, which concentrates the flavour. (The juices can come in useful though; Nigel Slater tops them up with sparkling water for a pretty pink drink, Nigella Lawson makes them into jelly, and I've gone for a deceptively innocent-looking gin-soaked granita.)

Though it's most often eaten as a dessert in this country, rhubarb's piercing astringency makes it an excellent accompaniment to rich savoury dishes too; classically paired with oily fish like mackerel, it will also cut through the natural fattiness of meats like pork, duck and lamb, and makes a killer partner for cheese.

Rhubarb loves ...

FLORAL FLAVOURS
Rose, orange blossom,
lavender

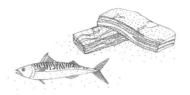

OILY FISH AND FATTY MEAT
Mackerel, pork belly,
black pudding, pâté

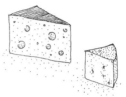

CHEESE
Nutty Cheddar
creamy ricotta

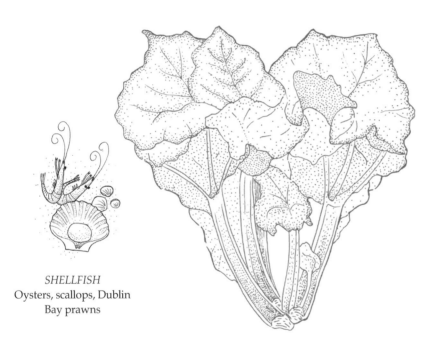

SHELLFISH
Oysters, scallops, Dublin
Bay prawns

SWEET THINGS
Demerara, honey,
maple syrup

DAIRY
Custard, ice cream,
Greek yoghurt, cream

AROMATIC HERBS
Rosemary and thyme

CITRUS
Especially oranges and pink grapefruit

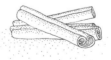

SWEET SPICE
Vanilla, cinnamon, ginger, chilli

Mackerel and samphire tartare with pickled rhubarb

serves 4 as a substantial starter

½ a small red onion, very finely chopped
4 very fresh mackerel fillets, skinned and boned
Juice of 2 limes
A small bunch of coriander, finely chopped
A dash of olive or rapeseed oil
A handful of samphire or 2 tablespoons capers

For the pickled rhubarb:
125g caster sugar
2 tablespoons coarse salt
½ teaspoon yellow mustard seeds
½ teaspoon peppercorns
1 dried red chilli
120ml cider vinegar
4cm piece of slim root ginger, peeled and thinly sliced
150g rhubarb, destringed if large, and thinly sliced

Apart from barbecued on the beach it was landed on, my favourite way to eat mackerel is raw; when super fresh, its oily flesh is almost creamily rich, making it (in my opinion) a better choice than the more usual salmon for the tartare treatment, though salmon makes a good substitute here if you prefer. Serve with a salad and some thin rye bread toasts.

1. Make the rhubarb pickle at least 24 hours before you want to serve it. Combine all the ingredients except the ginger and rhubarb in a small pan and bring to the boil, stirring to dissolve the salt and sugar. Add the ginger. Meanwhile, pack the rhubarb into a medium jar, then pour the hot pickling liquor over it to cover. Allow to cool slightly, then tighten the lid.

2. When you're ready to eat, soak the finely chopped red onion in iced water for 5 minutes while you prepare the rest of the tartare. Cut the mackerel into small dice, then squeeze over the lime and add the coriander and a dash of oil. Season and toss together with the well-drained onion and capers, if using them instead of samphire.

3. Scatter over the samphire fronds, if using, and add a generous helping of pickled rhubarb. Taste to check the seasoning, then serve immediately.

Pork rillettes with rhubarb chutney

serves 6

For the rillettes:
500g pork belly, skin removed
450g pork shoulder
2 teaspoons salt
1 bay leaf
2 garlic cloves, crushed with
     the back of a knife

For the rhubarb chutney:
100g soft light brown sugar
100ml cider vinegar
1 red onion, finely chopped
1 unwaxed orange, zest only
½ teaspoon salt
½ teaspoon fennel seeds
1 star anise
½ teaspoon Sichuan
     peppercorns
500g rhubarb, roughly chopped

Meltingly soft meat spread on crisp toast with a lightly spiced, sharp rhubarb chutney to cut through all that rich, creamy fat – an indulgent lunch indeed, but in small quantities this is also an excellent make-ahead starter for a dinner party.

Originally conceived as a method of preservation, if you seal them well, the rillettes should keep for a good few months, as will the chutney; the flavour certainly improves after 3 or 4 days if you can wait that long.

1. To make the rillettes, heat the oven to 170°C/fan 150°C/gas 3. Cut the pork into rough 4cm chunks and put into an ovenproof casserole dish with the other ingredients. Add about 600ml of cold water to just barely cover, then put on the heat and bring to a simmer. Cover and bake for 3–4 hours, until most of the fat has melted, and the meat is falling apart.

2. Meanwhile, for the chutney, put all the ingredients apart from the rhubarb into a large pan, bring to the boil, stirring to dissolve the sugar and salt, and boil for 5 minutes. Add the rhubarb, bring to the boil again, then turn down the heat and simmer until the rhubarb has broken down and the mixture is thick and jammy. Spoon into clean jars.

3. When the pork is ready, place a sieve over a large bowl and separate the solids from the liquid. Decant the liquid back into the pan and simmer, adding any remaining whole pieces of fat, then once this has melted, pour the liquid back into the same bowl, or a gravy separator if you have one. Meanwhile, shred the meat in the sieve into strands with a fork, or your fingers.

4. Once the fat has risen to the surface of the liquid, spoon it off into a fresh bowl, and pour the brown meaty juices beneath on to the meat. Check the seasoning of the meat and pack into ramekins or a jar or pot, then, once cool, pour the fat on top (you may need to reheat if it has solidified in the meantime). Refrigerate until ready to eat (if you want to keep it for longer than a few days, buy some lard, melt, and use to create a really solid seal on top of the ramekins or jars, which should mean it keeps for up to 4 months in the fridge.

5. Serve the rillettes at room temperature, with the rhubarb chutney and some crisp toast.

Persian lamb and rhubarb stew

Serves 4

3 tablespoons olive oil
1 large onion, finely sliced
½ teaspoon ground turmeric
500g boned shoulder of lamb, cut into bite-sized chunks
A large bunch of parsley, roughly chopped
A small bunch of mint, leaves only, roughly chopped
A generous pinch of saffron
4 stalks of rhubarb, cut into 4cm lengths
2 tablespoons honey, or to taste
2 tablespoons flaked almonds, toasted, to serve (optional)

A wonderfully vivid green dish where the sharpness of the rhubarb makes the perfect foil for the rich slow-cooked lamb, though you could substitute beef shin, or even chicken thighs if you prefer. Serve with basmati rice to soak up the turmeric yellow sauce, and a fresh herb salad.

1. Heat 2 tablespoons of oil in a casserole dish, and soften the onion with a pinch of salt. When golden, add the turmeric and cook for a couple of minutes, then turn up the heat and add the lamb, in batches if necessary, and brown, stirring so the onions don't burn.

2. Pour in 500ml of water and scrape the bottom, then bring to a simmer, cover, turn down the heat and simmer for 1 hour.

3. Heat the remaining oil in a frying pan and fry the chopped herbs for a couple of minutes until they wilt. Add to the casserole along with the saffron and cook for another 15 minutes.

4. Add the rhubarb, cover and cook for about 15 minutes, until broken down into the sauce. Stir in the honey and taste for seasoning – depending on your rhubarb, you may also want to add a little more honey if you find it too sour. Sprinkle with the almonds just before serving, if using.

Rhubarb Bircher muesli

makes 6 servings

550g rhubarb, cut into 4cm
  batons
200ml apple juice
4 tablespoons honey
125g jumbo rolled oats
150g natural yoghurt
30g shelled pistachios,
  toasted and roughly
  chopped
30g almonds, toasted and
  roughly chopped

More usually made with grated apples (there's a classic recipe in *Perfect Host*), this is the spring and summer equivalent.

For the sake of aesthetics, you can keep a few chunks of rhubarb back to top the dishes, but when I make this for myself at home, I just stir it all together. Muesli, after all, does mean 'mash'. This keeps well in the fridge for several days.

1. Put the rhubarb into a small pan with the apple juice and 3 tablespoons of honey. Heat gently, stirring to dissolve the honey, until the rhubarb has softened and begun to break down – some pieces should still be intact.
2. Meanwhile, toast the oats in a hot dry frying pan until fragrant. Allow the rhubarb to cool in the syrup, then tip into a sieve set over a bowl to collect the juices.
3. Put the oats into a large-ish bowl and tip over the rhubarb juices. Leave to soak overnight, then stir in the yoghurt, a pinch of salt, half the nuts and the rhubarb, reserving a few whole chunks to top. Refrigerate until ready to serve.
4. Serve with a couple of chunks of rhubarb in the middle, scattered with the remaining nuts and a drizzle of honey.

Rhubarb and marmalade sticky pudding

serves 6

1 stick of rhubarb, cut into 4cm
   lengths
6 tablespoons marmalade
   with peel
2 tablespoons golden syrup
150g softened butter, plus
   extra to grease
120g soft light brown sugar
2 eggs, beaten
100g spelt flour
50g plain flour
2 teaspoons baking powder
90ml milk

Rhubarb, marmalade and sticky steamed pudding; you'd be hard pressed to find a more British pudding than this, unless you served it with Bird's custard. Which, of course, you absolutely must.

1. Put the rhubarb, 3 tablespoons of marmalade and the golden syrup into a small pan and heat gently for about 5 minutes, until the marmalade and syrup have melted together and the rhubarb has begun to soften. Take off the heat and set aside.

2. Grease a 900ml pudding basin with butter, then spoon the contents of the pan into the base.

3. Beat together the butter and sugar with a pinch of salt until fluffy, then mix in the eggs. Fold in the flours and baking powder until well combined, then stir in the rest of the marmalade and taste – depending on what sort you use, you might want to add a little more for a stronger flavour. Add just enough milk so that the mixture drops easily from a spoon, then spoon it into the basin, leaving a couple of centimetres' gap at the top for the pudding to rise.

4. If your basin lacks a lid, cover with a pleated piece of parchment paper (again so the pudding has room to rise), then secure with a double layer of foil, and make a string handle if you'd like to make life easier for yourself later.

5. Put into a saucepan, pour in enough boiling water to come halfway up the basin, then bring back to the boil, cover and steam for 2 hours, topping up the water regularly.

6. Uncover, run a skewer round the edge of the basin and turn out on to a serving dish.

Rhubarb and custard trifle with an amaretto syllabub

serves 8–10

800g rhubarb
5 heaped tablespoons caster
   sugar
10 boudoir biscuits
12 amaretti biscuits
5 tablespoons amaretto liqueur

For the custard:
200ml milk
400ml double cream
1 vanilla pod, slit in half and
   seeds scraped out
6 egg yolks
3 tablespoons caster sugar
2 tablespoons cornflour

For the syllabub:
150ml amaretto liqueur
Juice of 1 lemon
1 tablespoon soft brown sugar
250ml double cream

I've never met a trifle I didn't like; this one is inspired by that classic school dinner combination, rhubarb and custard, razzed up with a generous slug of almond. The natural sharpness of rhubarb acts as a counterpoint to the sweetness of the other layers.

1. Heat the oven to 200°C/fan 180°C/gas 6. Destring the rhubarb if large and old (no need if slim) and cut into 4cm pieces, or smaller if thick. Arrange in a roasting tin with the sugar and 4 tablespoons of water, then cover with foil and bake for 25–45 minutes, depending on the thickness of your rhubarb, until soft but still holding its shape. It will be quite sharp, but don't worry, the custard will see to that.
2. Meanwhile, make the custard. Put the milk and cream into a heavy-based pan along with the vanilla pod and seeds, and heat gently to just below a simmer. Beat the yolks, sugar and cornflour together in a large heatproof bowl. Pour the simmering milk and cream into this bowl, beating all the time, then turn the heat down and pour the custard back into the pan.
3. Stir until it's thick enough to coat the back of a wooden spoon, being careful it doesn't overheat and turn into scrambled eggs (I often fill the sink a quarter full of cold water when making custard just in case – if it threatens to turn, plunge the pan into the sink and stir vigorously to see if it can be rescued). Allow to cool.
4. Line the base of a glass bowl with boudoir biscuits (you may not need them all), then crumble over half the amaretti biscuits and sprinkle with the 5 tablespoons of amaretto. Carefully spoon the rhubarb on top, along with its juices, making sure it looks pretty around the edge. Pour the cooled custard on top, and refrigerate, covered, until set.
5. To make the syllabub, whisk together the amaretto, lemon juice and sugar until the last has dissolved. Beat in the cream until it forms soft peaks, then spoon gently on top of the trifle. Decorate with the remaining amaretti, crushed, just before serving.

Rhubarb gin granita

serves 8

225g caster sugar
450g rhubarb, roughly chopped
50ml lemon juice
1 tablespoon rosewater
　(optional)
250ml gin

Sweet, pink and happily wicked, this is an excellent way to round off a heavy meal. As a bonus, it also produces enough stewed rhubarb for several breakfasts. Also great served in little shot glasses, with a dash more gin.

1. Put the sugar into a large pan with 950ml of water and heat, stirring, until dissolved. Add the rhubarb and the lemon juice and cook until the rhubarb has broken down completely. Allow to cool, then strain the pink juice into a large flat dish and set the stewed pulp aside for another use: it's pretty good with yoghurt or cereal.
2. Stir in half the rosewater, if using, and the gin and taste, adding more rosewater if you think it needs it (brands vary greatly in strength). Freeze for 1½ hours, until beginning to solidify, then run a fork through it, stirring the frozen bits from the edges back into the middle and breaking it all up.
3. Repeat every hour or so (the exact timings don't matter too much) until it's fully frozen, then cover.

is for Smoke

This chapter is dedicated to an ingredient you can't buy in the shops, or keep in the cupboard – indeed, you can't even hold it in your hand. There are other worthy candidates for the letter S, of course: shellfish and saffron, sausages and sandwiches (and indeed sausage sandwiches), but none of them has the same strange power to beguile. If I see the word 'smoke' on a menu, I want it.

The flavour of smoke is at once simple and impossible to describe; it tastes, of course, as it smells – of charred wood and bitter bonfires, both intensely savoury and deeply primeval. Our attraction to the pungent whiff of smoke is as ancient as our fascination with fire.

It's similarly universal too: the smoky flavours of the Merkén pepper used by the Mapuche Indians of Chile and the paperbark wrappings of the Australian Aborigines, the smoked mutton of Iceland and the smoked shrimp of West Africa – the whole world loves a smoke.

Smoke, the great preserver

We have been smoking food in these islands for thousands of years, and fish preserved in this way became particularly important in medieval Britain, when the numerous fast days dictated by the Church took meat off the menu for the few that could afford it in the first place.

The same technique was used to preserve meat; hams and bacons, yes, but also cold smoked mutton joints in upland areas, beef, duck and goat. (Hot-smoking, where the subject is subjected to heat as well as smoke, is far less effective at stopping spoilage, and is thus done only for flavour – and very nice the results are too.)

Almost anything can be smoked if you have a yen to do so; the only food I've tried that should have been left well alone was a smoked Stilton, which proved umami overload. But Cheddar and vodka, butter and garlic, almonds and apricots: all fair game.

Smoke without fire

You don't need actual smoke to get the flavour into your food though; here are a few slightly quicker alternatives:

— Smoked paprika: An easy way to add a touch of char to dishes, this mild, earthy paprika is made from peppers that have been dried, smoked and then ground into a powder. I use it for everything from tomato soup to sprinkling over a roast chicken.
— Chipotle chilli: These smoked jalapeño chillies, available whole, flaked or as a very versatile paste, are a hotter, richer alternative to smoked paprika, and an essential ingredient in chilli con carne and the like, as well as on eggs the morning after the night before.
— Liquid smoke: More popular in the States, though available online here, this smoke-infused liquid made by passing smoke through water is held in disdain by those with the space, time and equipment not to call on its services, but has its benefits for the rest of us. Though it's never going to transform a herring into a kipper, a drop or two added to some slow-roasted pulled pork, beans, burgers or a bourbon cocktail is quite transformative. Critics often carp on about its carcinogenic qualities, while ignoring the considerable health risks that come with too much smoke of any kind.

— Tea powder: Grind lapsang souchong tea to a powder and use as a smoky seasoning. It works particularly well on poultry, game and fish, but is also nice on stone fruits and creamy summery puddings. You can also use lapsang to hot-smoke with.

— Toast powder: See page 284 (Burnt toast powder, Toast).

— Charcoal infusing: See page 276 (Smoky black dal with eggs, Smoke).

See also: Sicilian almond and tomato pesto (page 19, Almond), Blackened jalapeño and avocado slaw (page 109, Hot), Mexican chilli chocolate mousse (page 116, Hot), Kentucky pulled lamb (page 273, Smoke).

Charred squash soup with zhoug and toasted pumpkin seeds

serves 4

1 medium butternut squash
Olive oil, to grease
40g pumpkin seeds (you can
    use some of the squash
    seeds if you like)
A squeeze of lemon juice
750ml chicken or vegetable
    stock

For the zhoug:
A large bunch of coriander,
    roughly chopped
A small bunch of flat-leaf
    parsley, roughly chopped
1–3 small green chillies,
    depending on heat and
    tolerance, deseeded and
    chopped
1 garlic clove, crushed
½ teaspoon ground cumin
½ teaspoon salt
10 tablespoons extra virgin
    olive oil

Almost any vegetable is improved by baking – the heat concentrates and intensifies the flavours, and if you take things a step further, as here, you get a hit of smokiness too.

Zhoug is a hot, aromatic Yemeni sauce which can be drizzled over the soup much like a pesto, but which is also fabulous on everything from potato salad to grilled fish, boiled eggs or a humble hunk of bread, so though the recipe below makes more than you'll probably need, you should have no problem finding other homes for it.

1. Heat the oven to 240°C/fan 220°C/gas 9. Peel the squash and cut into chunks about 5cm across, discarding the seeds and fibrous strands around them. Put on a lightly greased baking tray and toss with olive oil. Season well. Bake until the squash is soft and charred – about 45 minutes.

2. Meanwhile, make the zhoug by whizzing the herbs, chillies, garlic, cumin and salt to a purée in a food processor, then drizzling in oil to make a loose paste. Taste for seasoning.

3. When the squash is cooked, remove from the oven. Toss the pumpkin seeds on a baking tray with a little oil, salt and lemon juice and bake for about 3 minutes, until lightly toasted, then set aside and turn the oven off.

4. Put the squash into a pan, add a little stock and purée with a stick blender, adding more stock until you reach your desired consistency. Reheat and season to taste.

5. Serve drizzled with zhoug, and with pumpkin seeds scattered across the top.

Muhammara

serves 6–8

6 red peppers
150g walnut pieces
4 tablespoons white
    breadcrumbs
2 garlic cloves, crushed
2–4 tablespoons pomegranate
    molasses
2 tablespoons lemon juice
1 teaspoon smoked paprika
1 teaspoon salt

This smoky sweet and sour Syrian red pepper dip is utterly beguiling – it really knocks hummus, or even my beloved (and similarly smoky) babaganoush, into a cocked hat for flavour. Great with toasted flatbreads or crudités.

1. Heat the oven to 240°C/fan 220°C/gas 9. Pierce the peppers with a skewer in a couple of places, then put on a greased baking tray and roast until blackened and collapsed. Allow to cool, then peel and seed and roughly chop.
2. Toast the walnuts in a hot dry frying pan, then allow to cool slightly and put in a food processor. Whiz until coarsely ground, then tip out.
3. Put the peppers, breadcrumbs and garlic into the processor and whiz to a purée, then add the molasses, lemon juice, paprika and salt along with the walnuts. Whiz to combine, then taste and adjust the seasoning if necessary.

Smoked cod's roe and beetroot dip

serves 6

50g stale crustless white bread
Juice of ½ a lemon
170g smoked cod's roe
1 garlic clove, crushed
75g mascarpone cheese
50g Greek yoghurt
100g cooked and peeled
    beetroot (1 smallish one)
1 teaspoon grated or creamed
    horseradish (to taste)

This started off as a taramasalata, but after I'd gone beyond the slightly heretical, though at least Greek, yoghurt and added a soft Italian cheese and the very northern European horseradish, I decided it was a bit of a case of the philosopher's axe (or, at least, his dip). Authentic or not, it's pretty delicious. Roe varies in smokiness, so try it first, and if it threatens to overpower, soak it in cold water for an hour or so to soften the flavour.

1. Put the bread into a shallow bowl and squeeze over the lemon juice. Leave to soften while you prepare the rest of the ingredients.
2. Scoop the roe from the skin encasing it and put in a food processor or a large bowl (if you have a hand-held blender) along with the garlic, cheese and yoghurt. Roughly chop the beetroot, tear the bread into pieces and add both to the bowl. Whiz until smooth.

3. Stir in the horseradish and taste for seasoning, adding a little more lemon juice if necessary. Great with toasted rye bread, or crudités like radishes, carrot and cucumber batons, or cool baby new potatoes with dill.

Kentucky pulled lamb

serves 6

1.5kg lamb shoulder, bone in,
    at room temperature
1 tablespoon salt
1 tablespoon dark sugar
1 tablespoon smoked paprika
1 teaspoon liquid smoke
    (optional)

For the sauce (mop):
240ml water
2 tablespoons
    Worcestershire sauce
2 tablespoons cider vinegar
1 teaspoon dark brown sugar
¼ teaspoon ground allspice
1 teaspoon lemon juice

Barbecue in the States is a gloriously varied regional art, but they only seem to export the edited highlights. Pulled pork and burnt ends are, of course, undeniably delicious, but they're not the be-all-and-end-all, and there's no excuse for ignoring the Bluegrass State's particular speciality: slow-smoked mutton served with a thin, black, outrageously tangy sauce, bread, and often a thin spicy meat stew known as burgoo (got to love the idea of garnishing meat with more meat).

Mutton is still annoyingly hard to get hold of here, but if you can find a shoulder of that or hogget, by all means substitute it – you'll need to allow longer to cook, but the flavour will be its own reward.

1. Preheat the oven to 240°C/fan 220°C/gas 9. Put the lamb into a roasting tin. Combine the salt, sugar and paprika and rub into the meat, then cook for 20 minutes, until well browned. Remove from the oven and reduce the temperature to 150°C/fan 130°C/gas 2.
2. Pour 1 litre of water into the tin, cover with foil and bake for about 7 hours, until soft enough to pull off the bone and shred. Add the liquid smoke if using.
3. Towards the end of the lamb cooking time, make the sauce by putting all the ingredients into a small pan. Bring to the boil, then simmer for 10–15 minutes, until well reduced.
4. When the lamb is shredded, spoon the mop over the meat to taste.

Kichri-kedgeree

serves 4, generously

250g yellow moong dal
200g basmati rice
2 smoked haddock or other
    smoked firm white fish fillets
50g ghee
2 onions, finely sliced
2 teaspoons salt
Ground seeds of 5
    cardamom pods
1 tablespoon curry powder
1 teaspoon ground ginger
4 eggs
400g spinach

This satisfying supper dish is perhaps best thought of as Kedgeree: The Prequel – one of the many steps kichri might have gone through in its mutation from Indian dal and rice to Edwardian breakfast, boasting both the original pulses and the very British smoked fish, as well as some spinach, which happens to go beautifully with both.

1. Rinse the dal and rice well under running water, then leave to soak in lukewarm water for 30 minutes. Put the fish into a shallow pan on a low heat, cover with 1.25 litres of boiling water and leave to sit for 10 minutes.
2. Lift the fish out of the water (do not tip this away!) and break into large flakes.
3. Melt the ghee in a large saucepan over a medium-low heat. Add the onions and fry gently until golden brown. Scoop a third out and set aside as garnish. Stir in the salt and spices and fry for another couple of minutes, then stir in the drained dal and rice and the fish cooking water.
4. Bring to the boil, cover, and cook over a low heat for 25 minutes without lifting the lid. Meanwhile, put the eggs into a pan of cold water, bring to the boil, then turn down the heat and simmer for 6 minutes. Wash the spinach, drain and put into a large pan over a medium heat with no more water than still clings to the leaves. Cover and allow to wilt, then press out as much water as possible. Drain the cooked eggs and run under cold water to cool, then peel and cut in half.
5. When the rice is done, stir in the spinach and fish, add the eggs and scatter with the reserved onion to serve.

Smoky black dal with eggs

serves 4 as a main course

200g urad dal (black lentils),
    soaked overnight
4 eggs (optional)
3 tablespoons ghee or
    vegetable oil
1 onion, finely sliced
2 tablespoons ginger, grated
6 garlic cloves, crushed
2 small green chillies, sliced
    into thin rounds, seeds
    removed
4 black cardamom pods, seeds
    only, crushed
1 teaspoon ground cinnamon
1 teaspoon garam masala
1 x 400g tin of plum tomatoes,
    roughly chopped
2 tablespoons tomato purée
4 tablespoons Greek yoghurt
1 piece of natural charcoal
    (nothing impregnated with
    lighter fuel)

This is a slightly lighter, more tomatoey version of the outrageously rich Punjabi dal makhani, infused with the smoky flavour of black cardamom and lightly smoked before serving. If you don't have a gas hob, however, you can leave out step 6; it will still be delicious.

The eggs make it into quite a substantial main dish, but feel free to leave them out too if you'd prefer to serve it as a side.

1. Put the drained dal into a pan and cover with cold water. Bring to the boil, skim, boil hard for 10 minutes, then turn down the heat and simmer until very soft (how long this takes depends on the age of the pulses, but expect about an hour to an hour and a half). Do not drain.
2. Put the eggs, if using, into a pan of cold water, bring to the boil, then turn down the heat and simmer for 6 minutes. Drain and run under cold water to cool, then set aside.
3. Heat 2 tablespoons of ghee or oil in a frying pan (with a lid, as you'll need this later; if not, use foil) over a medium heat and cook the onion until soft and golden. Add the ginger, garlic and chillies and fry, stirring, for a further couple of minutes.
4. Stir in the crushed and ground spices and cook for another minute, still stirring, until you can smell them. Tip in the tomatoes and purée. Drain the dal over a bowl, retaining the cooking water, and add to the pan along with 300ml of its liquid. Bring to the boil, then turn down the heat to medium and simmer until the sauce has thickened and started to separate, and oil begins to pool around the sides of the pan. Meanwhile, peel and halve the eggs.
5. Turn the heat off, stir in the yoghurt and arrange the eggs on top, leaving a space in the middle for the next step.
6. Put a piece of charcoal on the flame of your hob, and heat until it glows red. Place a small metal dish in the middle of the frying pan. Using metal tongs (this is important, obviously), place the charcoal in the dish, and spoon over the remaining ghee or oil. Cover the pan tightly and leave for 5 minutes to infuse before checking the seasoning and serving, without the charcoal.

Smoked mackerel and charred cauliflower gratin with smoked chilli breadcrumbs

serves 2 (easily doubled)

1 small cauliflower
Oil, to grease
250ml double cream
100ml whole milk
2 small garlic cloves, crushed
2 smoked mackerel fillets
1 teaspoon smoked chipotle
   chilli paste (see intro)
A generous handful of
   breadcrumbs

This is an indulgent autumnal or winter supper; the smoky golden cream cloaks the white clouds of cauliflower in a dangerously seductive fashion, offset by the crunchy chipotle-spiked topping.

I am borderline obsessed with Gran Luchito smoked chilli paste, but if you don't have time to order any online, and can't find another brand in the shops, heat a little oil and fry a pinch of the more widely available chipotle chilli flakes for a minute or so before stirring in the breadcrumbs in step 3.

1. Heat the oven to 240°C/fan 220°C/gas 9. Break the cauliflower into large-ish florets and toss with a little oil and salt on a baking tray. Bake for about 20 minutes, checking regularly, until it's just turning golden and beginning to char round the edges.
2. Meanwhile, put the cream and milk into a small saucepan and bring to a simmer. Add the crushed garlic and flake in the mackerel in large chunks, removing the skin if necessary. Take off the heat and leave to infuse while the cauliflower cooks.
3. Heat the chilli paste in a frying pan and, when hot, stir in the breadcrumbs to coat. Take off the heat.
4. Take the cauliflower out of the oven and turn the heat down to 200°C/fan 180°C/gas 6. Tip it into the cream and mackerel mixture and stir to coat. Season to taste, then spoon into a shallow ovenproof dish.
5. Sprinkle over the breadcrumbs and bake for about 15–20 minutes, until bubbling.

Bacon and split peas with a quick mustard pickle

serves 6

1 tablespoon vegetable oil
   or lard
1 onion, finely chopped
1 leek, finely sliced
1 large carrot, finely diced
1 bay leaf
1.25kg smoked boneless collar
   of bacon
500g yellow split peas
2 tablespoons butter
2 teaspoons brown mustard
   seeds

For the pickle:
3 teaspoons soft light brown
   sugar
2 teaspoons salt
5 teaspoons mustard powder
120ml cider vinegar
1 large carrot, peeled and finely
   diced
2 spring onions, chunkily sliced

Before the potato ruled these isles, dried peas were the staple starch for the masses, and this recipe always gives me a pleasing sense of connection with the past. It's thrifty winter comfort food par excellence – the kind of dish to send you into a contented coma afterwards if you so much as dare to look at the sofa.

Ask your butcher, or consult the label on your bacon collar, to find out whether it needs pre-soaking overnight. The homemade pickle is very quick, but does need marinating time; piccalilli would work well if you don't have that luxury.

1. To make the pickle, whisk together the sugar, salt, mustard powder and vinegar until dissolved. Put the chopped vegetables into a small, clean jar and pour in the marinade to cover. Leave for at least 12 hours.
2. To cook the bacon and split peas, heat the fat in a large casserole dish. Soften the onion, leek and carrot with the bay leaf for a few minutes, then add the bacon. Pour over the split peas and 1.5 litres of water, cover and bring to the boil. Skim off any scum from the top, then cover and cook for about 1¾–2 hours, until the meat is falling apart and the peas are thick. Remove the meat from the peas.
3. Heat the butter in a small frying pan over a medium-high heat. Add the mustard seeds and cook until they sizzle and pop. Stir into the split peas and taste – they shouldn't need any further seasoning.
4. Carve the bacon (though it won't take much cutting) and serve in chunks with a spoonful of split peas and the pickles on the side. Some boiled greens wouldn't go amiss either.

is for Toast

In five years of writing my *Guardian* column, I've discovered one thing that holds true for every recipe. Post something simple online – or at least something that appears simple, given there are almost as many ways to fry an egg as there are to turn it into a soufflé – and some wag will always, without fail, respond underneath: 'What next, a recipe for toast?'

And, once in a blue moon, I reply, yes, yes please, I would dearly love to address the best way to toast bread. Because, though any fool can put a slice of bread in a toaster, it takes practice to get really superlative results out of it.

In my teenage years, I must have eaten a minimum of three slices a day. Even now, walking past certain caffs in the morning, the smell of cheap toast in quantity gives me a Proustian rush.

Nowadays, perhaps in reaction to the pasty sliced white of my schooldays, I like my toast aggressively crunchy, with enough structural integrity to bear the weight of several toppings, which generally means sourdough, though I have a soft spot for very seedy brown bread (of the sort on page 361) and a decent soft white bloomer, done well. But I also like the tangy flavour of sourdough, the way it keeps for ever in the bread bin, and the generous smattering of holes, just large enough for the butter to pool in as it melts. (Good toast also demands patience for this coming together of ingredients, the ingress of rich, salty fat into bread, before tucking in.)

Back to the toasting. Sliced bread is undoubtedly more convenient, especially for the cack-handed among us, but the rougher surface of the home-sliced kind gives a crisper result. Your call. The bread itself should be slightly stale, not just because fresh bread deserves to be eaten as such, but because the lower moisture content makes for better toast.

Call me nerdy, but I like to preheat the toaster by putting it on for a cycle before inserting the bread, and then flip the bread a couple of times, so it cooks evenly – whatever manufacturers claim, the middle of the toaster is always hotter than the walls. (And despite what you read online, those numbers on the dial do not usually represent minutes, a pernicious rumour that caused me to doubt my toasting prowess for about three weeks last year before I thought to test the theory out.)

Thicker items are better done under a grill to prevent the edges burning before the middle is heated through, and the crumpet, a specialist subject of mine, should be toasted face-side down until the base sounds hollow before being flipped over. (Mad as it sounds, I do not like to let anyone else cook my crumpets for me. I just can't trust them to take it seriously enough.)

But we can agree to disagree over the specifics – if you want it virtually raw, or charred and smoking, if you have an inexplicable attachment to cheap white sliced that gums and wads on the roof of your mouth, or like to bake loaves with a mother older than your own, feel free. Most of the recipes below will work well with almost any kind of bread.

Nothing soothes like toast. As an American blogger living here wrote: 'If I was depressed, I'd want something like a plate of meatloaf and a carton of Ben and Jerry's to cheer me up. If I was British, apparently you could appease me with a piece of toasted bread. It makes me think that maybe they're a bit simple.' And thank God, sometimes, for a little simplicity.

Quick ideas for toast

Breakfast:

— Muesli on toast. Sounds odd, but it works: spread toast (brown seems apt here) with a thick coating of Greek yoghurt, drizzle with honey and scatter with chopped dried figs or other fruit of your choice and nuts (I like almonds), mixed peel and seeds, and a pinch of salt.
— Ricotta, ripe figs or apricots, and honey
— Thick-cut marmalade, English mustard and bacon
— Marmite or peanut butter and ripe banana
— Tahini with honey and sea salt
— Ripe avocado, salt, chipotle honey (or honey and chipotle flakes)

Lunch and supper:

— Tinned sardines, mashed with a little lemon juice and Tabasco (an oldie but a goodie)
— Hard-boiled eggs mashed with a little butter, snipped chives, salt and lots of freshly ground pepper
— Cold roast meat topped with mayonnaise mixed with Dijon mustard, capers and green herbs
— Meat drippings and pickles (finely chopped gherkins, sauerkraut or kimchi)
— Steamed kale or sprouting broccoli, sautéd with a little garlic and lots of olive oil
— Washed rind cheese, sliced apple and chopped walnuts, grilled
— Chickpeas mashed with olive oil, seasoned and topped with smoked paprika
— A rub of garlic, squashed tomatoes and a sprinkle of sea salt and olive oil
— Mushy peas and shredded ham
— Melted cheese, mango chutney and a dusting of cayenne pepper
— Masala beans: Fry half a finely chopped onion and 2 crushed garlic cloves in a small pan until soft, then stir in a teaspoon of curry powder and ½ teaspoon of chilli powder. Cook for a minute or so, then add a tin of baked beans and simmer until thickened. Season to taste.

See also: Wild garlic bread (page 331, Wild).

Burnt toast powder

Not so much a recipe as a slightly crazed idea, burnt toast powder is madly popular in the States. I find it unpleasantly bitter in a savoury context, but surprisingly delicious on very sweet things, like ice cream, chocolate mousse or caramel tart, especially with a pinch of coarse salt.

To make it, burn a piece of stale bread until it's completely black all over (it's wise to open the windows and stick the extractor fan on), then leave to dry out overnight. Crumble into pieces, then grind into a powder and use as above.

White beans on toast

serves 4

225g dried cannellini or haricot
   beans, soaked overnight
   (or about 525g drained
   tinned white beans)
A knob of butter
4 rashers of dry-cured streaky
   bacon, finely chopped
2 shallots, finely chopped
2 sprigs of thyme, leaves picked
120ml dry white wine
150ml double cream
4 slices of sturdy bread

This recipe, for a richer, more savoury and yes, fancier version of the undisputed classic of quick lunches, doesn't mean I love the tinned sort any less, but a change is as good as a rest, as my granny used to say.

1. Drain the soaked beans if using, then put into a medium pan, cover with cold water and bring to the boil. Skim off the scum, turn down the heat and simmer for about 2 hours, until tender (the exact time will depend on the age of your beans, so check regularly). Drain.
2. Heat the butter in a medium pan over a medium-high heat and add the bacon. Fry for a couple of minutes, until the fat starts to melt, then add the shallots and thyme. Fry, stirring occasionally, until the bacon begins to brown, then stir in the wine, scraping the bottom of the pan clean. Simmer for about 7 minutes until most of the wine has evaporated, then stir in the cream. Season.
3. Stir in the beans. While they heat through, make the toast. Serve – well, you know how to serve beans on toast.

Duck and sherry pâté with pickled figs and pistachios

serves about 6
(or more as a snack)

10 dried figs
120ml red wine vinegar
2 tablespoons white sugar
25g shelled pistachios

For the pâté:
350g duck or chicken livers
100g butter, diced
1 shallot, finely chopped
1 teaspoon thyme leaves
Zest of 1 unwaxed orange
75ml Pedro Ximénez sherry
75ml double cream
½ teaspoon salt
½ teaspoon Chinese
   five spice

I very nearly didn't include this recipe, because pâté seemed such an embarrassingly obvious choice in a chapter about toast, but just like when confronted with a plate of crisp warm bread with a thick coating of rich, sweet meat, I couldn't resist. It's a classic for a reason.

1. To make the pâté, trim the livers of any sinewy or green bits and roughly chop. Heat a knob of butter in a frying pan over a medium heat and add the shallot. Fry until soft, then stir in the thyme and orange zest and fry for another minute or so. Turn up the heat and add the livers. Sauté for a couple of minutes, until golden brown on the outside, then tip into a food processor.

2. Pour the sherry into the pan, still on the heat, and scrape to deglaze. Allow to bubble until syrupy and reduced, being careful it doesn't start to burn, then pour into the machine along with the remaining butter.

3. Whiz until smooth, then add the cream, salt and five spice and whiz to combine. Taste for seasoning, then spoon into a bowl and allow to cool. Cover and chill for a couple of hours until set.

4. Meanwhile, put the figs into a small pan along with the vinegar and sugar and bring to a simmer, stirring to dissolve the sugar. Turn down the heat and simmer gently for about 30 minutes, until the figs are sitting in a sticky syrup (I'd recommend using the extractor fan during this process; it's pungent stuff). Spoon out of the pan and set aside.

5. When you're ready to serve, slice the figs and roughly chop the pistachios. Serve the pâté on toasts or biscuits, with a slice of fig on top (or two or three, depending on the size of the vehicle) and an artful scattering of pistachios.

Southern cheese on toast

serves 4

20 smallish tomatoes, or, if
 tomatoes are in season,
 enough ripe tomatoes of any
 size for 4
4 slices of robust bread
1 garlic clove, halved
2 burrata or buffalo mozzarella
 balls

For the basil purée:
25g basil
100ml extra virgin olive oil

By southern, I don't mean with zider and West Country Cheddar, or indeed Velveeta and cornbread, but soaked in the sunny flavours of the Mediterranean. Creamy mozzarella, sweet umami-rich tomatoes and a peppery green basil purée make this a treat indeed for a summer lunch, but I like it just as well with baked tomatoes when they're not quite up to eating raw, so feel free to make it with either.

1. If you're making this outside peak tomato season (or if your tomatoes turn out to disappoint), heat the oven to 210°C/fan 190°C/gas 7, then put the tomatoes on a greased baking tray (cut them in half if they're larger than a walnut) and bake for about 20 minutes, until they're starting to split.

2. Meanwhile, bring a small pan of salted water to the boil and put a large bowl of iced water next to it. Dunk the basil into the hot water for 15 seconds, then immediately scoop out with a slotted spoon and put into the iced water. Drain well and dry, then put in a small food processor, or use a stick blender or a pestle and mortar to blend with the oil, adding the latter gradually until you have a smoothish purée. Add salt to taste.

3. Toast the bread until golden, then rub with the cut garlic clove. Squish the tomatoes on top, drizzle with basil purée, add half a burrata or mozzarella (if you're using the former, do this on a plate so you catch any escaping cream), season and add a little more purée. Devour.

Salmon and coriander tartare with avocado and wasabi cream on toasted rye

serves 2

1 ripe Hass avocado (the brown knobbly ones)
2 teaspoons wasabi paste (if you're making it up from the powder, use 2 teaspoons powder to 1 teaspoon warmish water)
Juice of 1 lime
1 teaspoon soy sauce (preferably Japanese)
1 salmon fillet
A small bunch of coriander, chopped
A handful of pea shoots
1 tablespoon pumpkin seeds
A dash of pumpkin seed, extra virgin olive or avocado oil
2 slices of dark rye bread

Unapologetically dense and healthy, rye bread nevertheless makes surprisingly good toast – especially those crisply curling edges. Packed full of what are somewhat defensively known as 'good fats', avocado, salmon and pumpkin seeds are an aptly nutritious topping for an outrageously quick lunch that's guaranteed to keep you feeling full up until, well, at least the four o'clock coffee and cake break, if not longer.

Pumpkin seed oil isn't widely available here, more's the pity, but if you see some, snap it up: vivid green and nutty-tasting, it makes an excellent salad dressing. As you'll be eating the salmon raw, make sure it's very fresh. If you're worried, freeze it for 24 hours, then defrost before use.

1. Cut the avocado in half, remove the stone, then scoop out the flesh into a small bowl or mini chopper. Add half the wasabi along with the lime juice and soy sauce. Whiz until smooth (or mash as best you can, if you don't have a stick blender or mini chopper), then taste and season accordingly. I like to add the rest of the wasabi, but you may not.
2. Skin the salmon if necessary, then cut into small dice. Put into a small bowl with the coriander, season well, and toss together with the pea shoots, pumpkin seeds and a dash of oil.
3. Toast the bread until crisp, then spread with the avocado and top with the salmon and pea shoots. Eat immediately.

Mexican torta with black beans, chorizo, avocado and goat's cheese crema

makes 2

80g cooking chorizo
1 x 400g tin of black beans
60g soft goat's cheese
6 tablespoons crème fraîche
2 crusty rolls or chunky slices
of a thick baguette
Olive oil, to cook
1 ripe Hass avocado (the
brown knobbly ones)
Pickled jalapeños, to serve
A small bunch of coriander,
roughly chopped, to serve

Although the burrito has won hearts internationally, Mexican sandwiches aren't all about tortilla wraps – indeed, in the north of the country tortas, or filled rolls, are also known as *lonches*, due to their popularity at, you guessed it, lunchtime.

The bread used there is a local variation on the French baguette, so use any crusty rolls or wide baguette that looks good. The earthy flavour of the beans, enriched by the spicy orange fat of the chorizo, makes a lovely contrast to the creamy avocado and goat's cheese.

1. Slit the chorizo and scoop out the meat. Heat a frying pan over a medium heat and sizzle the meat until the fat has rendered, then stir in the drained beans. Cook for a couple of minutes until warmed through, then mash to a rough paste and season to taste.
2. Mash together the cheese and crème fraîche. Heat a griddle pan over a high heat and cut the rolls in half. Brush each cut half with a little oil, then, once the griddle is smoking hot, toast the cut sides until charred.
3. Divide the bean mixture between the bottoms of the rolls. Slice the avocado and arrange on top, followed by a scattering of jalapeños and coriander. Spread the tops with the goat's cheese crème fraîche and put the two halves together.

is for Umami

Famously known as the fifth taste, joining sweet, salty, bitter and sour at the flavour party rather belatedly at the beginning of the last century, umami is best described as savoury. Intensely savoury. Almost too savoury to bear, like soy sauce, or sun-dried tomatoes or a really mature Parmesan – in fact, just writing about it is making my tongue prickle slightly at the edges.

For centuries, we were at a loss as to how to describe this taste, which hovered on the edge of salty, but wasn't strictly that, was much richer, and deeper, and, well, less salty. It was the flavour of charred meat and old cheese, ripe tomatoes and fried mushrooms, meat stock and all sorts of good things, including, in Japan, dashi broth made from dried kelp and tuna flakes.

In a country where animal products were once considered taboo, this meat-free stock gave Japanese cuisine a much-needed injection of savoury richness, and it was this that intrigued chemist Kikunae Ikeda. There is, he wrote, 'a taste which is common to asparagus, tomatoes, cheese and meat but which is not one of the four well-known tastes'. After years of patiently distilling seaweed, veal stock and other likely candidates, in 1908 he found the secret ingredient that linked them all: glutamic acid.

But, as he discovered, glutamic acid doesn't taste of anything in its original form. It's not until it's broken down by heat, fermentation or time into something called an L-glutamate that our tongues can detect it – which is why raw meat doesn't have much in the way of umami, but a hamburger does (and explains why most of us add anchovy-rich Worcestershire sauce to steak tartare). Ikeda named this new flavour umami, or 'delicious taste' – often (nauseatingly) translated by modern sources as 'yummy'.

For many years, umami was thought to be something that simply enhanced the other flavours, but in fact, it doesn't seem to intensify sweetness or acidity, bitterness or even saltiness – it simply makes food taste 'more of itself'. The current thinking is that when we add umami to our food, whether by cooking it in a dashi or chicken stock, adding tomato ketchup or sprinkling over Parmesan, we're highlighting the small quantities of umami already present.

It wasn't until 2001, however, that umami taste receptors were identified on the human tongue, thus laying to rest, once and for all, the debate over its existence as a flavour in its own right.

Indeed, unlike the other flavours, which are sensed relative to each other (which is why we add a pinch of salt to sweet desserts, and serve cheese with fruit and sticky chutneys), umami alone can be detected on its own, probably because it's a protein – the human body makes up to 40g of glutamate a day, leaving it in constant search of a top-up of amino acids.

Umami-rich foods

MARMITE
1,960mg / 100g

WALNUTS
638mg / 100g

SOY SAUCE
782–1,264mg / 100g

PARMESAN
1,000–2,700mg / 100g

CURED HAM
337mg / 100g

OMATOES
0mg / 100g

OYSTERS
130mg / 100g

MARINATED ANCHOVIES
1,200mg / 100g

DRIED SHIITAKE
1,060mg / 100g

The truth about MSG

The year after Ikeda's discovery, he began commercial production of umami in the form of a more stable sodium salt of glutamic acid, otherwise known as the much-maligned MSG and sold today under a variety of brand names around the world, including the deliciously coy 'Ac'cent seasoning'. (In much of Asia it is known, more brazenly, as Gourmet powder.)

Though it took off almost immediately in Asia, MSG didn't make the leap into the Western diet until after the Second World War, when American soldiers returned from the Far East with a taste for the stuff. Initially they weren't quite sure what exactly they were missing, but once food scientists put two and two together, MSG became a key ingredient in all sorts of industrially produced foodstuffs in need of a flavour boost, from TV dinners to chewing gum, and proved an especially helpful addition to diet foods when fat fell from favour in the 1960s.

Not that you'll often see MSG listed as such on labels; it goes by many names, including autolyzed yeast extract, E621, natural beef or chicken flavouring, seasonings and hydrolyzed milk protein, none of which sound much more appetizing. I have no cod medical objections to MSG, but I'd prefer to get my umami from foodstuffs that are actually delicious in their own right, like cheese, just as I'd prefer to get my vitamin C from an orange rather than a tablet.

But the fact that the big bad wolf is nothing but a glutamate also produced in quantity by our own bodies has done nothing to allay the fears of those who believe themselves to be a victim of 'Chinese restaurant syndrome', a mysterious condition which has gained remarkable credence in the western world for the past forty years without anyone actually being able to find any evidence for it. Every single food testing authority in the world has deemed MSG completely safe for human consumption.

According to Jeffrey Steingarten's excellent essay 'Why Doesn't Everyone in China Have a Headache?', written in 1999, 90 million Americans claim to be affected by MSG. In China, where they consume 1.8 million tonnes of the stuff every year, they're too busy eating to worry about it.

Umami injectors

— Strong stock: Preferably beef. Those little jelly pots which are far too intense for normal use come into their own in an underwhelming meat stew; add a little at a time to taste, or do the same with a crumbled stock cube. Miso or Korean doenjang are good vegetarian alternatives.

— Marmite: Like stock cubes, this is best done behind closed doors, but the effects are just as magical, as well as being helpfully vegetarian friendly. Bovril, which does the same job, is not, of course.

— Anchovies: Lots of people think they don't like anchovies, but most of them (vegetarians excepted) are wrong. They just don't like the oversalted, hairy little things that infested every pizza up until 1988. Melt them down into a sauce, and anchovies don't taste fishy at all, they taste intensely, wonderfully savoury. (The potato, black kale and anchovy pie recipe on page 229 is a good way to prove this.) A discreet squirt of anchovy paste or Gentleman's Relish has rescued many a dish in my household.

— Soy sauce: If your stir-fry lacks pep, or your pork belly stew needs a bit of poke, a dash of soy sauce should do the trick. Don't overdo it though, as it can overwhelm other flavours.

— Worcestershire sauce: The sweet, spicy western equivalent to soy sauce. The classic kind is not veggie friendly, so check the label.

— Tomato or mushroom ketchup: I'm not a big fan of ketchup generally (I'm a mustard girl) but I do keep it for sneakily stirring into boring sauces.

— Cheese: If in doubt, add cheese. If you take one thing away from this book, let it be that.

See also: B is for Blue Cheese, Canederli alla tirolese with Parmesan broth (page 53, Dumplings), Bacon refried beans (page 83, Fat), Potato, black kale and anchovy pie (page 229, Potatoes), Pissaladière (page 357, Yeast).

Shrimp and grits with bacon and Parmesan

serves 2

500ml chicken stock
250ml milk
100g stoneground grits (see intro)
1 tablespoon double cream
40g Parmesan or Grana Padano, grated
2 rashers of smoked streaky bacon, finely chopped
10 large raw prawns, peeled and deveined, but tails left on
A small bunch of chives

Seafood and cheese is one of those combinations which the cognoscenti all know to be deeply wrong, but is happily quite the done thing down in Mississippi. Here the nutty sweetness of the prawns bounces beautifully off the salty savoury flavour of the cheese and bacon, with the creamy corn as a soothing backdrop.

If you can't find grits (and they are available online), you can substitute cornmeal or polenta, although the flavour won't be quite the same.

1. Combine the stock and milk in a medium saucepan and bring to a simmer, then pour over the grits, whisking vigorously to combine.
2. Turn down the heat to low and simmer for about 20–30 minutes, until the grits are thick and creamy, stirring regularly to make sure they aren't sticking.
3. Once they're ready, take off the heat and stir in the cream and cheese, then season to taste. Keep warm while you cook the topping.
4. Heat a dry frying pan over a medium-high heat and fry the bacon until crisp and beginning to brown. Scoop out with a slotted spoon and add the prawns. Sauté until pink on both sides, then scoop out and add to the bacon (if you leave them in the hot pan while you assemble the dish they will continue cooking).
5. Divide the grits between two shallow bowls. Top with the prawns, then scatter the bacon around them. Finally snip over the chives to serve.

Courgette fritters with bagna cauda hollandaise

serves 4 with extra sauce

450g courgettes
   (2 large-ish ones)
2 spring onions
50g plain flour
50g dried breadcrumbs,
   preferably panko
1 teaspoon chilli flakes
A whole nutmeg, to grate
1 egg
A small bunch of parsley,
   finely chopped
Oil, to fry

For the sauce:
3 fat garlic cloves
10 anchovies, rinsed if packed
   in salt
100ml olive oil
3 egg yolks
150g cold butter, cubed

Bagna cauda (rather wonderfully, 'warm bath') is an incredibly rich, salty, garlicky dip from Italy's Piedmont region, usually served with raw or boiled vegetables, but this thicker version makes a dangerous pairing with hot, crispy courgette fritters. The slightly sweet, almost creamy flavour of the squash proves the perfect foil for the anchovy umami bomb.

This is a lovely late summer lunch or light(ish) supper. Don't be shy with the oil; you need it for really crispy fritters, but you can negate that by serving them with an undressed green salad.

NB: the sauce is also great with crudités, toasts, poached eggs; in fact, almost anything.

1. Coarsely grate the courgettes into a colander in the sink. Salt lightly, toss, and leave to weep while you make the sauce.
2. Roughly chop the garlic and anchovies and mash together into a smooth paste. Heat a splash of oil in a small frying pan over a lowish heat, and gently fry the mixture until the garlic just smells cooked. Scoop out of the hot pan so it doesn't continue cooking.
3. Heat the olive oil to warm (I put the jug into a saucepan of hot water) and boil a small kettle of water. Put the egg yolks into a pan with 1 tablespoon of cold water and the butter and set over a low heat. Stir continually until the butter has melted and emulsified into a smooth, thickish sauce, then gradually but vigorously whisk in the warm olive oil. Turn up the heat slightly and whisk until thickened. If it threatens to separate, whisk in a little of the boiling water from the kettle, which should bring it back together. Once thickened, stir in the anchovy and garlic and set aside somewhere warm while you make the fritters, whisking it occasionally (I sit the pan in the larger pan of warm water previously occupied by the jug of oil).
4. Squeeze out the courgettes well. Finely slice the spring onions, then put into a large bowl with the courgettes, flour, breadcrumbs, chilli flakes and a pinch of nutmeg. Briefly beat the egg and mix in along with the parsley.

5. Heat enough oil in a frying pan over a medium-high heat to shallow-fry – if you only grease the pan, your fritters will be soggy. Once the pan is hot enough that a courgette strand sizzles as it hits the oil, add the mixture in spoonfuls, flattening out as you do so, and fry in batches until golden brown on both sides. Drain on kitchen paper, then serve with the sauce.

Ox cheeks braised in Marmite

serves 4

600g ox cheek, trimmed of any sinew and cut into large chunks
1 tablespoon seasoned flour
2 tablespoons oil or dripping
1 onion, thinly sliced
1 large carrot, diced
1 leek, diced
300ml porter or other dark beer
3 tablespoons Marmite, dissolved in 4 tablespoons hot water
1 tablespoon dark brown sugar

Although I'm convinced they've changed the recipe in recent years, I still love Marmite and (to others' embarrassment) have been known to take a jar on holiday to perk up hotel breakfasts. (There's no joy in cheap jam, wherever it was made.) But it's also a very useful ingredient to have in the kitchen to deliver a quick shot of savoury flavour to insipid stews and soups – in this recipe it's out and proud; gorgeously sticky and salty, and quite superb with some creamy mash and steamed greens.

1. Toss the meat in the seasoned flour and heat the fat in a large casserole pan over a medium-high heat. Brown the meat well in batches, then set aside.
2. Turn down the heat a little, then add the onion, carrot and leek to the pan and stir well. Cook for about 10 minutes, until softened, then pour in the beer and stir to deglaze the bottom of the pan. Heat the oven to 170°C/fan 150°C/gas 3.
3. Stir in the Marmite-y liquid, the sugar, the meat and 100ml of water, bring to a simmer, then put into the oven for about 2½–3 hours, until the meat is falling apart. Taste before serving – you can stir in more Marmite if you're a fanatic like me, or more sugar if you think it could do with toning down a bit.

Chargrilled Caesar salad

serves 4

2 smallish garlic cloves

150ml olive oil

2 chicken breasts or 4 boneless
skinless thighs

4 rashers of streaky bacon

4 slices of day-old white
sourdough bread

8 little gem lettuces

A large handful of finely grated
Parmesan

2 anchovy fillets, rinsed

1 egg yolk

Juice of ½ a lemon

I'm loath to mess with an undisputed classic of the genre, which, frankly, has suffered enough (there's a tofu kale Caesar online. Seriously), but I'd like to propose this as an adaptation: lettuce is vastly enhanced by a little charring, a process that delivers yet another dollop of umami on top of the anchovy-rich dressing. Add the fried bread and the bacon and it's basically a salad for a very sophisticated hangover – hell, there's even an egg yolk in there for good measure.

1. Crush the garlic and add to the oil. Leave to infuse for about an hour. Bash out the chicken until it's nice and thin. Heat a griddle pan on a high flame and cook the bacon until crisp and well charred.
2. Tear the bread into bite-sized chunks and dunk in the oil, then griddle until crisp.
3. Cut the lettuces in half through the core, and brush with oil. Griddle until charred, then sprinkle with Parmesan. Set aside.
4. Brush the chicken with garlic oil and griddle on both sides until chargrilled and cooked through.
5. Mash the anchovies to a paste in a jug, then beat in the yolk, and gradually the rest of the garlic-infused oil until you have a thickish dressing. Stir in the lemon juice and taste – season if necessary.
6. Snip the bacon into small shards and cut the chicken into slices. Arrange the lettuce halves on a platter and scatter over the croutons, chicken and bacon. Drizzle with dressing to serve.

Crunchy soy-braised pig's tails

serves 4

4 pig's tails
225g plain flour
2 eggs, beaten
50g panko breadcrumbs
Oil, to cook

For the marinade:
3cm piece of ginger, roughly
    sliced
3 spring onions, roughly
    chopped
3 small whole dried chillies
½ a star anise
1 tablespoon dark brown sugar
3 tablespoons dark soy sauce
3 tablespoons Shaoxing wine

I'm aware that this recipe is quite a niche one – either you can stomach the idea of nibbling on a curly-wurly little tail or you can't – but rest assured, if you can get past the cutesy Pigling Bland associations, it will repay your bravery. The slim little tail gives surprisingly good value, particularly as butchers will often give them away for free. (You'll probably need to order them specially, though.)

Slow-cooked until the rich, gelatinous meat falls from the bone, then crumbed and baked until crisp, tails make a strangely good snack – the kind of thing that goes very well indeed with a cold beer with adventurous friends.

1. Heat the oven to 200°C/fan 180°C/gas 6. Put the tails into an oven dish just big enough to hold them, add the marinade ingredients, then barely cover with water. Cover and bake for 3 hours, checking the tails are still submerged in liquid every hour or so, and topping up as necessary. Allow to cool slightly in the stock.
2. Turn the oven up to 220°C/fan 200°C/gas 7. Put the flour, egg and breadcrumbs into separate bowls. Cover the base of a roasting tin with oil and put on the hob over a medium-high heat.
3. While it's heating, lift the tails out of their marinade and roll each in flour, egg and breadcrumbs, then egg and breadcrumbs again, until well coated. Brown all over in the roasting tin, then roast for 20–25 minutes, turning them over halfway through. Eat immediately, while you're still feeling brave.

Broccoli and edamame salad with Korean dressing

serves 4–6

1 large head of broccoli
450g shelled edamame beans, defrosted
1 tablespoon toasted sesame seeds

For the dressing:
6 tablespoons groundnut or other neutral oil
3 tablespoons doenjang (see intro)
Juice of 2 limes
1 tablespoon rice vinegar
1 teaspoon sugar
1 red chilli, seeded and finely chopped
1 teaspoon freshly grated ginger

Broccoli salads are yet another great American idea – in fact, the many charms of this excellent vegetable seem better appreciated in general across the pond – but this salad, which makes much of its crunchy texture and slightly bitter flavour, has a distinctly Far Eastern fusion feel to it.

Doenjang, a salty rich paste made from fermented soy beans, is one of the cornerstones of Korean cooking, and packs as much umami as an anchovy and Parmesan fritter – you could substitute Japanese miso paste if that happens to be easier to come by, but it's available online, and lasts for ever, so it's a useful thing to have in the cupboard for adding a bit of umami oomph to soups, rice dishes, etc.

1. Cut the broccoli into bite-sized pieces. Bring a large pan of salted water to the boil and prepare a large bowl or sink full of iced water. Blanch the broccoli and edamame for about 45 seconds, then transfer to the iced water to cool.
2. To make the dressing whisk together the oil and doenjang until well combined. Whisk in the lime juice, vinegar and sugar until you have a smooth dressing, then stir in the chilli and ginger. Taste, and add a little more of any of the ingredients if you feel it needs it.
3. Combine the broccoli and edamame in a salad bowl and toss through the dressing. Sprinkle with sesame seeds to serve.

Dashi pickles

This slightly smoky, sweet and savoury pickle makes an addictive accompaniment to Japanese curries, but is also surprisingly good in a cheeseburger. The ingredients for the stock should be easy to find in an oriental supermarket or online, and will also come in useful for the noodle recipe on page 194.

Makes a 1.5 litre jar

For the dashi stock:
20g kombu (dried seaweed)
3g bonito (dried tuna) flakes
1 tablespoon sugar
1 tablespoon salt
200ml rice vinegar
1 teaspoon soy sauce
1 teaspoon togarashi seasoning

For the vegetables:
2 tablespoons fine sea salt
10 small radishes, halved
2 carrots, cut into batons
½ a cucumber, seeds removed,
cut into batons
¼ of a cauliflower, in florets

1. Put the kombu into a pan with 1 litre of water. Bring to the boil, then scoop out the kombu with a slotted spoon and discard or save to use again (when, like tea leaves, its flavour will be less strong). Add the bonito, bring up to the boil, then pass through a sieve. Allow to cool, then pass through a sieve back into the same pan. Add the sugar and salt and bring back to the boil, stirring to dissolve, then add the vinegar, soy sauce and togarashi and allow to cool completely.
2. Meanwhile, dissolve the fine sea salt in 900ml water. Put the vegetables into a large bowl and cover with the water, adding just as much as it takes to submerge them (add more water if necessary). Allow to soak overnight (or for 8 hours), then drain. Pack into jars and fill with the cool stock. Cover with a lid and chill for at least 3 days before serving.

Green lamb kebabs

serves 4

4 anchovies, rinsed if packed
    in salt
4 fat garlic cloves
400g minced lamb (not the
    leanest kind)
2 tablespoons capers, roughly
    chopped
1 small green chilli, deseeded
    and roughly chopped
2 large handfuls of parsley,
    thick stalks removed,
    roughly chopped
A large handful of basil,
    roughly chopped
1 tablespoon lemon juice
1 tablespoon Dijon mustard

This mash-up of a classic sharp salsa verde and herb-flecked Turkish kofte is the product of my taste for pairing intensely savoury, aromatic flavours with the rich sweetness of lamb. Feel free to shape the meatballs into any form you like – they're good with rice and roasted peppers, but they'd make a pretty wonderful burger too, perhaps topped with a little yoghurt and folded into a warm flatbread with salad, or even with some simply dressed new potatoes.

1. Mash the anchovies and garlic into a paste in a pestle and mortar.
2. Put all the ingredients, anchovy and garlic paste included, into a food processor and pulse until you have a green mixture. Season. Heat a small frying pan over a high flame and cook a small blob to check the flavours, adding more garlic, lemon or mustard if desired.
3. Shape into six cylinders and refrigerate until you're ready to eat, then heat a frying pan, griddle or barbecue greased with a little oil. Cook the kebabs until golden brown on all sides, and cooked through to your liking.

V

is for Violets and other edible flowers

We don't eat a lot of flowers these days, and when we do, they tend to be in consciously foreign preparations; delectable deep-fried *flor de zucchini* and sticky Middle Eastern pastries are fashionable in a way that violet creams and lavender vinaigrettes are very definitely not. (I must admit this often works in my favour; I always get both rose creams in the chocolate selection.)

Yet again, however, I find myself impressed by the adventurous tastes of our forebears. The ancient Greeks and Romans were great lovers of flowers, but so were earlier inhabitants of these chilly islands, who not only distilled them for medicinal purposes but used them in salads, sauces and baking too.

A seventeenth-century collection of recipes said to have come from the household of the exiled Queen Henrietta Maria includes instructions for such treats as an almond and rosewater set cream much like a modern panna cotta, eel in a wine and saffron sauce and veal pastries crammed with dried fruit and spice, and seasoned with rosewater.

The gay abandon with which these long-dead cooks used flowers is quite staggering; Frances Bissell's excellent book *The Scented Kitchen* mentions one rose syrup recipe that calls for 11 gallons of petals – or an entire acre of bushes.

Although floral flavours began to fall from favour in Victorian times, coltsfoot wine, dandelion salads and elderflower vinegars all feature in collections of recipes compiled by the redoubtable Women's Institute right up to the present day.

But the urban population has rediscovered the charming possibilities of flowers in the kitchen in recent years as well – our growing taste for, and familiarity with, the flavours of the Indian subcontinent and the Middle East has made flower waters and saffron far easier to come by.

Although many perfectly edible examples are so very subtle that it's hardly worth the trouble of chewing, the best flowers impart delicate but haunting fragrance to food, somewhat like the elusive scent of warm jasmine on a summer's evening, or an old-fashioned rose in full fig in June.

And, if you think you don't like eating flowers, if you're not keen on artichokes, or capers, or cauliflower, do bear in mind that they're a vital ingredient in many dishes which don't shout about their floral content; creamy korma, for example (see page 20), and fragrant biryani both betray the Mughal fondness for rosewater, while North African spice mixes often feature rose petals, and orange blossom water perfumes many a meaty Moroccan tagine. Not so sickly sweet after all then.

Practicalities

The best flowers to eat will always be those you have grown yourself, for only then can you be absolutely sure that they haven't been sprayed with anything potentially unpalatable or, worse still, poisonous. However, if, like me, you're not lucky enough to have acres of flower beds at your disposal, it's possible to buy flowers grown for the purpose online; see page 384 for stockists. (This also has the distinct advantage, in many cases, of ensuring that the flowers have been selected for scent, rather than beauty – even if you grow roses at home, there's no guarantee that they're the right sort, and you may be disappointed.)

I try and wash flowers as little as possible as they're so delicate, but use your own judgement as to whether they require wiping with a damp cloth – shaking them a little to release any tiny stowaways is always a good idea, however.

If you're foraging for flowers, bear in mind the guidelines on page 324, especially when it comes to identification; no gorgeous cascade of sugared petals is worth a trip to A&E.

Many of the recipes in this chapter call for flower waters and essences, which can be found in Indian or Middle Eastern and baking specialists respectively. Essences will be much stronger than waters, and even within these categories the pungency varies widely between brands, so never add the quantity suggested all at once, but do so to taste.

See also: Chicken korma (page 20, Almonds).

Crab with ricotta and lemon zest and an elderflower and cucumber salad

**serves 2
(with plenty of vinegar
left over)**

2 dressed crabs
6 tablespoons ricotta
1 unwaxed lemon

For the elderflower vinegar:
1 head of elderflower, plus 1
    more after the first week
350ml white wine or cider
    vinegar

For the cucumber salad:
120ml elderflower vinegar
Juice of 1 lemon
2 tablespoons sugar
1 teaspoon salt
½ a cucumber, thinly sliced
1 teaspoon pink peppercorns
    (optional)

Brown crab and fragrant elderflower: two ingredients that sing the siren call of early summer for me, here combined in one vaguely Scandinavian lunch or light dinner. You can buy elderflower vinegar online, but it's very easy to make yourself – you'll just need to allow at least a week for it to infuse before you can reap the rewards, but in the meantime, the crabs will obligingly be growing bigger and fatter, ready for the pot, which can't be a bad thing.

1. To make the vinegar, shake the elderflowers to dislodge any tiny hitchhikers, then break into small flower sprigs. Tip a little of the vinegar out of the bottle into a mug, to use for some other purpose, then push the sprigs into the bottle. Seal and put somewhere nice and sunny for about a week.

2. Strain the vinegar into a jug and discard the flowers, then pour it back into the bottle and add the new flowers. You can now use it immediately or leave it in a dark place until you're ready to make the salad.

3. Whisk together the vinegar, lemon juice, sugar and salt until the last two have dissolved, then pack the cucumber into a clean jar with the peppercorns if using, and pour over this dressing. Leave to sit for at least 3 hours, but a few days is fine.

4. When you're ready to eat, scoop the brown meat out of the crabs and mix with the ricotta, the finely grated zest of the lemon and its juice. Season to taste, then replace in the shells. Serve with the cucumber salad and some crispbreads.

Fig and goat's cheese olive oil flatbread with lavender honey

serves 6

A small jar of clear honey
7 sprigs of lavender, plus a
    few extra to finish
225g plain flour
½ teaspoon baking powder
1 teaspoon salt
75ml olive oil, plus extra
    to brush
2 tablespoons semolina,
    cornmeal or polenta
5 ripe figs
120g log of soft, rinded goat's
    cheese

Lavender, to me, is the smell of holidays past; arriving in the Friday evening dark, and breathing in a warm, scented lungful of Provence.

This recipe, which makes an excellent lunch with a green salad, is also a good thing to have on the table while you're working your way through a couple of bottles of well-chilled rosé, or indeed a sticky bottle of pastis on a summer evening.

1. Tip the honey into a small pan and stir in 6 sprigs of lavender. Bring to the boil, then turn off the heat and allow to cool. Remove the lavender and pour back into the jar, adding one of the remaining sprigs. Heat the oven to 220°C/fan 200°C/gas 7.
2. Put the flour, baking powder and salt into a mixing bowl and whisk to combine. Whisk the oil with 125ml of warm water, then stir this into the dry ingredients and bring together into a soft dough.
3. Grease a small baking tray and sprinkle with the semolina, then use your fingers to gently prod the dough out to cover the tray, making it thinner in the middle and leaving a slightly thicker crust around the edge. Brush with a little oil and bake for 15 minutes.
4. Meanwhile, thinly slice the figs and goat's cheese. Arrange on top of the dough, drizzle with honey and return to the oven until the cheese bubbles and browns a little and the edges of the dough are golden. Sprinkle with a few more lavender flowers, being careful not to overdo it, and serve warm.

Geranium and apple snow

serves 4

50–75g white sugar
10 large, unsprayed geranium
    leaves, washed
500g cooking apples, peeled,
    cored and roughly chopped
3 egg whites
1 tablespoon icing sugar

This easy autumnal pudding is inspired by the subtly fragrant stewed apple with geranium often found on the Ballymaloe House breakfast table in season – it sounds an odd combination, but it works beautifully, and as even the worst gardener can keep a geranium alive, it's an easy way into cooking with your own flowers (make sure the leaves haven't been sprayed with anything noxious, though). If you don't happen to have any suitable geraniums, a splash of rosewater is a good substitute.

If you want, you can fold in some whipped double cream as well to make a more substantial, fool-like dessert, but I like the delicate texture of this fat-free version as it is (or with a little custard).

1. Put 50g of the sugar and 75ml of water into a small pan over a medium-high heat. Stir to dissolve, add the geranium leaves, bring to the boil, then simmer for a couple of minutes.
2. Remove the leaves, add the apple chunks, turn down the heat, cover and cook until they break down into a smoothish purée. Whisk to get rid of any remaining lumps, taste and add more sugar if needed, then allow to cool.
3. Whisk the egg whites until they hold soft peaks, then whisk in the icing sugar until glossy. Fold in the apple purée, a little at a time. Once it's all incorporated, taste and add more sugar if necessary.

Marzipan violets

makes about 25

80g icing sugar, plus a little
    extra to dust
80g caster sugar
1 egg
A few drops of almond extract
A few drops of violet essence
175g ground almonds, whizzed
    in the food processor if
    coarse
100g dark chocolate
Crystallized violets or coloured
    sugar, to decorate

At the very real risk of sounding like Miss Marple, I can think of few better companions for a winter's afternoon than a box of Fortnum & Mason violet and rose creams and a good book. I'm a big fan of the delicate perfume of violets in particular, which marries beautifully with sweet almonds in this nutty take on the classic sweet – don't be tempted to leave out the salt, it really makes them.

1. Bring a pan a third full of water to a simmer and sift the icing sugar into a heatproof bowl large enough to sit above, but not touching, the water. Run a little cold water into the sink. Stir the caster sugar and egg into the icing sugar, then set over the pan and whisk for at least 10 minutes, until thick and puffy.
2. Put the bowl into the sink, add a couple of drops of both flavourings and a pinch of salt and whisk until cool, then taste; the violet should be the dominant flavour, so add more if necessary, plus more salt if you like.
3. Stir in the ground almonds until you have a smooth paste, using your hands if necessary, then dust a tray with a little icing sugar and roll the marzipan into roughly quail's egg sized balls and arrange on the tray. Put in a cool place, or the fridge, to firm up a little – an hour should do it but longer won't hurt.
4. Melt the chocolate in a bain-marie (as above) or in the microwave, then dunk each ball in it to coat and put back on the tray, topping each with a violet or a sprinkle of sugar before it sets. Use any extra chocolate to touch up any thin bits, then set aside for the chocolate to harden.

Scandi saffron buns

makes 7 large buns

245ml milk
¼ teaspoon saffron threads
425g plain flour
10g active dried yeast
75g caster sugar, plus 1
    tablespoon to glaze
½ teaspoon salt
120g cold butter
1 teaspoon rosewater
A whole nutmeg, to grate
50g mixed peel
150g currants

For the filling:
¼ teaspoon saffron threads
A splash of milk
75g butter, softened
50g soft light brown sugar

A word of warning to any true-bred Cornwallahs out there; though I've taken the lead on ingredients from my beloved 1923 copy of *Cornish Recipes Ancient and Modern* from the WI, which includes saffron cake inspiration from as far back as 1805, the form of these is borrowed from the distinctly Scandinavian cardamom version – because a ring of sticky buns puts a smile on everyone's face. Fluffy, but undeniably substantial, they make a generous afternoon tea in themselves.

1. Heat the milk for the buns to hand-hot. Crush the saffron to a powder in a pestle and mortar and then tip this into the milk and leave to infuse for a few minutes.

2. Put the flour into a large mixing bowl with the yeast, 75g of sugar and the salt. Stir together with a whisk to break up any lumps, then grate in the butter and rub in with your fingertips until it resembles coarse crumbs. Add the rosewater and a grating of nutmeg to the milk, then pour it into the flour and stir until it comes together into a soft dough.

3. Lightly grease a work surface and knead the dough for about 10 minutes (it will be very sticky) until it starts to feel more like a coherent ball than a mess. Knead in the peel and currants. Wipe out the mixing bowl, grease and then return the dough to it. Cover and put in a draught-free place until doubled in size (this will probably take a couple of hours at least).

4. Meanwhile, to make the filling, grind the remaining saffron to a powder and pour in a splash of milk. Beat the butter and sugar together with a pinch of salt, then stir in the saffron-infused milk. Lightly grease a 23cm springform cake tin.

5. Knock back the dough by punching the air out of it, then pull or roll out on a lightly floured work surface into a rough 35 x 25cm rectangle, long edges parallel to you. Spread the butter over the top, stopping short about 1cm before the bottom of the rectangle, then roll up the dough, starting at the long edge closest to you, into a tight sausage.

6. Cut the sausage into seven pieces and arrange evenly around the tin, with the smallest in the middle. (Don't worry that they look a bit lonely; they'll expand.) Cover and leave to prove for about 30 minutes, until the dough springs back when prodded. Heat the oven to 220°C/fan 200°C/gas 7.

7. Bake for about 25–30 minutes, until golden brown. Meanwhile, stir the remaining tablespoon of sugar into a tablespoon of boiling water, then brush this on to the buns when they come out of the oven. Leave to cool slightly before tearing into them.

Shrikhand, or spiced saffron and pistachio yoghurt

serves 4

500g whole Greek yoghurt
½ teaspoon saffron
2 tablespoons milk
50–75g soft light brown sugar
1 tablespoon rosewater
4 tablespoons shelled
  pistachios, roughly chopped

A *Guardian* reader introduced me to this rich, fragrant Indian dessert, and I'll be forever grateful to them – it's very simple to make, but tastes incredibly special. You don't have to hang the yoghurt if you don't have time, because with Greek yoghurt most of the work has already been done for you, but it will make it even thicker and more luxurious.

1. If time permits, scoop the yoghurt into some muslin, secure with string, and hang to drain for a couple of hours (I suspend it from the arm of my food mixer so the whey drips into the bowl).

2. Pound the saffron in a pestle and mortar until powdered. Warm the milk up and pour into the mortar (this will make it much easier to get the saffron out too – it tends to stick to the base of mine). Leave to infuse for 5 minutes.

3. Mix the sugar into the yoghurt to taste, then the rosewater, a little at a time – they vary greatly in strength, so you may need more or less depending on your brand. Stir in the saffron-infused milk and serve with the nuts sprinkled on top.

Rose petal vodka

makes 700ml

4 fragrant, unsprayed roses
    (2 needed for each stage of
    the process)
1 medium bottle of vodka
    (about 700ml)

This is simplicity itself to do, and makes a lovely blush-pink long drink with tonic, as well as being gorgeous over ice.

1. Shake the roses to dislodge any insects, then carefully pick off the petals. Decant the vodka into a large jar or wide jug.
2. Put the petals of 2 roses into the jug and stir once, then seal with a lid or clingfilm and leave it somewhere sunny for 3 or 4 days; the vodka will turn a beautiful pink colour (unless your roses are yellow or white, of course).
3. Strain to remove the petals, then repeat the process with the second lot of roses (if you prefer a subtler infusion, you can skip this second step). Strain and pour back into the bottle. You can add fresh petals just before serving if you'd like it to look even prettier.

W

is for Wild

I won't claim I'm one of those people who's out every weekend combing the hedgerows for free food – for one, the hedgerows near me are likely to yield more kebab boxes than berries, and for another, frankly, much of the stuff on offer in my many foraging books doesn't seem worth the effort. (No one will convince me, for example, that nettles aren't considered weeds for a reason.)

That said, there are treats out there, for free, that are far superior to anything you can buy in the shops. Aromatic, grassy wild garlic has a quite different flavour to the bulb, while damsons are far tarter and richer than the sweet-natured common or garden plum.

There's also the very real benefit of feeling inordinately smug when serving up something you've harvested yourself, for nothing; not all of us have the space, or (admit it) the patience, to coax potatoes from the ground, or spend hours on the riverbank toiling for one tiny trout, but anyone can go down to the park with a plastic bag and spend a happy hour picking, and eating, blackberries.

There's a certain quiet satisfaction in dipping into the hunter-gatherer lifestyle for an afternoon, then going home and making the fruits of your labour even more delicious with some stuff you've foraged from more conventional sources. It's one of the luxuries of modern life.

The rules

It may be obvious that you shouldn't gather food from the side of busy roads, and should treat anything at cocked-leg height with caution in parks frequented by dogs (i.e. all parks), but look out as well for signs of chemical use in both town and country; if the leaves are yellowing, or clumps of plants are dead, then the area may well have been treated with insecticide, and you should leave well alone. Wash anything gathered well in fresh water before eating.

In terms of your rights and responsibilities, the law allows you to pick food on public land, or along a right of way, but you must have the landowner's permission to uproot any whole plants (usually a bad idea anyway, given you'll kill them), or indeed to cross from the footpath to that fruity-looking damson tree at the edge of the wood. Few landowners would mind you taking a handful for your own use, but nevertheless it's polite to ask if possible, and to avoid stripping the tree completely.

In fact, that's a good maxim in general when foraging; if you're too greedy, then others will be disappointed, and indeed with some species you risk killing the plant off completely for next year. Only take what you need, and be careful to cause as little damage as possible to the surrounding area while doing so.

The tools

A good identification guide (Richard Mabey's classic *Food for Free* is still the best to my mind) is the only must if you're getting any more adventurous than the bramble, but a supply of clean carrier bags, and a small pair of stout scissors or secateurs, will come in handy.

Wild garlic – March to June
Woodlands and hedgerows

Probably the easiest of all wild foods to identify, because you'll likely smell a clump of wild garlic before you see it, these broad green spears, with their star-shaped white flowers, can be found from March (in southern areas) to June in damp woodland and other shady places. Although there are other plants which look similar, only ramsons, as they're also known, have that distinct alliaceous whiff. Ideally use scissors to harvest them to avoid pulling the plants up by the roots, and go for younger, smaller leaves rather than tougher, darker old-timers. The flowers, which are also edible, make a pretty garnish, though the leaves will be more tender before the plant has flowered.

It's a very easy plant to make use of; it'll work pretty much anywhere you might use garlic or chives, and has a milder flavour than you might expect from its pungent smell. Fold it into mayonnaise, crème fraîche or scrambled eggs, mash it into butter, or snip it on top of salads, fish, and so on – you can even make a punchy pesto with it.

Samphire – June to September
Coastal marshes and salt flats

Properly known as marsh samphire, and found on tidal mudflats and salt marshes, the minerally, salty flavour of this leaves you in no doubt that it is a sea vegetable.

Young stalks are great tossed raw into salads, but any you've picked yourself will need washing thoroughly first to rid them of any grit. Steamed until al dente, samphire can be eaten like asparagus, dipped in melted butter, and pulled from its woody stems with the teeth, but if you're going to serve it as a vegetable, remove these fibrous lower portions before cooking.

Cobnuts – August to October
Woods, hedgerows and wasteland

On my way to the greengrocer to find cobnuts (a type of hazelnut) to test the meringue recipe in this chapter, I was amazed to find myself stepping over piles of the things on an unlovely London pavement – they look like spiky little corn husks with pale green or brown shells inside, depending on their age, and the hazel tree or bush that bears them has broad, serrated green leaves with a slightly furry underside.

People rave about the milky joys of raw green cobnuts, but though they're nice enough, the flavour really comes out when you toast them.

Of course, they're great simply roasted and salted, but they're also delicious wherever you might use hazelnuts otherwise: in a seasonal apple and blue cheese salad, popped into a chocolate brownie, or stirred through sautéd cabbage.

Blackberries – August to October
Woodland, wasteland, parks, hedgerows and heaths

These need little introduction, but I have discovered a couple of new things about this familiar fruit in recent years – the ripest berries will always be the lowest on the stem, and these are said to be the best of all, while those towards the top will be ready to eat last, and may be a bit sour (and thus, perhaps, better for cooking than eating raw).

Damsons – September to October
Hedgerows, parks, woods and edges of gardens

These diminutive blue-black plums, about the size and shape of a large olive, with a slightly chalky-looking skin, aren't common in our hedgerows, but I've happened upon them more than once by accident, and if you find a bullace, or wild plum (similar in size, but rounder), you can use the fruit in much the same way.

Like their relative the sloe, they're too bitter to eat raw, but when cooked with sugar they have a far fuller, richer flavour than you'll get from a dessert plum – and they're also excellent candidates for steeping in booze. (Freeze, use to half fill an empty bottle, then top up with vodka, gin or whisky and leave to mature for a few months before straining and sweetening to taste.)

See also: German plum bread with almond cream (page 360, Yeast).

Roast new potatoes with wild garlic dressing

serves 2

500g small waxy new potatoes
130ml olive oil
50g wild garlic leaves, well
    washed (reserve any flowers
    as garnish)
1 egg
2 tablespoons lemon juice
100ml sunflower oil

Inspired by patatas bravas (or at least my version of it, which includes a garlicky aïoli-like sauce as well as the fiery tomato sort), this makes a great tapas dish, but would also be a very welcome accompaniment to grilled fish or roast chicken. Helpfully, wild garlic pops on to the menu about the same time as the first new potatoes from Jersey – spring on a plate.

1. Heat the oven to 220°C/fan 200°C/gas 8. Cut the potatoes into rough 2cm chunks. Put a roasting tray with 2 tablespoons of the olive oil into the oven and leave to heat for 5 minutes, then take out, toss the potatoes in the hot oil, and bake for about 45 minutes, until crisp and golden.

2. Bring a pan of water large enough to hold the wild garlic to the boil, and prepare a large bowl or sink full of iced water. Blanch the wild garlic for 30 seconds, then dunk in the iced water to cool. Squeeze out well, then use a stick blender to blitz with the remaining olive oil to make a purée.

3. Put the egg and lemon juice into a food processor and whiz to combine. With the motor still running, drizzle in the sunflower oil until it comes together into a loose emulsion. Stir in the wild garlic purée and season to taste.

4. To serve, transfer the potatoes on to a serving plate and drizzle with the green mayonnaise. Sprinkle with sea salt and top with any flowers you may have trimmed from the garlic.

Scrambled eggs with crab and samphire

serves 2

2 thick slices of white
  sourdough bread
20g butter
A large handful of washed and
  trimmed samphire
4 eggs, lightly beaten
1 tablespoon brown crab meat
2 tablespoons crème fraîche
A generous 2 tablespoons
  white crab meat

This is a happily indulgent breakfast (or lunch, or supper), especially if you're on holiday by the seaside and want to eat local seafood three meals a day. And, even if you aren't, this will take you there, minus the shrieking seagulls and refreshing sea breezes. It would also be lovely with black pudding instead of the crab (you could even use both if you're really in the holiday mood).

1. Stick the bread in the toaster, or under the grill, as you wish.
2. Melt half the butter in a small frying pan and sauté the samphire briefly until well coated. Set aside. Butter the toast with a little of the remaining butter.
3. Pour the eggs into a medium, heavy-based saucepan off the heat. Add the remaining butter and a generous pinch of salt and place over a medium-high heat. Stir briefly, then leave alone for 10 seconds, and repeat until they're beginning to set, when you can start stirring continuously until they're nearly done to your liking (nearly!).
4. Whip off the heat and stir in the brown crab meat and crème fraîche, followed by the sautéd samphire. Season well with black pepper and dollop on to the buttered toast. Top with the white crab meat and serve immediately.

Wild garlic bread

**makes 2 slices but very
easily scaled up**

20g butter, at room temperature
2 tablespoons chopped
    wild garlic
A squeeze of lemon juice
1 tablespoon grated pecorino
    or hard goat's cheese
2 thick slices of robustly
    textured bread

I love garlic bread. I love wild garlic. This recipe is the only
sane conclusion to draw from both of these facts. If you want
to make an entire loaf of baguette or ciabatta, you'll need
about five times as much of the wild garlic butter, but you
won't regret it.

1. Mash the butter and garlic together with the lemon juice
and cheese, and season to taste.
2. Toast the bread, spread with the butter, allow it 30 seconds
to melt deliciously into the holes, then devour.

Michaelmas mess

serves 4–6

400ml double cream

For the cobnut meringues:
80g shelled cobnuts (about
    250g unshelled)
100g caster sugar
2 egg whites
A pinch of salt

For the damson compote:
300g damsons
75g caster sugar

An autumnal take on a classic summer pudding starring two of my favourite seasonal fruits, the cobnut and the damson – I think they have a more interesting flavour than their cultivated counterparts, but if you can only find ready-shelled hazelnuts and ordinary plums, worry not, it'll still be pretty delicious. (If you have more damsons left, then the plum and almond cake on page 360 is another possibility.)

1. Start with the meringues. Heat the oven to 170°C/fan 150°C/gas 3 and roast the cobnuts for about an hour, until hard, dry and brown. They will go scarily soft during cooking, but don't worry, they'll firm up again. Allow to cool slightly, then roughly chop.
2. Tip the sugar on to a baking tray and heat for about 5 minutes, then turn the oven down to 130°C/fan 110°C/gas ½. Meanwhile, whisk the egg whites with a pinch of salt in a large bowl to soft peaks. Tip the hot sugar, still whisking, into the egg whites and continue to whisk until the mixture is glossy and thick. Gently fold in the chopped cobnuts, being careful not to knock all the air out as you do so.
3. Dollop spoonfuls of the mixture on to a lined baking tray and bake for 2 hours, until firm. Leave to cool in the oven, then break into large shards.
4. Meanwhile, put the damsons into a pan with the sugar and heat, gently, covered, until the fruit has broken down. Push through a sieve until all you're left with in the sieve are the stones and skins.
5. When you're ready to serve, whip the cream to soft peaks, then gently fold through the compote and meringue.

Almond rice pudding with blackberry and apple compote

serves 6

50g butter
50g soft light brown sugar
100g pudding rice
600ml whole milk
A dash of almond extract
Flaked almonds, to serve

For the compote:
1 unwaxed lemon
550g apples, cooking or tart
    eating, peeled, cored and
    diced
1 tablespoon caster sugar,
    plus extra to taste
1 cinnamon stick
150g blackberries
A whole nutmeg, to grate

Even rice pudding haters will love this: inspired by a medieval favourite made with almond milk, and served with a fragrant seasonal compote that stretches those hard-won brambles a little further, it's the perfect autumnal dessert. (If you'd like to make it dairy free, substitute unsweetened almond milk here.)

1. Melt the butter in a medium pan and stir in the sugar and a pinch of salt, then, a minute later, the rice. Stir to coat, and cook, still stirring, for a couple of minutes.

2. Stir in the milk, add a few drops of almond extract, then bring to a simmer. Cover, leaving the lid slightly ajar. Stir regularly for about 45–55 minutes, until the rice is cooked. Taste and add more almond if necessary. Allow to cool to warm before serving.

3. Meanwhile, peel two long strips of zest from the lemon and put them into a pan with the apples, sugar, cinnamon stick and 1 tablespoon of water. Cook over a medium-low heat, covered, shaking the pan regularly so the apples don't stick.

4. Once they've begun to break down, add the blackberries, replace the lid, and continue to cook, shaking occasionally, until you have a smoothish purple purée. Taste and add more sugar if necessary, plus a good grating of nutmeg. Remove the cinnamon stick and lemon zest if you can find them.

5. Serve the rice pudding warm, rather than hot, with a generous dollop of compote and a sprinkle of flaked almonds on top.

Bramble old-fashioned

makes 1

5 large blackberries or 10 small
  ones
2 teaspoons soft brown sugar
2 tablespoons lemon juice
60ml peated whisky
Ice cubes, to fill

A fruity, slightly saline and very British take on the American classic. Note the exact amounts of sugar and lemon juice will depend on your blackberries, so use this as a rough guide only.

1. Mash the fruit in the bottom of a rocks glass with the sugar, lemon juice and the merest splash of water to help dissolve the sugar.
2. Add the whisky and a generous amount of ice and stir well to combine and chill. Serve immediately. Drink slowly.

is for Xmas

Like Wizzard, sometimes I wish it could be Christmas every day – in the kitchen at least. I adore everything about the food at this time of year, right up to the hundredth crumbly, buttery mince pie. I love the overload of sweetly spiced, faintly medieval dried fruit, the juxtaposition of thick, creamy bread sauce and salty little pigs in blankets, the vivid tangerines and glossy piles of nuts, and perhaps best of all, the excuse to drink sherry in your pyjamas and fill the house with the scent of mulled wine before the sun is over the yardarm. Even that cheap Advent calendar chocolate has its charms.

Bleak midwinter or not, the shops are bursting with lovely things in December – the zingy citrus season is well under way, inspiring fresh fruity salads and sticky, sugary candies; pomegranates, those lethally juicy garnet grenades, add a touch of pink sparkly glamour to everything they touch (including your new Christmas jumper), and cheeses made with rich summer milk are coming up from the cellar and into their own.

There are neat little sprouts and sweet fluffy parsnips, toasted chestnuts and salty oysters, plus a whole ark full of animals which have been fattening all autumn ready for this very moment. (Christmas isn't the jolliest of times for them, I'll admit.)

Planning

If you're in charge of the cooking this Christmas, don't panic; remember, it's just a Sunday roast with silly paper crowns. In fact, it's probably easier than your average roast, because most people will already be stuffed to the gills, and half pickled with booze by the time they sit down to eat, making them blessedly easy to please. But this isn't to say you shouldn't make an effort; it is Christmas, after all.

Having already dealt with the best way to cook a roast potato and a turkey, I won't repeat myself here, though I have sneaked in a modest spin on the classic bread sauce, just because I love it too much to leave out. Instead, the recipes in this chapter are a non-conformist celebration of the flavours of the season – an alternative Christmas message for cooks, if you like.

Bread and walnut sauce

serves 4 bread sauce lovers, 6 ordinary people

1 garlic clove, unpeeled
5 black peppercorns
1 bay leaf
550ml whole milk
100g shelled walnuts
A couple of stems of sage, leaves only
100g fresh white breadcrumbs
50g butter

I am a complete sucker for bread sauce. I love the stuff, and every Christmas I wonder why I don't eat it all year round (answer, because not all clothes are as forgiving as woolly jumpers). It's impossible to improve upon perfection, but this recipe, inspired by a Ligurian walnut sauce, gives it a jolly good go. The walnuts add a toasty, slightly bitter depth of flavour which works beautifully with turkey.

1. Squash the garlic with the back of your knife, skin and all, and put it into a medium saucepan with the peppercorns, bay leaf and milk over a medium heat. Bring to a bare simmer, then take off the heat and leave to infuse for 30 minutes.
2. Meanwhile, toast the walnuts in a dry frying pan until fragrant, then allow to cool slightly before whizzing to fine crumbs in a food processor; be careful not to overdo this last bit or you'll get walnut butter.
3. Scoop the garlic, bay leaf and peppercorns from the milk and discard. Finely chop the sage leaves. Put the milk back on a low heat and stir in the breadcrumbs, then cook until the sauce begins to thicken, stirring occasionally. Stir in the walnuts, butter and most of the sage, and season to taste. Top with the remaining sage and serve.

Georgian aubergine rolls with walnut sauce and pomegranates

makes about 15

100g walnuts

¼ teaspoon dried fenugreek seeds

½ teaspoon coriander seeds

10g coriander leaves, roughly chopped

1 tablespoon dill, roughly chopped

1–2 small garlic cloves (depending on your tolerance for raw garlic)

½ teaspoon paprika

1 tablespoon red wine vinegar

4 tablespoons olive oil

1 tablespoon pomegranate molasses

½ teaspoon fine salt, or to taste

Seeds of ½ a pomegranate

1 large-ish aubergine, preferably fairly long rather than wide

Oil, to grease

Nutty, sweet and sour, with subtle spicing courtesy of the characteristic Georgian combo of fenugreek and coriander, these simple rolls make very handsome little vegetarian canapés, especially as they have the great benefit of sitting happily at room temperature for a few hours. They're also very good with the cheesebread on page 354.

1. Toast the walnuts in a dry frying pan until fragrant, then allow to cool slightly. Repeat with the fenugreek and coriander seeds, then grind these to a powder.

2. Grind the walnuts to a coarse rubble in a food processor, then add the herbs, garlic and spices and whiz, adding the vinegar, olive oil, molasses and salt as you do so. Stir in the pomegranate seeds, keeping a handful back for decoration, then taste and adjust the seasoning if necessary.

3. Very thinly slice the aubergine lengthways – a mandoline is ideal for this if you have one. Heat a griddle pan on a high heat and brush the aubergine slices with oil, then cook in batches until lightly charred on both sides, and soft and floppy.

4. Put a scant teaspoon of walnut mixture on to the narrow end of an aubergine slice and roll it up around it, then put on a plate, seam down. Repeat with the rest of the slices, then serve scattered with the remaining pomegranate seeds.

Brussels sprout, hazelnut and lemon zest salad with goat's cheese

serves 4–6 as an accompaniment

500g Brussels sprouts
75g hazelnuts
1 unwaxed lemon
4 tablespoons neutral oil
2 tablespoons hazelnut oil
1 small log of fresh, soft goat's cheese (optional)

Sprouts still get a bad rap in this country, though given the remarkable renaissance of kale, I have high hopes they'll rise again in time, because, done properly, they really are lovely little things. Nutty sweet and wonderfully crunchy, they're far nicer in a fresh salad than boiled into submission with the turkey – just make sure you cut them really thinly so they aren't too chewy.

1. Pick the outer leaves from the sprouts, discarding any discoloured ones, and put into a serving bowl, then finely shred the inner leaves by holding each at the stalk end and slicing thinly until you reach the hard core. Alternatively, use a food processor if you can be bothered to find all the bits.
2. Toast the hazelnuts in a hot dry pan, being careful not to burn them, then roughly chop. Zest the lemon into a small bowl along with the juice and both oils. Season well and whisk to combine.
3. Toss the sprouts, hazelnuts and dressing together in a salad bowl and season to taste, paying particular attention to plenty of black pepper.
4. Top with chunks of crumbled goat's cheese, if using.

Spiced pumpkin and Parmesan pie with chestnuts

serves 6

For the pastry:
170g spelt flour
A pinch of salt
100g cold butter
1 tablespoon finely chopped
    sage leaves
1 egg yolk

For the pie filling:
1 small pumpkin (preferably a
    variety designed for cooking,
    not decoration, e.g. Crown
    Prince) or medium butternut
    squash
2 tablespoons maple syrup
¼ teaspoon ground cinnamon
¼ teaspoon ground ginger
½ teaspoon ground nutmeg
2 eggs, beaten
100ml double cream
50g Parmesan (or vegetarian
    alternative), finely grated
A knob of butter
150g chestnuts
100ml Madeira or port

This would make a good meat-free main course for Christmas dinner, or indeed a centrepiece for any of the big meals over the Christmas period – the rich sweetness of the roasted pumpkin and chestnuts is well balanced by the salty umami notes of the cheese, and both work fantastically well with the nutty spelt pastry. Serve with a green salad.

1. Heat the oven to 220°C/fan 200°C/gas 7. Cut the pumpkin or squash in half or quarters depending on the size, and scoop out the seeds and fibres inside. Place skin-side up in a roasting dish with a couple of tablespoons of water. Roast for about half an hour, until tender.
2. Allow to cool slightly, then peel off the skin and scoop the flesh into a food processor. Whiz until smooth, then put into a fine sieve or piece of muslin suspended over a bowl and drain for at least an hour, squeezing out the last of its liquid towards the end.
3. Meanwhile, make your pastry. Sift the flour into a mixing bowl, stir in the salt, then grate in the butter. Rub in using your fingertips until it resembles breadcrumbs, then stir through the chopped sage. Mix the egg yolk with 2 tablespoons of iced water, sprinkle half over the mixture, then stir with a knife until it comes together into a paste, adding a little more liquid if necessary.
4. Bring the mixture together with your fingertips, then roll out on a floured surface to the thickness of a £1 coin. Use it to line a 20–21cm tart tin and prick with a fork in several places. Cover with clingfilm and chill for 30 minutes. Heat the oven back up to 220°C/fan 200°C/gas 7.
5. Line the pastry case with greaseproof paper and fill with baking beans. Bake for 15 minutes, then remove the paper and beans and bake for another 5 minutes, until the base is pale golden. Remove from the oven and turn it down to 200°C/fan 180°C/gas 6.

6. Meanwhile, put 320g of pumpkin purée into a large bowl, discarding the excess liquid, and stir in 1 tablespoon of maple syrup and the spices, followed by the eggs. Gradually stir in the cream and cheese until you have a thick, creamy consistency, and season to taste (unless you prefer to steer clear of raw eggs), adding the remaining syrup if you like. Pour into the pastry case.

7. Bake for about 30 minutes, until the filling is set, but still slightly wobbly in the centre. Meanwhile, heat the butter in a small pan and add the chestnuts. Fry over a medium-hot heat until slightly coloured, then add the Madeira or port and reduce until sticky and glossy.

8. Ten minutes before the end of cooking, take the pie out of the oven, arrange the chestnuts on the top and return to the oven. Allow to cool on a wire rack for at least an hour before serving.

Turkey mole poblano

serves 4–10 depending on the size of your turkey

For the turkey (or use cooked leftovers and about 1.4 litres of chicken or turkey stock):
2 litres chicken stock
45g butter
1 carrot
2 celery sticks
1 bay leaf
A handful of peppercorns
1 turkey crown (you can use a whole turkey if you have a pot large enough)

This is a corker of a turkey recipe – not only an excellent way to use up the Christmas leftovers, but a very fitting dish for the big day itself, especially as you can make the sauce and poach the turkey a day or so ahead and combine the two before reheating.

The mole sauce, which comes from the mountainous Mexican state of Puebla, is fairly labour-intensive, but it's not difficult, and its richly spicy and bittersweet flavour repays the blood, sweat and tears. (While we're on the subject of sweat and tears, though tongue-tingling, it's not as fiercely fiery as the number of chillies in the recipe suggests, I promise.) The chillies and tomatillos are easily sourced online.

I like it with toasted corn tortillas, a crunchy salad (the Brussels sprout one in this chapter does nicely) and a dollop of soured cream to take the edge off the heat, but it would also be good with rice – and, when turkey isn't available, it will of course work with chicken too.

1. Put all the ingredients for cooking the turkey, apart from the turkey itself, into a large pan. Bring to a shiver, so the water trembles, but no bubbles break the surface, then add the turkey and poach gently for 15 minutes per 450g, until a thermometer poked into the thickest part of the breast reads 65°C. Allow to cool in the liquid.
2. Meanwhile, heat 75g of lard in a frying pan and fry the whole chillies, in batches if necessary, until fragrant. Tip them into a bowl, cover with warm water and leave to soak for an hour, then drain, saving the soaking water. Tip 225ml of this liquid back into the bowl with the chillies, and purée the chillies until smooth. Heat 75g more

For the mole sauce:

200g lard

10 mulato chillies

6 ancho chillies

6 pasilla chillies

½ teaspoon cloves

1 cinnamon stick

1 teaspoon black peppercorns

¼ teaspoon aniseed

¼ teaspoon coriander seeds

½ teaspoon Mexican oregano

4 tablespoons sesame seeds

5 garlic cloves, roughly
  chopped

3 tinned tomatillos, roughly
  chopped

2 tinned plum tomatoes,
  roughly chopped

50g raisins

50g almonds

40g pumpkin seeds

1 stale corn tortilla

1 slice of stale white bread

150g dark chocolate, finely
  chopped

5 tablespoons soft dark brown
  sugar

lard in the frying pan and fry the chilli purée for 10 minutes, then set aside (in the frying pan if you have another one for steps 3 to 5 – if not, scoop out the chillies and wash the pan before continuing).

3. Toast the cloves, cinnamon, peppercorns, aniseed and coriander in a dry frying pan until fragrant, then tip them into a pestle and mortar and add the oregano. Toast the sesame seeds until slightly golden, then add 3 tablespoons of them to the spices and set the remainder aside. Grind the contents of the pestle to a fine powder (alternatively you can use a spice grinder, if you have one).

4. Heat a little more lard in the pan, and fry the garlic, tomatillos and tomatoes until soft and pulpy, then set aside.

5. Clean the pan, then grease with lard and fry, in turn, the raisins, almonds, pumpkin seeds, tortilla and bread, greasing as necessary and tipping each out into the tomato mixture as soon as it's golden and toasted (raisins, which will not of course go golden, should be fried for about 20 seconds), and breaking the toasted tortilla and bread into small pieces once toasted, but before adding to the rest. Add the ground spices to the mixture and purée it all together until smoothish.

6. Put the purée into the frying pan with the chilli purée and stir in. Heat gently, then add the chocolate, and enough of the turkey cooking liquid to make it into a sauce – about 8 ladlefuls should do it. Stir in half the sugar, and simmer for an hour.

7. Meanwhile, strip the meat from the turkey. Once the sauce has been cooking for an hour, taste and season, adding the rest of the sugar if you think it needs it, and fold in the turkey. Cook for another half an hour before serving.

Tangerine and pomegranate salad with spiced Pedro Ximénez syrup and Marcona almonds

serves 4–6

100ml Pedro Ximénez sherry
5 tablespoons honey
1 cinnamon stick
8 tangerines
A whole nutmeg, to grate
½ a pomegranate
25g blanched Marcona
    almonds, roughly chopped

Though I love Christmas pudding, there comes a point when even I crave something lighter. This vaguely Moorish number celebrates two fine seasonal fruits, the tangy tangerine and the sweet, crunchy pomegranate, doused in a sticky, spicy syrup – because it's still Christmas, after all. It can be made well ahead of time, and kept in the fridge until its big moment.

NB: do try and get tangerines if possible; this won't work as well with bland, puffy satsumas, but clementines, or indeed larger oranges, will do at a pinch.

1. Put the sherry and honey into a small pan and heat gently, stirring to dissolve the honey. Add the cinnamon stick, bring to a simmer, and reduce for about 5 minutes until slightly thickened and syrupy. Take off the heat.
2. Peel the tangerines and slice horizontally. Remove any seeds you come across and tip any juices on to the serving plate on which you are arranging the tangerine slices.
3. Pour the syrup over the tangerines and grate over a little nutmeg. Cover and chill for at least an hour. Scatter over the pomegranate seeds and almonds just before serving.

Y

is for Yeast

The most alchemic of all ingredients, before science identified it as a fungus, yeast was naturally assumed to be a blessing from above. Only with the advent of the microscope in the seventeenth century did we discover that we had something physical to thank for all that bread and booze, but it wasn't until the nineteenth century, and the pioneering work of Louis Pasteur, that its role in the fermentation process was fully understood.

So, for much of human history, yeast remained a happy mystery, which is certainly how it still appears to many of us less scientifically minded bakers today. It would be a jaded soul indeed who failed to feel a little flutter when, on peeping underneath the tea towel, they found a swelling mass of living dough in place of the tight little ball of an hour before. Simple, everyday magic perhaps, but magic nonetheless.

There's an element of jeopardy to working with yeast that you just don't get with other leavening agents: chemicals, like baking powder, may be more reliable, but they're a lot less fun (and the results just don't compare). Yeast is amazing, and that's that. Without it we wouldn't have bread beyond the dense soda and cornbread kind (and, come to think of it, we wouldn't have any alcohol or chocolate either. It's frightening to think that human happiness depends so heavily on one tiny microorganism) or pizza or hot cross buns, doughnuts or bara brith, croissants, rum babas or even (shock horror) a decent crumpet. Life without yeast is a dull prospect indeed.

The chemistry

Though it's always nice to have a bit of magic in your life, it's often easier to cook with ingredients if you understand at least the basics of how they work. Here follows a very simplified explanation.

Yeasts are single-celled, microscopic fungi. In order to reproduce, they need energy. To get that energy they feed on the sugars and starches in bread dough, producing carbon dioxide and alcohol as by-products. As long as you've kneaded your dough to develop the gluten in it, it will be strong enough to trap this carbon dioxide in tiny pockets of gas, which will gradually cause the dough to rise.

But where does this sugar come from in the first place? Well, the magic starts the minute you begin mixing. As soon as flour and water come together, the broken starch cells in the flour begin to absorb the water, prompting enzymes to digest their starch and turn them into sugar – food for the yeast.

Note that yeast is very fussy about temperature; it's at its most active at about 35°C, but a slower fermentation gives more interesting results. Roughly speaking, 27°C is about as warm as you should go, and those of us with chilly kitchens will be pleased to know that many professionals prefer a long, slow fermentation, even leaving the dough overnight in the fridge to develop its flavour. It's best not to have too many plans when you're working with yeast, because, like animals and children, it can be unpredictable. (Unlike animals and children, it doesn't like too much salt or sugar, so don't overdo it.)

Once the dough has been stretched to its elastic limit by the air inside, it's time to bake. As it heats up in the oven, those air pockets expand, and the alcohol and water within evaporates, producing yet more gas, and causing the loaf to rise. Once a stiff crust has formed around the loaf, it stops rising, and when the interior temperature gets up near 100°C, it's baked.

Types of yeast

There's understandable confusion about the different types of yeast available, and how they work. See page 384 for information about conversion between different sorts.

— Fresh yeast: Comes in small brown putty-like cubes which need refrigeration. It's more powerful than dried forms, but has two distinct disadvantages: first, it only lasts a couple of weeks, which means a lot of wastage unless you eat a lot of bread, and second, it can be difficult to find. Look in wholefood shops and bakeries or ask at the bakery counter of supermarkets.

— Active dried yeast: Small brown granules of dormant yeast cells which are reactivated by soaking in warm water, often with some sugar for extra encouragement, before they are added to the dough. Many recipes are a bit vague about how you know if your yeast is ready to use – a few stray bubbles are not enough. Wait until the surface of the water is covered with a mass of beige froth. If that doesn't happen, either your water was too cold or your yeast is old – check the use-by date on the packet.

— Quick yeast: As the name suggests, more modern processing methods mean that this is more lively than active dried yeast, and can be added to dough without the need for any reactivation. Probably the easiest kind to use.

— Wild yeasts: If you're feeling brave, you can catch your own yeasts from the atmosphere in your home by making a sourdough starter, or mother. It will need more regular care and attention than a pot of dry stuff though.

Bear in mind that, though it might be tempting to add more yeast than the recipe suggests to speed up the rising time, in fact, the less you can get away with, and the slower your fermentation, the better the flavour of the end result. Yeast has a strong taste of its own which you don't want to be the dominant one in your bread.

Georgian cheesebread (khachapuri)

serves 8

10g active dried yeast
130ml warmish water
A pinch of sugar
300g plain flour, plus extra
    to dust
1 teaspoon salt
70ml plain whole milk yoghurt
1 tablespoon olive oil, plus extra
    to brush
200g firm mozzarella (of the
    kind used for pizza)
200g feta
1 teaspoon black onion seeds
    (optional)

My favourite culinary discovery of recent years is the food of Georgia, the former Soviet state whose cooking combines southern ingredients with a certain northern heartiness. Khachapuri is the love-child of a cheese pie and a deep-dish pizza – molten cheese barely encased in an ever-so-slightly fluffy crust, and best devoured as soon as it's cool enough to handle.

If you ever find any suluguni cheese, the authentic choice, snap it up – but the mix below makes a decent substitute.

1. Mix the yeast, a little of the water and the sugar into a loose paste. Leave until the surface is covered with tiny bubbles, indicating the yeast has begun its work.
2. Meanwhile, put the flour and salt into a mixing bowl and whisk together to combine. Once the yeast is ready, mix it with the remaining water, the yoghurt and oil and stir into the flour to make a soft dough.
3. Knead the dough on a clean work surface or in a mixer fitted with a dough hook until smooth and bouncy; this should take 5–10 minutes. Cover and put in a draught-free, warmish place for about an hour and a half, or until roughly doubled in volume.
4. Scoop the risen dough on to a clean work surface, punch the air out of it, then cover and leave until doubled again, which should take about 40 minutes.
5. Meanwhile, grate the cheeses and heat the oven to 200°C/fan 180°C/gas 6.
6. Roll out the dough on a lightly floured surface into a rough 30cm circle. Put the cheese in the centre, then bring one edge of the dough into the middle, fold one edge of that edge into the middle and continue this all the way round, pinching it together to seal. Slide on to a lightly greased baking tray. Brush with olive oil and scatter with onion seeds if using, then bake for about 35–40 minutes, until golden.

Buckwheat pikelets

makes 6 small or 3 large

180ml milk
1 teaspoon quick yeast
70g buckwheat flour
40g plain flour
½ teaspoon soft light brown or
    caster sugar
1 egg, beaten
½ teaspoon salt
Butter, to grease

Pikelets are a free-form Welsh variety of crumpet – made without the customary rings, they tend to be thinner and more flexible than the ordinary sort. This recipe, inspired by the buckwheat pancakes popular in Brittany and Belgium, has a richer, earthier, more savoury flavour than the white kind – I love them for breakfast (you can make the batter the night before), often with a fried egg and some spinach.

If you have buttermilk left over from the butter recipe on page 82, you can use it to replace some of the milk. Of course, the butter itself would be very welcome on top.

1. Warm the milk. Meanwhile, whisk together the yeast, flours and sugar in a large bowl, then whisk in the milk followed by the egg; the mixture should be a very loose dough or thickish batter. Cover and leave in a warm place for a couple of hours, until the surface is covered in tiny bubbles.
2. Whisk in the salt. Grease a small frying pan on a medium-high heat with butter, tipping off any excess for re-use. Test the temperature with a little of the batter; it should sizzle as it hits the pan.
3. Add ¾ of a ladleful to the pan for smaller pikelets, or a generous ladleful for larger ones, and cook until the base is dark and the the top dry and covered with small holes; this will take between 3 and 5 minutes. Flip and toast the top for a couple of minutes until golden, then serve or keep warm while you repeat with the rest of the batter.

Pissaladière

A Niçoise take on a pizza (it's only 30km from the Italian border, after all), this is an irresistible combination of crunchy flatbread base, salty anchovies and sweet onions. And make no mistake: those onions should be piled on top like a Chicago pizza pie, rather than scattered delicately in the Neapolitan manner – this is one time you'll be thankful you invested in a mandoline.

serves 8–10

1.5kg onions
4 tablespoons olive oil
A pinch of sugar
1 teaspoon herbes de Provence
100–200g anchovies in oil
  (depending on the strength
  of your love for anchovies)
2 small garlic cloves
A handful of stone-in black
  olives
1 red chilli, sliced

For the base:
450g strong white flour
5g quick yeast
1 teaspoon sugar
1½ teaspoons fennel seeds
1 teaspoon salt
60ml olive oil, plus extra to
  grease
About 240ml warm water
Polenta/cornmeal, to sprinkle

1. To make the base, whisk the flour, yeast, sugar, fennel seeds and salt together in a large mixing bowl. Make a dip in the middle, pour in the olive oil and enough of the water to make a dough, then turn out on to a lightly greased work surface and knead for about 10 minutes, until it feels smooth and elastic. Rub the bowl with oil and turn the dough in it to coat, then cover and leave in a draught-free place until doubled in size – about 1½–2 hours.

2. Meanwhile, get to work on the onions. Finely slice, which will take some time (I use a mandoline); then heat the oil in a large frying pan over a medium heat and add the onions and a generous pinch of sugar. Cook, stirring often, until very soft and golden, but not at all brown. Season lightly and stir in the herbs.

3. Put the anchovies and garlic into a pestle and mortar and mash until fairly smooth. Pound in the oil from the anchovies, a little at a time, to make a paste. Grease a large baking tray and sprinkle with cornmeal.

4. Once the dough has doubled in size, tip out of the bowl, knock back, then stretch or roll into a rectangle to fit the baking tray, pressing out any air. Heat the oven to 240°C/fan 220°C/gas 9.

5. Spread the anchovy paste over the dough, then top with the onions. Arrange the olives and chilli rings on top and bake for about 20 minutes, until the edges are golden.

Marmite and cheese mini doughnuts

makes about 18

225g strong white flour, plus extra to dust

7g quick yeast

5g caster sugar, plus extra to dust

20g unsalted butter, at room temperature, chopped, plus extra to grease

2 tablespoons Marmite

65ml milk

1 egg, beaten

40g Parmesan or other very hard cheese

100g mature Cheddar, grated

40g Gouda, grated

1 tablespoon cornflour

2 tablespoons whole milk

2 litres vegetable or sunflower oil, to cook

Killer party food – if the idea of savoury doughnuts troubles you, just think of them as slightly more substantial versions of that classic French nibble, the gougère. Best served warm, while the cheese is still gorgeously gooey.

1. Combine the flour, yeast and sugar in a large bowl and mix well. Put the butter and Marmite into a small pan with the milk and 45ml of water, and heat gently, stirring until they have melted. Pour this into the mixing bowl, along with the egg, and stir until it comes together into a dough: it should be soft and slightly sticky.

2. Tip on to a lightly floured surface, or (better still as the mixture is soft) into a mixer fitted with a dough hook, and knead until smooth and elastic (about 10 minutes in a mixer, more by hand). Put into a lightly greased bowl, cover with a damp tea towel, and leave in a warm place until doubled in size (about an hour). Meanwhile, finely grate the Parmesan and spread out on a plate to dry out slightly.

3. Shape the dough into balls of about 20g each, folding each side tightly into the centre in turn, rotating as you go, then turn the ball over and put it on a lightly floured baking tray or board, spacing them well apart. Cover and leave to rise again for 45 minutes.

4. Meanwhile, toss the grated Cheddar and Gouda with the cornflour, and put in a medium pan over a low heat. Add the whole milk and allow the cheeses to melt, stirring regularly, until smooth. Keep warm.

5. Heat the oil in a large pan or deep-fat fryer to 160°C. Cook the doughnuts in batches for about 2 minutes on each side, until golden, then blot with kitchen paper and sprinkle with Parmesan. Make a small hole in the side of each, and use a piping bag to inject a splodge of cheese. Eat immediately, while they're still warm.

German plum bread with almond cream

makes a 23cm cake

115ml whole milk
7g active dried yeast
25g caster sugar
250g plain flour
¼ teaspoon ground nutmeg
5g salt
30g butter, at room temperature
1 egg, beaten
25g mixed peel
Oil, to grease

For the almond cream:
125g butter, at room
    temperature
65g soft light brown sugar
60g caster sugar
100g ground almonds
25g plain flour
2 eggs, beaten
25g flaked almonds
2 tablespoons whisky, brandy
    or rum

To top:
6 plums
1 tablespoon demerara sugar

Cake doesn't quite do this defiantly bready, almost savoury fruit number justice. Based on the German *pflaumenkuchen*, but with added almonds and a touch of very British peel and spice, this is hearty afternoon tea territory, rather than any delicate dessert. I'd describe it as the love-child of a hot cross bun and a fruit tart.

If you happen to come across any yellow plums, a mixture of them and the purple sort looks very pretty here – traditionally it would be made with damsons, in which case increase the amount of demerara sugar at the end.

1. Heat the milk to blood temperature, then whisk some of it into a loose paste with the yeast and ½ teaspoon of the sugar. Leave until the surface of the paste is covered with a froth of tiny bubbles.
2. Meanwhile, whisk together the remaining sugar with the flour, nutmeg and salt and cut the butter into it in small pieces. Rub the butter into the dry ingredients. When the yeast is ready, stir in the remaining milk, then stir the whole lot into the flour, followed by the egg, to make a softish dough.
3. Once it comes together, tip on to a clean surface and knead until smooth and springy (roughly 5–8 minutes). Scatter the peel over the work surface and knead into the dough until evenly distributed. Oil the bowl lightly, turn the dough in the oil, then cover and leave for about an hour and a half, until doubled in size.
4. Meanwhile, beat the butter for the almond cream until softened, then beat in the sugars and a pinch of salt until the mix is light and fluffy. Mix in the ground almonds and flour until well combined, followed by the eggs, a little at a time. Finally stir in the flaked almonds and the booze.
5. Cut the plums in half, remove the stones, then cut each half into wedges. Grease a 23cm springform tin. Knock the air out of the risen dough, then put the dough into the tin and use your fingers to spread it out evenly across the base.
6. Top the dough with the almond cream, followed by the plum wedges (I favour two concentric circles), then cover with a clean tea towel and leave for 40 minutes. Meanwhile, heat the oven to 200°C/fan 180°C/gas 6.

7. Sprinkle the demerara sugar on top of the plums and bake for about 40–45 minutes, until golden, then allow to cool slightly before serving.

Wholesome loaf

makes 1 loaf

2 tablespoons treacle
(about 55g)
325ml tepid water
7g active dried yeast
300g very strong wholemeal
flour
140g rye flour
10g salt
100g seeds of your choice
Oil or butter, to grease

Though I love the robust chewiness of sourdough, sometimes I crave the workaday, brown nuttiness of the seed-strewn breads that are ordinary fare in Germany and Scandinavia, but frustratingly hard to find here. This one is lovely with soup, and makes outstanding cheese on toast, but, most importantly of all, it's fabulous with a generous wodge of butter.

1. Dissolve a teaspoon of the treacle in the water, then whisk in the yeast. Leave in a warmish place until the top is copiously frothy. Meanwhile, whisk together the flours and salt in a large bowl. Stir the remaining treacle into the yeasty water to dissolve and then stir this into the flours to make a soft, sticky dough – if it feels at all dry, add a little more water.
2. Tip on to a clean work surface (no need to flour) and knead until the dough starts to feel silky and elastic (and springs back when prodded), then scatter the seeds on the work surface and work into the dough until evenly distributed. Form the dough into a ball and put into a lightly greased bowl. Cover and leave in a draught-free place (I use a cold oven) until doubled in size.
3. Grease a roughly 20 x 10cm (1lb) loaf tin. Flatten the dough into a rough rectangle, short side parallel to you, then fold the bottom third into the middle, the top third down on top of it, then fold the whole thing over once more. Pinch the fold closed with your fingers around the bottom and the sides, then put into the loaf tin, seam-side down. Cover and leave to rest in the same place for about an hour to an hour and a half, until slightly risen (it won't double, being rye).
4. Heat your oven as high as it will go. Put a baking tray or pizza stone in there if you have one, and a roasting tin in the bottom. Boil a little water in a kettle. Put the loaf into the hot oven and immediately pour the hot water into the roasting tin underneath. Bake for 5 minutes, then turn the temperature down to 220°C/fan 200°C/gas 7 and bake for 45 minutes, rotating once. Allow to cool in the tin.

Z

is for Zest

You might guess citrus zest would taste bitter, like the pith on a sloppily peeled orange, but the reality is intensely aromatic, even zingy, at once somehow fresher, and more complex – often almost floral – than the fruit itself, which can be one-dimensional in its acidity.

Each of the citrus zests has its own unique flavour, as different as the fruits themselves. Lime is fruitier and slightly more bitter than the fragrant lemon, orange is rich and marmaladey, while grapefruit has a peppery freshness and the pomelo is almost too perfumed for its own good – the connoisseur's choice, perhaps. The elusive bergamot, available for only a few weeks every year, is very much like Earl Grey tea (unsurprisingly, given that fine brew gets its flavour from the oil of this sour sort of orange).

Once you discover citrus zest, there's no limit to its uses, both sweet and savoury, whether that's adding some lightness and sunshine to a rich meat stew, like the lemon zest and parsley gremolata traditionally served with osso bucco; a touch of bitter depth to a sugary icing; or as a highly perfumed, sticky piece of confectionery in its own right in the form of candied peel.

The anatomy of citrus peel

It may have been the smell of citrus zest that first attracted us to the fruit, long before selective breeding led to the introduction of sweet eating varieties. The flesh, nowadays largely considered the important bit, is protected by a thick spongy layer called the albedo, but better known as pith, which cushions the delicate collection of tiny juice sacs within.

Importantly for our purposes, surrounding the pith is a thin colourful layer of glands that secrete and store volatile oils, which are responsible for the distinctive scent and taste of the zest. If you've ever squeezed a twist of lemon peel over a martini, and seen beads of fragrant oil collect on the surface, you'll know this already – and if you haven't, then you should probably stop reading and go and do so at once.

Most citrus these days is waxed after picking, to stop the evaporation of moisture and keep it fresh for longer. To avoid ingesting this (harmless, but not particularly pleasant-tasting) substance, go for the unwaxed sort, which are available in most greengrocers and supermarkets, or choose organic fruit, which isn't treated in this way. If you can only get the ordinary stuff, a scrub with wire wool under hot water helps.

Tools

When removing zest, avoid taking any of the bitter pith with it unless you're making candied peel or marmalade. This means using a fine grater (for small pieces that will blend easily with other ingredients), a citrus zester (for long thin strips of the kind you might want to drape over a salad, or some pasta), or a vegetable peeler (for long strips you might use to garnish a drink with, or for a marinade). At a pinch, you can use a sharp knife, but this requires a very steady hand.

See also: Spotted dick (page 61, Dumplings), Crab with ricotta and lemon zest and an elderflower and cucumber salad (page 312, Violets), Brussels sprout, hazelnut and lemon zest salad with goat's cheese (page 343, Xmas), German plum bread with almond cream (page 360, Yeast).

Slow-roast tomato pasta with lemon salt, ricotta and basil

serves 4

10 medium tomatoes
Extra virgin olive oil, to drizzle
320g squid ink spaghetti,
    linguine or other long pasta
200g ricotta
A small bunch of basil

For the lemon zest salt:
60g flaky sea salt
Zest of 2 unwaxed lemons

OK, so this takes a while for what is, essentially, a very simple pasta, so feel free to substitute semi-dried tomatoes packed in oil if you prefer – I like to do a big batch of tomatoes and use them over several days on toast, in salads and in dishes like this, which makes it worthwhile. The lemon salt is well worth the effort, though; you'll be finding uses for it for ages, from fish to ice cream (try it).

Essentially, however, even if you buy in the tomatoes and mix salt with fresh lemon zest, this dish is still worth a go; it's so much more than the sum of its few parts. You can use ordinary pasta, but the colour of the ricotta, tomatoes and herbs is far more striking against the black of the squid ink variety – don't be tempted to toss it all together or you'll spoil the effect; it's for the diner to mess up.

1. Start by making the salt. Heat the oven to 120°C/fan 100°C/gas ½ and mix the salt and zest together well. Spread out on a lined baking sheet and bake for an hour. Remove, but leave the oven on.
2. Cut the tomatoes in half and brush with olive oil. Sprinkle with some of the lemon salt and bake for 4 hours.
3. Cook the pasta in plenty of boiling salted water until al dente, then drain and toss with olive oil and a good pinch of the lemon salt. Divide between bowls and arrange the tomatoes, a few spoonfuls of ricotta and some basil leaves artistically on top, together with a final pinch of lemon salt. Serve immediately.

Mediterranean ceviche

serves 2

½ a small red onion, finely
    sliced
300g skinless sea bass or sea
    bream
Juice of 4 limes
4 tangerines or clementines
1 small red chilli, deseeded and
    finely chopped
1 small head of fennel, finely
    sliced
3 tablespoons finely chopped
    candied peel
A handful of mint leaves, torn

Candied peel in ceviche is an idea I shamelessly nabbed from my friend Hen, who once had a sideline running a pisco and ceviche bar in a Turkish-Cypriot social club in Hackney. As you do. The bittersweet flavour works surprisingly well with the creamy fish and peppery mint – and once I'd added orange, my mind began to run along more Mediterranean-type flavours, like aniseedy fennel. They might not recognize it in Lima, but I bet the Turks would dig it.

1. Cover the onion with cold water and leave to soak for 5 minutes, then drain well. Meanwhile, cut the fish into large bite-sized pieces and sprinkle with ½ teaspoon of salt.
2. Stir the lime juice, the juice of 2 of the tangerines and the chilli into the fish, then add the drained onion and leave for 10 minutes.
3. Meanwhile, peel the remaining tangerines and cut into thin slices, and finely slice the fennel. Add to the fish along with the candied peel and mint leaves, reserving a little of these as garnish, and toss together well. Divide between plates, garnish and serve immediately.

Peach and mozzarella salad with crispy lemon zest and basil

serves 2 (easily scaled up)

1 large unwaxed lemon
6 tablespoons olive oil
2–3 fairly ripe peaches or
  nectarines
1 ball of buffalo mozzarella
4 sprigs of basil

Frying something as fresh and aromatic as lemon zest may sound counter-intuitive, but in fact it only enhances the flavour, releasing all sorts of lovely volatile oils and rendering it deliciously crisp in the process. I love the combination of creamy, lactic mozzarella with sweet, slightly acidic fruit – for a more robust dish, swap the peaches for ripe tomatoes and serve the lot on sourdough toast.

1. Peel the zest from the lemon in strips, keeping them as thin as possible to avoid the bitter white pith. Scrape any pith off the peel with a sharp knife, then cut the strips into long thin lengths. Put a plate lined with kitchen paper by the hob.
2. Heat the oil in a small frying pan and, when hot, fry the zest for about 30 seconds, until just beginning to crisp and colour. Use a slotted spoon to scoop on to the paper to drain, and allow the oil in the pan to cool.
3. Juice the lemon and whisk the cooled oil into 2 tablespoons of the juice. Season to taste.
4. Slice the peaches and divide between two small plates in a circle. Sprinkle with a little dressing, then tear the mozzarella over the top. Spoon over a little more dressing, season, and sprinkle with the lemon zest strips and torn basil leaves to serve.

Candied peel

**makes enough to fill
a 2 litre jar**

1 pomelo (or add an extra
    grapefruit and orange)
1 grapefruit
1 orange
1 lemon
1 lime
500g sugar

I'm on a one-woman crusade to rescue candied peel from
its seasonal niche. Though it's pretty great in Christmas
cakes and hot cross buns, its aromatic bittersweet flavour is
also welcome in everything from workaday British dishes
like porridge and spotted dick (page 61) to more exotic fare
like ceviche (see page 366). Or you can just serve it as a little
something after dinner with coffee.

1. Cut the base off the pomelo and stand it upright, then take off the
peel in long wide strips, getting a good amount of pith with it (this
means the finished peel will be tender, rather than hard and chewy).
Cut into slimmer strips (unless you'd prefer to keep them in larger
pieces), then repeat the process with the other fruit.
2. Put the peel into a large pan and cover with cold water. Bring to
the boil and simmer until soft – this should take about an hour. Drain,
cover with fresh water, bring to the boil and simmer for a further 15
minutes, then drain again.
3. Put the sugar into the pan with 250ml of cold water and bring to a
simmer, stirring to dissolve the sugar. Add the peel, then turn down
the heat and simmer until the peel has absorbed most of the syrup –
this should take about an hour and a half. Be careful it doesn't stick
towards the end.
4. Scoop out on to a rack set above something easy to clean (to catch
any drips), and leave somewhere dry and fairly warm to harden
overnight.

Pistachio and pink grapefruit cake

makes a 20cm cake

150g shelled unsalted
   pistachios
200g golden caster sugar
1½ pink grapefruits
50g polenta
2 teaspoons baking powder
½ teaspoon ground cardamom
A pinch of salt
4 eggs
200g extra virgin olive oil
3 tablespoons honey
10g shelled salted pistachios
   (about 20), roughly chopped

Fresh and bittersweet, this gluten-free cake is a very spring-like affair, and the syrup means it keeps well for a week.

1. Grease a 20cm loose-bottomed cake tin. Whiz the unsalted pistachios in a food processor until fairly finely ground. Add the sugar and the finely grated zest of the grapefruits and whiz briefly to combine, then stir in the polenta, baking powder, cardamom and salt.
2. Whisk together the eggs and oil and stir these into the dry ingredients. Scrape into the tin. Put into the oven and turn it to 200°C/fan 180°C/gas 6 (trust me, you don't need to preheat it for this one). Bake for 40–50 minutes until set on top.
3. Towards the end of the cooking time, heat the honey in a small pan with the juice of the half grapefruit. Bring to a simmer, then take off the heat.
4. Put the cake, still in its tin, on to a plate with a rim and pour over the syrup, a little at a time, adding more once each lot has been absorbed. Leave to cool before turning out and sprinkling with the chopped salted pistachios.

Chocolate orange cheesecake

serves 8

60g butter
250g dark chocolate digestives
3 tablespoons cocoa powder
75g dark chocolate chips
   or chunks
500g ricotta
200g cream cheese
5 tablespoons honey
2 blood oranges (see intro)
1 tablespoon marmalade

A fresher, lighter take on the traditional baked cheesecake, which, if I'm honest, has never really won me round, this uncooked ricotta-based version balances creamy cheese with a bittersweet dark chocolate base and juicy, ice-cold orange slices. Blood oranges are the ideal when in season, but if not the ordinary variety will do just fine.

1. Melt the butter, and bash the biscuits up roughly. Put them into a food processor and whiz into coarse crumbs, then pour in the melted butter and whiz until smooth. Mix in the cocoa powder and a good pinch of salt, then stir through the chocolate chips.
2. Grease a 20cm loose-bottomed cake tin, and press the base mixture into it, pushing down firmly. Refrigerate while you make the topping.
3. Drain the ricotta well in a sieve, then put into a bowl, beat in the cream cheese, and stir in honey to taste. Zest one of the oranges into the mixture, then spoon on top of the biscuit base, cover and chill for an hour or so.
4. Heat the marmalade gently until liquid. Peel the oranges and remove as much pith as possible. Thinly slice into rings and arrange on top of the cheesecake, then brush with the marmalade. Return to the fridge and chill for at least 2 hours, until ready to serve.

Pomelo sour

makes 1

50ml gin
75ml pomelo juice (freshly
    squeezed)
2 teaspoons sugar syrup
10ml egg white
A healthy shake of bitters
½ teaspoon finely grated
    pomelo zest, plus 1 thin strip
    of zest to garnish

Since belatedly discovering this massive fruit in south-east Asia, I've fallen in love with its perfumed flavour, which works beautifully in this lighter take on the classic whisky cocktail. If you can't find pomelo, you can substitute grapefruit, though you may need to add more sugar depending on the colour.

Sugar syrup is easy to make: dissolve sugar in an equal weight of water, then bring to the boil and simmer for about 5 minutes, until reduced and syrupy. Allow to cool before using.

1. Put all the ingredients apart from the strip of zest into a cocktail shaker with plenty of ice. Shake vigorously, then strain into a cold glass and top with a twist of the zest.

Acknowledgements

Thanks to: as ever, my fabulous editor Juliet Annan for her tireless enthusiasm and great patience, and Anna Steadman for her infinite calm. Much gratitude is also due to Helen Cathcart and River Thompson for making my food look so very beautiful, with more than a little help from Sophie Missing, an immensely talented cook and food stylist (and an invaluable source of trashy coffee and *Archers* conspiracy theories) – thank you all for making it so much fun (and for the canine first aid).

Sarah Ballard and Zoe Ross, for all the important stuff, and for being generally kind and wonderful in the face of the odd meltdown.

Annie Lee for her eagle eyes, Giulia Garbin for the lovely illustrations and design, James Blackman and Ellie Smith for managing everything with such aplomb.

All at the *Guardian*, especially Susan Smillie for putting up with my excuses, and for always making me laugh, Bob Granleese for the *vieille prune* (well, I did promise), and Mina Holland for her wise advice.

Caroline Stafford and Phill Price for their very patient help with my muddled chemistry, Hen Clancy for her ceviche generosity, Phillip Souta for his expertise in the matter of Eastern European dumplings, Jot Davis for help with Italian translation, Vanessa Maurice-Williams and her hens for finishing the first triple chocolate malt cake before I'd even fetched a knife, and Alex Matts and Claire Cohen for feeding me wine until the alphabet made sense.

Richard and Gemma for keeping a roof over my head (and more importantly, a kitchen under my feet) while writing this, and Pam and John for their immense generosity and generous dogsitting. Also, of course, to all my other friends who have kindly allowed themselves to be guinea pigs, and provided such wonderful support and sympathetic ears throughout the process, including Aimee, Alastair and Swanley, Alice and Emily, Anna and Jot, Ali and Iain, Ed, Emma and Tim, Greg, Helen and Jonathan, Ian and Beth, Jacqueline, James, Jemma and Curtis, Julia and Jay, Kelda, Lily and Marcus, Lorna, Lucinda, Matt, Olivia and Nick, Pia, Phillip and Anna and Tiffany and Sam, and everyone I've no doubt forgotten, plus all the nice people on social media for cheering me up on a daily basis.

My whole family, especially my parents, for everything. And, lastly, thanks to Wilf, who has simultaneously driven me mad and kept me just about sane: no more kale chips, I promise.

Index